AMERICAN MORNINGS

Favorite Breakfast Recipes
From Bed & Breakfast Inns

W0006845

Tracy & Phyllis Winters

Winters Publishing
P.O. Box 501
Greensburg, Indiana 47240

(812) 663-4948

PHOTO & ART CREDITS
Front cover: From The William Catlin House, Richmond, VA
Back cover: From Ironhedge Inn B&B, Dundee, IL

The information about the inns and the recipes were supplied by the inns themselves. The rate information was current at the time of submission, but is subject to change. Every effort has been made to assure that the book is accurate. Neither the inns, authors, or publisher assume responsibility for any errors, whether typographical or otherwise.

Library of Congress Card Catalog Number 92-63198
ISBN 0-9625329-6-7

Dedication

With gratitude to our families,
who have helped and supported
us in so many ways.
We love you all.

With love to our daughters,
Rebekah Ann, age 4,
and
Rachel Ann, age 1,
whose patience and
"good behavior"
made it possible
for us to compile and
publish this book.

A special thanks to
Rebekah,
who helped number
the pages on
the computer.

Acknowledgement

Many thanks to all of the innkeepers
who took valuable time to select recipes
and fill out questionnaires.
It is because of their efforts that we
were able to make this book a reality.

Preface

This book is a follow-up to a book that we published three years ago, *BREAKFAST COOKBOOK*. Recently our inventory started to run low. Rather than reprint, we decided to compile a new book featuring different recipes and updated information about the inns. This book is the result.

Although *AMERICAN MORNINGS* is primarily a cookbook, we have used a format which features details about each inn supplying a recipe. This was done not only to give credit to the inns, but also to provide you with a directory of fine Bed & Breakfast establishments across the country to assist you in selecting accommodations when you travel. An index at the rear of this book lists the inns by state.

If you decide to stay at one of the inns we have included, please call ahead to check on room availability and to verify the rates and other information. Although the rates listed were accurate at the time of submission, they are subject to change.

AMERICAN MORNINGS includes many inns that were in the first book, as well as a number of new ones. Since publishing *BREAKFAST COOKBOOK*, we have also compiled and published five cookbooks featuring recipes from inns in a particular state. (See page 320 for information about these state B&B cookbooks.) This edition marks the second or third time we have worked with some of the innkeepers, and we have made some good friends, even if it's only over the telephone. The recipes they have submitted feature the best of what is available at inns around the country. We hope they help brighten your *AMERICAN MORNINGS*.

CONTENTS

MUFFINS

ALPEN GLOW MUFFINS

2 cups white flour	1 cup raisins
2 cups whole wheat flour	1 cup chopped pecans
2 1/2 cups sugar	1 cup shredded coconut
4 teaspoons baking soda	2 cups grated apple
4 teaspoons cinnamon	(3 apples)
1 teaspoon salt	6 large eggs
4 cups grated carrots	1 1/2 cups vegetable oil
(1 lb.)	4 teaspoons vanilla

Sift first five ingredients into large bowl. Stir in carrots, raisins, nuts, and apples. In another bowl, beat eggs, oil, and vanilla. Stir into flour mixture until just combined. Spoon into greased muffin tins. Bake at 350° for 25 minutes. Makes 2 dozen muffins.

Submitted by:

Mountain View Inn	Full breakfast
RFD Box 69	7 rooms, 7 private baths
Waitsfield, Vermont 05673	Children allowed
(802) 496-2426	No pets
Fred & Suzy Spencer	Restricted smoking
$45.00 to $65.00 per person	

An old farmhouse located in Vermont's Green Mountains in the heart of ski country. Breakfast served around a large pine harvest table where guests can visit and plan the day's activities. Guest rooms are decorated with handmade quilts and braided rugs.

APPLE MUFFINS

1 cup sugar
1/2 cup oil
2 eggs
1 teaspoon vanilla
21 oz. can apple pie
 filling

2 cups flour
1 teaspoon cinnamon
1 teaspoon baking
 powder
1 teaspoon baking soda
1/2 teaspoon salt
Walnuts or raisins (opt.)

Topping:
1/2 cup brown sugar
3 tablespoons sugar
1/4 cup butter

3 tablespoons flour
1 tablespoon cinnamon
1/2 cup nuts

Mix sugar, oil, eggs, and vanilla. Add apple pie filling. Combine all dry ingredients, and nuts if desired. Add to apple mixture. Fill muffin tins half full. Mix together topping ingredients, and add to top of muffin batter. Bake at 350° for 15 - 20 minutes. Makes 2 dozen.

Submitted by:

The Rivertown Inn B&B
306 West Olive St.
Stillwater, Minnesota 55082
(612) 430-2955
Chuck & Judy Dougherty
$49.00 to $149.00

Full breakfast
9 rooms, 9 private baths
Children, over 12
No pets
No smoking
Mastercard, Visa, Am Ex

Beautifully restored, 1882 3-story lumberman's mansion. Charming guest rooms decorated with fine Victorian antiques, some double whirlpools & fireplaces, and central a/c. Overlooks St. Croix River Valley. 4 blocks from Historic Main Street. Stillwater's oldest B&B!

APPLE-RAISIN OATMEAL MUFFINS

1 egg
1/2 cup oil
3/4 cup milk
1 cup raisins
1 apple, finely chopped
1 cup quick oats
1/3 cup sugar

1 cup flour
3 teaspoons baking powder
1 teaspoon salt
1 teaspoon nutmeg
2 1/2 teaspoons cinnamon

Beat egg. Add rest of ingredients and stir thoroughly. Bake at 400° for 15 - 20 minutes. Muffins do not get brown on top. Can be made the night before.

Submitted by:

Tunnel Mountain B&B
Route 1, Box 59-1
Elkins, West Virginia 26241
(304) 636-1684
Anne & Paul Beardslee
$50.00 to $60.00

Full breakfast
3 rooms, 3 private baths
Children, over 13
No pets
Smoking allowed

Charming 3-story fieldstone home nestled on five private wooded acres. Rare wormy chestnut and pine woodwork, fireplace in common room. Antiques and collectibles extend warm, friendly atmosphere. Hiking, skiing, canoeing, fishing, restaurants, national forest & historic sites all nearby. Enjoy WV hospitality at it's finest.

APPLESAUCE MUFFINS

1/2 cup softened butter	1 teaspoon ground allspice
1 cup sugar	1/2 teaspoon ground cloves
1 egg	1/2 teaspoon salt
1 cup unsweetened applesauce	1 teaspoon baking soda
1 1/2 teaspoons ground cinnamon	2 cups all-purpose flour
	1/2 cup chopped nuts

Cream butter and sugar. Add egg. Stir in applesauce and spices (chunky applesauce adds a little extra zip). Sift together salt, soda and flour. Add to applesauce mixture, and beat until mixed. Do not overmix batter. Stir in nuts. Fill greased muffin tins 2/3 full. Sprinkle a few Grape Nuts cereal on top. Bake at 350° for 8 - 10 minutes (or 25 - 30 minutes if muffin mix has been refrigerated). Recipe will keep several days in the refrigerator, and can be doubled without problems. Makes about 15 - 3" muffins.

Submitted by:

The Gingerbread Mansion	Continental plus breakfast
400 Berding Street	9 rooms, 9 private baths
Ferndale, California 95536	Children, over 10
(707) 786-4000	No pets
Ken Torbert	No smoking
$95.00 to $175.00 (seasonal)	Mastercard & Visa

Northern California's most-photographed inn, we boast twin, claw-footed tubs for "his & her" bubble baths, fireplaces, bicycles, 4 guest parlors, afternoon tea and colorful gardens. Attention to detail, elegance and warm hospitality make this the ultimate special experience.

BANANA-NUT MUFFINS

2 cups unsifted,
unbleached flour
1 1/4 cups sugar
1 teaspoon baking soda
1 teaspoon ground
cinnamon
1/2 teaspoon salt

2 eggs, lightly beaten
2/3 cup oil
4 oz. crushed, undrained
pineapple
1 1/2 cups diced
bananas
1 cup sliced almonds

Combine dry ingredients in large bowl. In medium bowl whisk together eggs, oil and pineapple. Combine with flour mixture, stirring only until moist. Batter will be thick. Stir in bananas and almonds. Spoon into muffin cups. Garnish with sliced almonds. Bake at 350° for 50 - 60 minutes. Makes 12 muffins.

Submitted by:

Aaron Burr House
80 W. Bridge St.
New Hope, Penn. 18938
(215) 862-2343
Carl Glassman &
Nadine Silnutzer
$75.00 to $155.00

Continental plus breakfast
6 rooms, 6 private baths
Children allowed
Pets allowed
No smoking
Am Ex

1854 Victorian home with canopy beds, fireplaces, hardwood floors, original art, and a/c. In Historic District, convenient to reach from Philadelphia, NYC, and Washington, D.C. But our Victorian splendor and unhurried atmosphere make us seem "worlds away." Mobil guide and AAA approved.

BANANA-WHITE CHOCOLATE MUFFINS

1 egg	1/4 cup sugar
1/4 cup vegetable oil	2 tablespoons baking
1/2 cup bananas,	powder
pureed (1 large)	1/3 cup grated white
1/2 cup milk	chocolate
2 cups flour	1/3 cup ground pecans

In bowl, blend egg, oil, bananas, and milk. In larger bowl mix well flour, sugar, baking powder, white chocolate and ground pecans. Make well in center of dry ingredients. Pour in milk mixture. Stir until moistened. Do not overmix. Fill muffin cups 3/4 full. Bake at 400° for 15 - 20 minutes until tops are golden brown. Makes 16 muffins.

Submitted by:

Glynn House Inn	Full breakfast
43 Highland St.	4 rooms, 4 private baths
Ashland, N.H. 03217	Children allowed
(603) 968-3775	No pets
Betsy & Karol Paterman	Restricted smoking
$65.00 to $75.00	Mastercard & Visa

Queen Anne Victorian fully restored, and decorated in period antiques. Located in the lakes and White Mountains of New Hampshire. Just 2 hours from Boston, I-93, Exit 24.

BLUEBERRY-BROWN SUGAR MUFFINS

3 cups flour
1/2 cup sugar
3/4 cup dark brown
  sugar
4 teaspoons baking
  powder

1 teaspoon salt
1 teaspoon cinnamon
2 eggs, lightly beaten
1/2 cup oil
1 cup milk
2 1/4 cups blueberries

Mix dry ingredients together. Mix wet ingredients together. Fold the dry mix into the wet mix. Add blueberries. Bake in greased muffin pans at 400° for approximately 20 minutes. Makes 24 muffins.

Submitted by:

The Golden Plough Inn
Peddler's Village
Rte. 202 & Street Road
Lahaska, Pennsylvania 18931
(215) 794-4004
Donna Jamison
Gen. Mgr.: Robert Cassidy
$95.00 to $250.00 for 2
  people. $15.00 charge for
  additional guests over 1 year

Continental plus breakfast
60 rooms, 60 private baths
Children allowed
No pets
Smoking allowed
Mastercard, Visa, Am Ex,
  Discover

Luxurious 18th century country inn located along the old stagecoach route between New York & Philadelphia. Jacuzzis, a/c, canopy beds, fireplace, balconies. Near specialty shops, superb dining, antiques.

BLUEBERRY LEMON YOGURT MUFFINS

4 eggs	2 teaspoons baking
2 cups plain yogurt	powder
2/3 cup freshly	1 1/2 teaspoons baking
squeezed lemon juice	soda
2 cups sugar	1 teaspoon sugar
4 cups flour	2 cups fresh blueberries

Beat eggs. Add yogurt, lemon juice, and sugar, and beat. Mix in dry ingredients. Fold in blueberries. Bake at 375° for 15 - 20 minutes until golden. Makes 2 dozen muffins.

Submitted by:

200 South Street Inn	Continental plus breakfast
200 South Street	20 rooms, 20 private baths
Charlottesville, Virginia 22901	Children allowed
(804) 979-0200	No pets
Brendan Clancy	Smoking allowed
$85.00 to $160.00	Mastercard, Visa, Am Ex

Two restored 19th century houses in Historic District of downtown Charlottesville. All rooms feature English and Belgian antiques. Fireplaces, whirlpool tubs, canopy beds, sitting rooms. Less than 1 mile to University of VA, 4 miles to Monticello. Afternoon tea & wine.

BLUE CORN MUFFINS

3/4 cup softened butter
(1 1/2 sticks)
1/2 cup sugar
5 eggs
1/2 cup milk
4 tablespoons minced
jalapeno peppers
1 cup corn

1 cup grated Monterey
Jack cheese
1 cup grated Cheddar
cheese
1 cup all-purpose flour
1 cup blue cornmeal
2 teaspoons baking
powder
1 teaspoon salt

Cream butter and sugar. Combine eggs and milk, and add to butter mixture. Add peppers, corn and cheeses. In separate bowl combine flour, cornmeal, baking powder, and salt. Slowly add dry ingredients to wet ingredients and blend. Pour into greased muffin tins and bake 20 - 25 minutes at 375°.

Submitted by:

Hennessey House, Inc.
1727 Main St.
Napa, California 94559
(707) 226-3774
Lauriann Delay &
  Andrea Weinstein
$85.00 to $150.00

Full breakfast
10 rooms
No pets
No smoking

Breakfast served in dining room featuring hand-painted, stamped, tin ceiling. Some rooms with whirlpool tubs and fireplaces. All rooms furnished in antiques. Some canopy beds or luxurious feather beds.

BONNIE'S CHOCOLATE ZUCCHINI MUFFINS

1 cup brown sugar	1 cup mini chocolate
1 cup white sugar	chips
3 cups flour	1/2 cup nuts (opt.)
1 teaspoon baking soda	3 eggs, beaten
1 teaspoon baking	3 teaspoons vanilla
powder	1 cup oil
1 teaspoon salt	2 1/2 cups grated
1 teaspoon cinnamon	zucchini
3 oz. grated Hershey bar	

Preheat oven to 425°. Mix together sugars, flour, soda, baking powder, salt, cinnamon, Hershey bar, chocolate chips and nuts. In separate bowl mix eggs, vanilla, oil, and zucchini. Then add this to dry ingredients. Fill muffin cups about 3/4 full. Bake for 18 - 20 minutes. Don't overbake! Makes 26 - 28 muffins.

Submitted by:

White Lace Inn
16 N. Fifth Avenue
Sturgeon Bay, Wisconsin
  54235 (Door County)
(414) 743-1105
Dennis & Bonnie Statz
$66.00 to $148.00

Continental plus breakfast
15 rooms, 15 private baths
Children, over 10
No pets
Restricted smoking
Mastercard, Visa, Am Ex
  Discover

Three turn-of-the-century homes surrounding landscaped gardens and gazebo. Each wonderfully inviting guest room furnished with lovely antiques: four poster or ornate Victorian beds, cozy down comforters, and a double whirlpool tub or fireplace in most rooms.

BRAN MUFFINS

2 cups boiling water
2 cups Nabisco 100% Bran cereal
2 1/2 cups white sugar
1 cup oil
5 cups plain flour
5 teaspoons soda
1 1/2 teaspoons salt
4 eggs
1 quart buttermilk
4 cups Kellogg's All Bran cereal
1 lb. raisins

Pour boiling water over Nabisco 100% Bran cereal, and let set until cool. Cream together white sugar and oil. Sift together flour, soda and salt, and set aside. Add eggs, one at a time to creamed sugar and oil. Beat after each addition. Add buttermilk and Nabisco 100% Bran that has cooled. Add dry ingredients, Kellogg's All Bran and raisins. Fold in only until moist. Store in 5 quart airtight container in refrigerator and use as needed. Dip out into greased muffin pan and bake at 375° about 20 minutes. Never stir mixture, just dip! Will keep 3 - 4 months in refrigerator.

Submitted by:

Dry Ridge Inn
26 Brown Street
Weaverville, N.C. 28787
(704) 658-3899
John & Karen Vander Elzen
$45.00 to $55.00

Full breakfast
5 rooms, 5 private baths
Children allowed
No pets
Restricted smoking
Mastercard, Visa, Discover

Farm house over 100 years old, located 10 minutes north of Asheville. Large guest rooms with antiques and handmade quilts. Gift shop featuring crafts from Blue Ridge Mountains. Interesting Civil War history. "Welcome to Grandmother's home."

CAROB CHIP MUFFINS

1 egg, slightly beaten	1/3 cup sugar
1/3 cup margarine or butter, softened	1/3 cup brown sugar
	Pinch of salt
1/2 cup milk	1/2 teaspoon nutmeg
1/2 cup sour cream	1/2 teaspoon cinnamon
2 1/2 cups flour	1/2 teaspoon ginger
1 tablespoon baking powder	1 cup carob chips

Topping:
1/2 cup chopped walnuts   Honey to taste

Preheat oven to 400°. Cream together egg, butter, milk, and sour cream. In separate bowl combine flour, baking powder, sugars, and spices. Add dry mixture to egg mixture. When completely mixed, add carob chips. Evenly divide mixture into 12 well-greased muffin tins. Top with chopped walnuts, and sprinkle a little brown sugar or drizzle honey over the top of muffins. Bake for 25 - 30 minutes or until done and lightly brown. Makes 12 muffins.

Submitted by:

Holden House - 1902 B&B Inn	Full breakfast
1102 W. Pikes Peak Avenue	5 rooms, 5 private baths
Colorado Springs, CO 80904	No children
(719) 471-3980	No pets
Sallie & Welling Clark	No smoking
$65.00 to $95.00	Mastercard, Visa, Am Ex, Disc.

Historic storybook Victorian and carriage house, with mountain views, antiques, feather pillows, turn-down service, and family heirlooms. Romantic retreat with suites boasting fireplaces, "tubs for two" and more! Warm hospitality in atmosphere of yesteryear. Near Pikes Peak area. Friendly resident cats "Mingtoy" & "Muffin" are the official greeters.

CARROT CAKE MUFFINS

1 3/4 cups all-purpose flour	1 teaspoon ground cinnamon
2/3 cup brown sugar	1/2 cup crushed pineapple, undrained
1 teaspoon baking powder	1/2 cup vegetable oil
1/2 teaspoon baking soda	1 egg, lightly beaten
1/2 teaspoon salt	1 1/2 teaspoons vanilla
	2 cups shredded carrots
	1/2 cup raisins

Preheat oven to 400°. Grease 12 muffin cups. In large bowl, mix together dry ingredients. In separate bowl, mix pineapple, oil, egg and vanilla, until blended. Make well in center of dry ingredients. Add pineapple mixture and stir just to combine. Stir in carrots and raisins. Spoon batter into muffin cups. Bake 15 - 20 minutes. Cool 5 minutes. Remove muffins from cups. Makes 12 muffins.

Submitted by:

Captain Dexter House of Edgartown	Continental plus breakfast
35 Pease's Pt. Way, Box 2798	11 rooms, 11 private baths
Edgartown, Mass. 02539	Children, over 10
(508) 627-7289	No pets
Tenee & Jim Casaccio	Restricted smoking
$75.00 to $180.00	Mastercard, Visa, Am Ex

Beautifully restored 1840's home in country Colonial style. Most rooms have canopied beds and fireplaces. Lovely landscaped garden areas for sunning. Short stroll to harbor & town. Homebaked breakfasts, and afternoon aperitif or lemonade. Great hospitality!

COUNTRY BREAKFAST MUFFINS

1 large egg
1 cup sour cream
2 tablespoons sugar
1 tablespoon shortening
1 1/3 cups flour

1 teaspoon baking
powder
1/2 teaspoon baking
soda
1/2 teaspoon salt

Preheat oven to 400°. Grease muffin cups. In large bowl, beat egg until light and frothy. Whisk in sour cream, sugar, and shortening. Sift together dry ingredients. Stir into egg mixture. Do not overmix. Pour into greased muffin cups. Bake 20 - 25 minutes, or until golden brown. Serve hot. Makes 1 dozen muffins.

Submitted by:

Brookside Farm
1373 Marron Valley Road
Dulzura, California 92017
(619) 468-3043
Edd & Sally Guishard
$65.00 to $85.00

Full breakfast
9 rooms, 9 private baths
No children
No pets
No smoking
Mastercard & Visa

Restored 1927 farmhouse and stone barn. Inn is in rural setting - gardens, birds, farm animals. Owner is a professional chef. Recipes have been published in San Diego Home & Garden.

CURRANT MUFFINS

2 cups sifted flour	1 teaspoon salt
4 teaspoons baking powder	1/4 cup shortening
	2/3 cup currants
1/3 cup granulated sugar	2 eggs
	3/4 cup milk

Rinse currants and drain. Mix together flour, sugar, baking powder and salt. Cut in shortening. Stir in currants. Beat eggs lightly and add milk. Turn into dry mixture and stir only until flour is moistened. Fill greased muffin tins 2/3 full. Bake at 375° 20 - 25 minutes. Makes 12 - 15 medium muffins.

Submitted by:

The Stacked Arms	Full breakfast
R.R. #2, Box 146	6 rooms, 1 private bath
Birch Point Road	Children, over 5
Wiscasset, Maine 04578	No pets
(207) 882-5436	Restricted smoking
Dee, Pat & Sean Maguire	Mastercard, Visa,
$40.00 to $90.00	Discover

Country setting, beautiful gardens, and hand-stenciled rooms with orthopedic queen or twin beds, ceiling fans, and small refrigerators. Centrally located in mid-coast Maine for many day trips. Train and boat rides from our village.

FRESH LEMON MUFFINS

1/2 cup vegetable oil (or olive oil)	1 teaspoon baking soda
1 cup sugar	1 cup plain lowfat yogurt
2 eggs or 3 egg whites	2 cups flour
1 1/2 teaspoons nutmeg	1/4 cup freshly squeezed lemon juice
Grated peel from 2 fresh lemons	2 tablespoons sugar

Preheat oven to 375° and grease muffin tins. Beat oil and sugar together. Add eggs one at a time with nutmeg and lemon peel. Stir baking soda into yogurt. It will start to bubble and rise. Fold flour and yogurt into egg mixture, scoop into muffin tins and bake 18 - 20 minutes, or until springy to the touch. While muffins bake, mix lemon juice and sugar. When muffins are done, cool 3 minutes in tins, then remove and dip top and bottom in lemon juice and sugar mixture.

Submitted by:

Captain Freeman Inn
15 Breakwater Rd.
Brewster, Mass. 02631
(800) 843-4664
Carol Covitz
$65.00 to $185.00

Full breakfast
12 rooms, 9 private baths
Cildren, over 10
No pets
No smoking
Mastercard, Visa, Am Ex

Located in historic Brewster on Cape Cod. Antique-filled, elegant Victorian sea captain's mansion. Wraparound porch, in-ground pool. Walk to beach. Fireplaces, jacuzzis, sumptuous breakfast.

GOOD MORNING MUFFINS

List 1:
1 cup flour
2 teaspoons baking powder
1 teaspoon baking soda
1/2 cup bran
1/2 cup wheat germ
1/2 cup oatmeal
1/2 cup cornmeal
1/2 cup raisins

1/2 cup sugar
1/2 cup walnuts
1 teaspoon cinnamon
1/2 teaspoon ginger
1/2 teaspoon nutmeg
List 2:
1 cup buttermilk
1 Golden Delicious apple
1/3 cup melted butter
1 egg, beaten

Preheat oven to 400°. In large bowl, mix ingredients in List 1. In food processor, blend ingredients in List 2 until smooth. Combine both mixtures, stirring to blend them thoroughly, but without overmixing. Coat 2" muffin pans with nonstick spray, and fill each muffin cup 2/3 full. Sprinkle with additional oatmeal, and let the pans rest 5 to 7 minutes before placing in oven. Bake on middle-level rack for 20 minutes. Makes 18 muffins. An original, popular recipe.

Submitted by:

Ashton Country House
1205 Middlebrook Road
Staunton, Virginia 24401
(703) 885-7819
Sheila Kennedy &
Stanley Polanski
$65.00 to $80.00

Full breakfast
4 rooms, 4 private baths
Children, over 16
No pets
No smoking

Greek Revival brick home, circa 1860, on 20 peaceful acres at the outskirts of Staunton. Guest rooms are comfortably furnished with queen-size or double bed. Breakfast and afternoon tea are prepared by a professionally trained chef, and often accompanied by live piano music. Historic attractions and fine dining are nearby.

HEALTHFUL WHOLE GRAIN MUFFINS

2 sticks margarine, melted	1 box or 7 cups All Bran cereal
2 cups warm water	5 cups unbleached flour
3 cups sugar	2 cups oatmeal
3 teaspoons salt	5 teaspoons baking soda
4 beaten eggs	1 quart buttermilk

Mix first 8 ingredients together. Add baking soda to buttermilk and stir with wire whip. Beat into first mixture and let rest in refrigerator overnight. Bake at 400° for 20 minutes. Remainder can be stored in tight container in refrigerator for up to 3 weeks. Makes 6 dozen muffins.

Submitted by:

The Kingsley House	Full breakfast
626 West Main Street	7 rooms, 7 private baths
Fennville, Michigan 49408	Children, over 12
(616) 561-6425	No pets
David & Shirley Witt	Restricted smoking
$75.00 to $125.00	Mastercard & Visa

Elegant 1886 Victorian home built for prominent Kingsley family. Third floor getaway suite with jacuzzi & sitting room. Family antiques, bicycles available. Minutes from Saugatuck, Holland, and Lake Michigan. Chosen one of top 50 B&B's in America by Inn Times.

HOMESTEAD BREAKFAST MUFFINS

1 1/2 cups flour
1/2 cup sugar
2 teaspoons baking powder
1/2 teaspoon salt
1/2 teaspoon nutmeg
1/2 teaspoon cinnamon
1/2 teaspoon baking soda
1 teaspoon poppy seeds (opt.)
1/2 cup oil
2 small eggs
1/2 cup milk

Carefully mix all dry ingredients with a whisk. Beat eggs with milk and oil. Add to dry ingredients, don't overmix. Pour into 12 paper baking cups in a muffin tin. Sprinkle top with cinnamon-sugar mixture if desired. Bake at 400° for 18 minutes. Don't overmeasure liquids, and don't overbake. Makes 12 muffins.

Submitted by:

Homestead Inn B&B
Route 1A, Box 15
York Beach, Maine 03910
(207) 363-8952
Dan & Danielle Duffy
$49.00 to $59.00

Continental breakfast
4 rooms, 1 private bath
Children allowed
No pets
Restricted smoking

Built in 1905, inn offers quiet rooms with ocean views, breakfast served in our barn board dining room or on private deck out back. Walk to 2 beaches and famous Nubble Lighthouse. Seashore, sunsets, and serenity included.

JAM MUFFINS

2 cups all-purpose flour	1 egg
2/3 cup sugar	1 teaspoon vanilla
2 teaspoons baking powder	1/4 teaspoon almond extract
1/2 teaspoon salt	3/4 cup shredded coconut
1 cup milk	
1/2 cup margarine, melted	1/2 cup jam (your choice)
	1/2 cup sliced almonds

In large bowl, combine flour, sugar, baking powder & salt. In another bowl, mix milk, melted margarine, egg and vanilla. Pour over flour mixture and stir until just combined. Gently stir in coconut. Spoon half the batter into greased muffin tins. Top with a small amount of jam and cover with remaining batter. Sprinkle sliced almonds over the top. Bake at 400° for 15 - 20 minutes. Makes 9 - 12 muffins.

Submitted by:

Glacier Bay Country Inn
P.O. Box 5
Gustavus, Alaska 99826
(907) 697-2288
Al & Annie Unrein
$54.00/child AP to $198.00/
   double AP

Full breakfast
9 rooms, 8 private baths
Children allowed
No pets
No smoking

Whimsical, rambling wooden structure built with lumber logged & milled right on the property, surrounded by meadows, rain forests, delightful mountain views, with a wonderful feeling of peace and seclusion. Friendly personalized service, homemade breads.

MARMALADE MUFFINS

1/4 cup butter or margarine
1 cup sour cream
1/4 cup milk
1 egg
1/2 teaspoon vanilla
1/4 cup sugar
1/2 teaspoon salt

1 1/2 cups all-purpose flour
2 teaspoons baking powder
1/2 teaspoon baking soda
1 cup sweet marmalade

Grease 12 muffin cups. In saucepan melt butter. Remove from heat and add sour cream and milk. Blend well. Beat in egg and vanilla. In separate bowl combine dry ingredients. Add butter mixture to dry ingredients and stir until just moistened. Add marmalade and mix again. Spoon batter into prepared muffin cups. Bake at 350° for 15 - 20 minutes. Makes 12 muffins.

Submitted by:

Greenvale Manor
Route 354, Box 70
Mollusk, Virginia 22517
(804) 462-5995
Pam & Walt Smith
$65.00 to $95.00

Full breakfast
6 rooms, 6 private baths
No children
No pets
Restricted smoking
Mastercard & Visa

Romantic, relaxing 1840 Waterfront plantation, with sweeping views of Rappahannock River & Greenvale Creek. Antiques, a/c, fireplaces in 2 suites. Beach, pool, dock, bicycles, and boats for rent. Watch a river sunset from our veranda & unwind on 13 acres of rural privacy.

MARTY'S MARVELOUS MUFFINS

1/2 cup whole wheat flour	1 egg, beaten
1 1/2 cups unbleached white flour	1/4 cup corn oil
1/2 cup sugar	7/8 cup orange juice
1 tablespoon baking powder	1 cup blueberries, fresh or frozen
Pinch of salt	1 cup raspberries, fresh or frozen

Preheat oven to 425°. Combine dry ingredients in large bowl. In separate bowl, combine the liquid ingredients with the berries. Pour this mixture into the dry mix and stir gently with a rubber spatula. Do not overmix. Spoon into greased muffin tin (we use an ice cream scoop) 2/3 full. Bake until golden brown about 25 minutes. Makes 12 small or 8 large muffins.

Submitted by:

Applebrook Bed & Breakfast
75 Liberty St. (Route 115 A)
Jefferson, N.H. 03583
(800) 545-6504
Sandra Conley & Martin Kelly
$40.00 to $60.00/room

Full breakfast
8 rooms, 4 private baths
Children allowed
Pets allowed
No smoking
Mastercard & Visa

Taste our mid-summer raspberries while enjoying spectacular mountain views. Fresh baked raspberry-blueberry muffins are part of the country breakfast awaiting you at our comfortable, casual Victorian farmhouse. Venture from our peaceful rural setting to hike, fish, bike, swim, go antiquing. or ski downhill or cross-country.

MINCEMEAT MUFFINS

1 cup vegetable oil	1 cup whole wheat flour
1 cup brown sugar	1 cup white flour
3 eggs	2 teaspoons baking soda
1 cup mincemeat	1/4 teaspoon baking
1/2 teaspoon lemon	powder
extract	1/2 teaspoon salt

Mix first 3 ingredients. Add mincemeat and lemon extract. Combine dry ingredients and add to wet mixture. Bake at 350° for 20 minutes. Makes 1 dozen muffins.

Submitted by:

The Stephen Potwine House
84 Scantic Road
East Windsor, Conn. 06088
(203) 623-8722
Bob & Vangi Cathcart
$55.00 to $75.00

Full breakfast
4 rooms, 1 private bath
No pets
Restricted smoking

Charming country farmhouse overlooks a pond, flowers and willow trees. On picturesque open property surrounded by acres of farmland and fields. Historic homestead house is decorated with artwork, collectibles and antiques. Convenient to many attractions.

NANCY'S CHOCOLATE CHOCOLATE CHIP MUFFINS

2 eggs
1/2 cup oil
1 cup milk
1 teaspoon vanilla
1 3/4 cups flour
1/2 cup sugar

1/4 cup cocoa
1 tablespoon baking powder
1/2 cup chocolate chips (the secret is to double this amount)

Preheat oven to 400° and grease muffin tin. In large bowl add eggs, oil, milk and vanilla, combine well. In smaller bowl mix flour, sugar, cocoa, baking powder and chocolate chips, combine well. Combine two mixtures, stirring just to moisten. Place in muffin cups and bake for 15 minutes. Makes 12 medium-size muffins.

Submitted by:

Saratoga Rose
4174 Rockwell St.
P.O. Box 238
Hadley, N.Y. 12835
(518) 696-2861
Anthony & Nancy Merlino
$75.00 to $135.00

Full breakfast
4 rooms, 4 private baths
Children, over 12
No pets
Restricted smoking
Mastercard, Visa, Discover

1885 Queen Anne Victorian mansion, in the southern Adirondacks. Purchased & renovated in 1988 by the Merlinos 2 weeks after their marriage, it became their honeymoon. Garden room has outside deck & jacuzzi. Romantic Queen Anne Room has cozy corner fireplace. Wonderful cuisine by Chef Anthony in candlelit restaurant.

NO-CHOLESTEROL PUMPKIN MUFFINS

1/4 cup vegetable oil
1/4 cup applesauce
1 cup sugar
4 egg whites
1 cup canned pumpkin
1/2 cup skim
  buttermilk
2 cups all-purpose
  flour

2 teaspoons baking
  powder
1 teaspoon baking soda
1 1/2 teaspoons ground
  cinnamon
1/2 teaspoon ground
  allspice
3/4 cup chopped walnuts
1 cup raisins

Preheat oven to 350°. Mix together first 6 ingredients. Add dry ingredients and beat until batter is smooth. Stir in walnuts and raisins. Spoon into greased muffin tins, 3/4 full, and bake 30 minutes. Makes 16 - 18 muffins.

Submitted by:

Stone Lea B&B
40 Newton Avenue
Narragansett, R.I. 02882
(401) 783-9546
Carol & Ernie Cormier
$60.00 - $125.00 (seasonal)

Full breakfast
6 rooms, 6 private baths
Children, over 10
No pets
No smoking
Mastercard & Visa

Ocean-front Victorian home on National Historic Register, built in 1884, on 2.2 acres overlooking rocky Atlantic coastline. Watch the ocean traffic from our sun porch or patio, sunbathe on beautiful lawn or rocks, play pool in commons area or listen to player piano. 25 minutes to Newport.

PEACH-NUT MUFFINS

1/2 cup butter, room
  temperature
1/3 cup sugar
1/2 cup light brown
  sugar
1 egg
1/2 cup sour cream
1/2 teaspoon almond
  extract

1 3/4 cups all-purpose
  flour
2 teaspoons baking
  powder
1 teaspoon cinnamon
1 cup chopped
  peaches
1/2 cup chopped
  walnuts

Preheat oven to 375°. Beat together first 6 ingredients until blended. Stir in dry ingredients just until moistened. Drop into muffin tins lined with paper cups. Sprinkle tops with cinnamon-sugar mixture. Bake until tops of muffins spring back when touched, about 15 - 20 minutes.

Submitted by:

The Oak House
Seaview Ave., P.O. Box 299
Martha's Vineyard,
Oak Bluffs, Mass. 02557
(508) 693-4187
Betsi Convery-Luce
$110.00 to $220.00 (summer)

Continental breakfast
10 rooms, 10 private baths
Children, over 10
No pets
Smoking allowed
Mastercard, Visa, Discover

Romantic seaside Victorian mansion, with spectacular ocean views & some private balconies. Elegant oak interior furnished with antiques. Originally Mass. Gov. Claflin's summer home. Homebaked breakfast, afternoon tea on glassed-in sunporch. Walk to town, tennis, biking and the beach.

PINEAPPLE CREAM MUFFINS

2 cups all-purpose flour
2 teaspoons baking powder
1/2 teaspoon baking soda
3 1/2 oz. pkg. instant French vanilla pudding

2/3 cup brown sugar
1 egg, well beaten
1 cup sour cream
8 3/4 oz. can crushed pineapple with juice
1/2 cup oil

Prepare muffin pan. In large bowl sift together flour, baking powder, baking soda, and pudding mix. Stir in brown sugar. In separate bowl combine egg and sour cream. Fold in pineapple and oil. Add mixture to dry ingredients, stirring until moistened. Bake at 425° for 15 minutes. Makes 16 muffins.

Submitted by:

Carrington's Bluff B&B
1900 David St.
Austin, Texas 78705
(512) 479-0638
Gwen & David Fullbrook
$60.00 to $75.00

Full breakfast (gourmet)
8 rooms, 6 private baths
Children allowed
No pets
Restricted smoking
Mastercard, Visa, Am Ex, Disc.

Located downtown on an acre, tree-covered bluff. 35' front porch with rockers, tables & chairs faces garden & bluff. Antique-filled rooms, English country decor with Laura Ashley fabrics. Close to University of Texas, State Capitol, restaurants & shopping, hike & bike trail.

RASPBERRY MUFFINS

1 1/2 cups flour
1/2 cup sugar
2 teaspoons baking
powder
1 egg

1/2 cup milk or
buttermilk
1 cup crushed frozen
raspberries, red or
black

Preheat oven to 325°. Mix first five ingredients. Do not overmix. Add raspberries. Mix slightly. Pour into greased muffin cups. Bake 15 minutes or until golden brown. Serve warm with butter. Makes 1 dozen.

Submitted by:

Crescent House B&B
459 Beach Road
Sarasota, Florida 34242
(813) 346-0857
Paulette Flaherty
$50.00 to $105.00

Continental breakfast
4 rooms, 2 private baths
Children allowed
No pets
Restricted smoking

Fully restored home, over 70 years old, furnished with comfortable antiques. Fresh Florida orange juice, homemade muffins, scones & freshly ground coffee for breakfast. Sunbathe, or cool off in the Gulf of Mexico. Walking distance to Siesta Village & Pavilion, with restaurants, shops, & public beach. European service & hospitality.

RHUBARB PECAN MUFFINS

2 cups flour
3/4 cup sugar
1 1/2 teaspoons baking
  powder
1/2 teaspoon soda
3/4 cup chopped pecans

1 1/4 cups fresh rhubarb
1 egg
1/4 cup oil
3/4 cup orange juice
2 teaspoons grated
  orange rind

Preheat oven to 350°. Grease or spray muffin tins. Combine all dry ingredients. Mix pecans and rhubarb together with dry ingredients to coat. Whisk egg, oil, juice and rind together. Add egg mixture to dry ingredients. Stir just until moist. Bake until golden brown. Makes 12 muffins.

Submitted by:

Michael Cahill Bed & Breakfast
1106 Walnut Blvd.
Ashtabula, Ohio 44004
(216) 964-8449
Patricia & Paul Goode
$35.00 to $50.00

Full breakfast
4 rooms, 3 private baths
Children allowed
No pets
Restricted smoking

1887 "stick-style" Victorian home in Harbor Historic District. Within walking distance to shopping on Bridge St., Marine Museum, charter boat fishing, tennis & Walnut Beach. Nine room home, 3 large sitting rooms and open porches to serve guests.

SLEEPY HOLLOW'S ORANGE BLOSSOM MUFFINS

1 box white cake mix
  with pudding
3 eggs
1/4 cup vegetable oil
1/3 cup water
2 drops each yellow &
  red food coloring

2 - 5.5 oz. pkgs. sugared
  orange slice candy,
  finely minced
11 oz. can mandarin
  oranges, drained &
  chopped

Preheat oven to 350°. In large bowl mix all ingredients into white cake mix. Coat muffin tins with no-stick cooking spray. Fill cups about 2/3 full and bake for 15 minutes. Note: Candy is sticky when chopped, but will separate when stirred into batter. If small muffin tins are used (1 1/2" across bottom and 2 1/4" across top), yield is 48 muffins.

Submitted by:

The Son's Shady Brook B&B
P.O. Box 551
Coleman, Florida 33521
(904) PIT STOP
Jean Lake Martin
$50.00 to $60.00

Full breakfast
4 rooms, 4 private baths
No children
No pets
No smoking
Mastercard, Visa, Am Ex

Come for a refreshing change; modern house on 21 wooded acres overlooking spring-fed creek offering solitude & tranquility with therapeutic, picturesque surroundings. Beautifully decorated, a/c, piano, fireplace, library, homemade bread. Within an hour from Orlando & Tampa. Good fishing nearby.

SOUR CREAM OATMEAL MUFFINS

2 cups quick oats	2 teaspoons baking powder
2 cups sour cream	1/2 teaspoon salt
2/3 cup unsalted melted butter	1 teaspoon baking soda
4 eggs	Granulated sugar
2 cups light brown sugar	Quick oat flakes
2 cups flour	

Combine oats and sour cream. Add butter, eggs, and brown sugar. Sift together flour, baking powder, salt and baking soda. Stir into wet mixture. Fill muffin cups. Top with sugar and oat flakes. Bake at 350° for 17 - 20 minutes. Makes 24 muffins.

Submitted by:

Albonegon Inn
Capitol Island, Maine 04538
(207) 633-2521
Kim Peckham
$48.00 (sgl.) to $115.00 (sui.)

Continental breakfast
15 rooms, 3 private baths
Children allowed
No pets
No smoking

Perched on the rocks of a small private island four miles from Boothbay Harbor. Wraparound porches with spectacular views of surrounding islands and wildlife.

SPICY SOUR CREAM & RAISIN MUFFINS

2 large eggs
1/2 cup sour cream
1/2 cup milk
2 tablespoons instant
  coffee
3/4 cup raisins
1 1/2 cups flour

1/2 cup oatmeal
1/2 cup sugar
2 teaspoons baking
  powder
1/2 teaspoon cinnamon
1/2 teaspoon cloves
1/2 teaspoon allspice

Whisk eggs, sour cream, milk, and instant coffee in bowl until well-blended. Stir in raisins. Let stand 5 minutes. Stir. Preheat oven to 375° and grease 12 muffin cups. Mix dry ingredients and spices into large bowl. Add sour cream mixture and fold in until dry ingredients are moistened. Scoop batter into muffin cups. Sprinkle with oatmeal flakes. Bake 20 - 25 minutes until browned. Serve hot. Yield: 12.

Submitted by:

High Meadows Vineyard Inn
Rte. 20 S.   Route 4, Box 6
Scottsville, Virginia 24590
(804) 286-2218
Peter Sushka & Jae Abbitt
$75.00 to $130.00

Full breakfast
12 rooms, 12 private baths
Children allowed
Pets allowed, with prior notice
No smoking
Mastercard & Visa

19th century architectural two-period historic landmark evokes old-world ambience. Romantic gardens, on 23 acre pastoral setting for relaxing walks, European evening supper baskets at pond, gazebo, or vineyard. Terrace & fireside breakfasting. Near Charlottesville, Monticello and University of Virginia.

SWEET POTATO MUFFINS

1 3/4 cups flour	3/4 cup chopped pecans
1/4 teaspoon baking	or walnuts
powder	2 eggs
1 teaspoon baking	1/2 cup oil
soda	1 1/2 cups sugar
1 teaspoon allspice	1 cup canned sweet
3 teaspoons cinnamon	potatoes
2 teaspoons nutmeg	1/3 cup water

In a large bowl, sift together flour, baking powder and soda. Add spices and nuts. In a second bowl, beat together the eggs, oil, sugar, sweet potatoes, and water. Combine the mixtures into one bowl. Pour combined mixture into greased muffin tins, 3/4 full. Bake at 375° for 20 to 25 minutes. Makes 12 muffins.

Submitted by:

The Mason Cottage	Full breakfast
625 Columbia Avenue	4 suites, all private baths
Cape May, New Jersey 08204	Children, over 12
(609) 884-3358	No pets
Dave & Joan Mason	Restricted smoking
$85.00 to $165.00	Mastercard & Visa

An elegant Victorian B&B built in 1871, the inn is French Second Empire with a curved mansard roof. The parlor and guest rooms are appointed with historic Victorian patterned wallpapers and restored antique furniture. Many pieces are original to the inn.

WILD BLACKBERRY OATMEAL MUFFINS

2 cups rolled oats	2 teaspoons baking
2 cups buttermilk	powder
1/2 cup canola oil	1 teaspoon salt (or
1/2 cup honey	Salt Sense)
2 eggs or 4 egg whites	1 teaspoon baking
2 cups whole wheat	soda
flour	2 cups blackberries

Grease bottom of muffin tins using oil or Pam. Soak oats in buttermilk overnight. Mix in oil, honey and eggs. Mix well. Blend dry ingredients and add to batter. Fold in blackberries and fill muffin tins 2/3 full. Bake in 400° oven for 30 minutes. Makes 12 Texas-size muffins.

Submitted by:

Bear River Valley B&B
03636 Bear River Rd.
Petoskey, Michigan 49770
(616) 348-2046
Russ & Sandra Barkman
$48.00 to $60.00

Continental plus breakfast
3 rooms, 1 private bath
No children
No pets
No smoking

A Northwoods retreat in the heart of MI's finest outdoor recreational area. Enjoy rustic charm and natural beauty in our spectacular sylvan setting. Close to lakes, beaches, shops, galleries, restaurants, and outdoor sports. Healthy breakfast of juice or fruit, whole grain breads, cereals, pastries, & homemade jams. Authentic Finnish sauna.

YOGURT GRANOLA MUFFINS

1 1/2 cups packaged
  biscuit mix
1 cup granola or
  lowfat granola
1/4 cup packed brown
  sugar

2 beaten eggs
8 oz. honey-vanilla
  yogurt (or any fruit-
  flavored yogurt)
2 tablespoons cooking
  oil (canola oil is good)

Grease 12 muffin cups, line with paper baking cups, or spray with non-stick spray coating. In large mixing bowl stir together biscuit mix, granola, and brown sugar. Make a well in the center. In small mixing bowl stir together eggs, yogurt and oil. Add egg mixture all at once to granola mixture. Stir just until moistened. (Batter should be lumpy.) Fill prepared muffin cups 2/3 full. Bake at 400° for 16 - 18 minutes or until golden. This is an excellent moist muffin.

Submitted by:

Elizabeth Street Guest House
202 E. Elizabeth
Fort Collins, Colorado 80524
(303) 493-2337
John & Sheryl Clark
$43.00 to $65.00

Full breakfast
3 rooms, 1 private bath
Children, over 10
No pets
No smoking
Mastercard, Visa, Am Ex

1905 post-Victorian American 4-square home, 1 block east of Col. State University. Antiques, 3-story miniature house, leaded windows and oak woodwork. Near restored downtown area. Easy access to Rocky Mountain National Park and Anheuser-Busch Brewery.

COFFEE CAKES
&
OTHER CAKES

APFEL KUCHEN (AUSTRIAN APPLE BREAKFAST CAKE)

2 1/2 cups flour
1 cup ground hazelnuts
3 teaspoons baking
powder
2 cups sugar
1 cup vegetable oil
5 eggs
1/4 cup orange juice

2 1/2 teaspoons vanilla
extract
4 medium apples,
peeled, cored & sliced
2 1/2 teaspoons
cinnamon mixed with
5 tablespoons sugar

Preheat oven to 350°. Combine flour, nuts, baking powder, sugar, oil, eggs, juice, and vanilla. Mix well. Pour half of batter into greased and floured spring form pan. Arrange half of the apple slices on top and sprinkle with half of the cinnamon-sugar mixture. Pour remaining batter into pan. Arrange remaining apples on top. Sprinkle with rest of cinnamon-sugar mixture. Bake 1 - 1 1/2 hours. Makes 1 large cake.

Submitted by:

Alpen Rose Bed & Breakfast
P.O. Box 769 Winter Park
Winter Park, Colorado 80482
(303) 726-5039
Robin & Rupert Sommerauer
$65.00 to $95.00

Full breakfast
5 rooms, 5 private baths
Children, over 10
No pets
No smoking
Mastercard, Visa, Am Ex

Surrounded by aspens and pines, and a magnificent view of the front range. Furnished with antiques and Austrian accessories. 2 miles from Winter Park ski area. Hiking, fishing, mountain biking, rafting and golfing in summer. Memorable breakfast with Austrian specialties.

APPLE ALMOND BREAKFAST CAKE

2 cups all-purpose flour
1 teaspoon baking soda
1 teaspoon salt
1 teaspoon cinamon
1 1/2 cups sugar
1 cup safflower oil

3 eggs, beaten
1 teaspoon vanilla
extract
1/2 cup sliced almonds
1 1/2 cups peeled &
seeded apples

Sift dry ingredients together. Add wet ingredients. Add almonds, and apples. Bake at 350° until toothpick comes out clean.

Submitted by:

Ventana
Highway 1
Big Sur, California 93920
(408) 667-2331 or
(800) 628-6500
Robert Bussinger
$165.00 to $785.00 (dbl.)

Continental plus breakfast
62 rooms, 62 private baths
No children
No pets
Restricted smoking
Mastercard, Visa, Am Ex,
Discover

Surrounded by 240 acres of meadows & forests, nestled in the hills above a rugged coastline & crashing sea. Guest rooms seem rustic, but inside are decorator-perfect with country ambience & pretty views. Some terraces & private hot tubs. 2 lounges & 2 - 75' pools.

BISCUIT COFFEE CAKE

1/2 cup sugar
1 teaspoon cinnamon
2 - 10 oz. cans refriger-
ated flaky biscuits
3 oz. cream cheese,
cut into 20 pieces
1/4 cup butter, melted

1/3 cup chopped walnuts
Glaze:
1 cup sifted powdered
sugar
1 - 1 1/2 tablespoons
water
1/2 teaspoon vanilla

Combine sugar and cinnamon. Separate biscuit dough. Roll each piece into 3" circle. Place 1 piece cream cheese and 1 teaspoon cinnamon sugar in center. Pinch edges together, form into ball, set aside. Repeat with remaining dough. Place butter in bottom of 10" ring mold or bundt pan; sprinkle with remaining sugar and walnuts. Layer balls of dough, seam side up. Bake at 350° for 35 minutes or until golden brown. Invert onto plate. Combine glaze ingredients. Stir until smooth, drizzle over coffee cake. Serves 8 - 10.

Submitted by:

Peacock's "Inn on the Sound"
313 Grand Ave., P.O. Box 201
Falmouth, Mass. 02541
(508) 457-9666
Phyllis & Bud Peacock
$65.00 to $115.00 (double)

Full breakfast (gourmet)
10 rooms, 10 private baths
Children, over 14
No pets
Restricted smoking
Mastercard, Visa, Am Ex, Disc.

Spectacular ocean view, attentive hospitality, warm country charm, & spacious rooms combine to provide a perfect setting for your next vacation escape. Walk to beach & Martha's Vineyard ferry. Exciting, varied day trips. Honeymoon package. Reservations recommended.

COFFEE CAKE

2 cups flour
1 teaspoon salt
2 teaspoons baking
  powder
1 cup sugar
2 teaspoons cinnamon
1 cup chopped nuts
2 eggs
1/2 cup vegetable oil

Topping:
8 oz. cream cheese,
  softened
1/3 cup sugar
1 beaten egg
Dash of salt
1 teaspoon vanilla
1 can cherry or blueberry
  pie filling

Mix flour, salt, baking powder, sugar, cinnamon, and nuts in bowl with wooden spoon. Add eggs and oil, mix again. Pat mixture into 9" x 13" greased glass baking dish. Preheat oven to 350°. Combine all topping ingredients except pie filling, and mix with mixer. Spread topping over flour mixture. Bake approximately 1 hour. Warm pie filling in microwave, and after cutting coffee cake, top with pie filling. Note: Pie filling can be placed on cake prior to baking.

Submitted by:

Oak Tree Inn
Vinegar Hill & Hwy. 110 West
Heber Springs, Ark. 72543
(501) 362-7731
Freddie Lou Lodge
$70.00 to $80.00

Full breakfast
6 rooms, 6 private baths
Children in condos & river
  cabins only
No pets
Restricted smoking

Recapture the warmth of a bygone era for nonsmoking adults. Warm to a crackling wood fire and the charm of planked oak floors. Whirlpool baths, queen beds, tennis court, and pool. Condos and river cabins for smokers and children. Friendly, personal service.

COFFEE SWIRL YOGURT CAKE

2 cups sifted flour
1/2 teaspoon salt
1/4 teaspoon baking soda
1/4 teaspoon baking powder
1 stick butter, room temperature

1 1/4 cups sugar
1 teaspoon vanilla
3 eggs
1 cup plain yogurt
1/4 cup powdered instant coffee (any flavor- Dutch mint, Hazelnut, Mocha, etc.)

Preheat oven to 350°. Grease loaf pan. Combine dry ingredients in large bowl. Beat butter, sugar and vanilla until fluffy. Add eggs one at a time, beating after each addition. Beat in flour mixture and yogurt alternately. Remove 1 cup of batter and add instant coffee, mixing well. Pour half the plain batter into pan. Drop spoonfuls of coffee batter on top. Add remaining plain batter and swirl with a spoon handle. Bake until toothpick comes out clean, about 1 1/4 hours. Makes 12 servings.

Submitted by:

Sundial Inn
48 Beach Ave.-P.O. Box 1147
Kennebunk Beach, Maine
 04043
(207) 967-3850
Kenny Family
$60.00 to $140.00

Continental plus breakfast
34 rooms, 34 private baths
Children, over 13
No pets
Restricted smoking
Mastercard, Visa, Am Ex

Oceanfront inn offers quiet setting with beach access. Cable TV, a/c, designer linens, antiques, some ocean views, whirlpool tubs. Dining room overlooks ocean. Living room with chintz-covered sofas, wicker furniture & fireplace. Elevator & h/c accessible. Large porch overlooking the ocean. Near many attractions.

COUNTRY CHOCOLATE CAKE

1 cup sugar	1/4 teaspoon red food
1 1/2 cups flour	coloring
Dash of salt	1 teaspoon baking soda
5 tablespoons cocoa	1/4 cup salad oil
1 tablespoon vinegar	1 1/2 teaspoons vanilla
	1 cup cold water

Mix all ingredients together until smooth. Bake in ungreased 8" pan at 350° for 35 minutes. Enjoy warm with ice cream to top it off! Makes 12 servings.

Submitted by:

Jefferson Inn	Full breakfast
Route 171	6 rooms, 3 private baths
Thompson, Penn. 18465	Children allowed
(717) 727-2625	Pets allowed
Doug & Marge Stark	Restricted smoking
$25.00 to $50.00	Mastercard & Visa

Situated in the rolling hills of Northeast Pennsylvania, our 1871 inn offers uniquely decorated rooms and a warm atmosphere. Near fishing, boating, skiing, snowmobiling, horseback riding, golfing, and deer and turkey hunting.

COUSIN MARY'S SOUR CREAM COFFEE CAKE

1 cup butter
2 cups sugar
2 eggs
1 cup sour cream
1/2 teaspoon vanilla
   extract
2 cups flour
1/4 teaspoon salt

1 1/2 teaspoons baking
   powder
2 tablespoons brown
   sugar
1/2 cup chopped walnuts
   or pecans
1 teaspoon cinnamon

Preheat oven to 350°. Cream butter and sugar Add eggs and mix until light and fluffy. Fold in sour cream and vanilla. Fold in flour, salt, and baking powder. Pour half of the batter into greased bundt or angel food cake pan. Mix brown sugar, nuts and cinnamon. Sprinkle half of this mixture over batter. Add remaining batter, and sprinkle again with brown sugar mixture. Bake for 50 minutes. Serves 12.

Submitted by:

Thatcher Brook Inn
P.O. Box 490, Rt. 100 North
Waterbury, Vermont 05676
(800) 292-5911
Kelly & Peter Varty
$75.00 to $160.00

Full breakfast
24 rooms, 24 private baths
Children allowed
No pets
Restricted smoking
Mastercard, Visa, Am Ex

A full-service country inn listed in Vermont Register of Historic Buildings. Guestrooms decorated in a Laura Ashley-style. Some fireplaces and whirlpool tubs. Restaurant features country French cuisine, served in 4 candlelit dining rooms, one designated "couples only" - romantic!

CRANBERRY COFFEE CAKE

1/2 cup butter
1 cup sugar
2 eggs
1 teaspoon baking
   powder
1 teaspoon baking soda
1/4 teaspoon salt

2 cups flour
1 teaspoon almond
   extract
1 cup dairy sour cream
1/2 can (8 oz.) cranberry
   sauce
1/2 cup chopped walnuts

Cream butter and sugar. Add eggs, beat well. Mix dry ingredients, add to creamed mixture. Blend in extract and sour cream. Pour half of the mixture into greased tube pan. Place cranberries and nuts over batter. Repeat layers. Cut through mixture with a knife to swirl. Bake at 350° for 55 - 60 minutes. Makes 9 - 12 servings.

Submitted by:

Custer Mansion B&B
35 Centennial Drive
Custer, S.D. 57730
(605) 673-3333
Mill & Carole Seaman
$45.00 to $75.00

Full breakfast
6 rooms, 2 private baths
Children, over 6
No pets
No smoking

Historic 1891 Victorian home, with individually decorated guest rooms in country charm and Victorian elegance. We specialize in friendship, and clean, comfortable rooms, with delicious home cooking recommended by Bon Appetit.

CREAM CHEESE COFFEE CAKE

Batter:
3 cups flour
1 teaspoon baking powder
1 teaspoon baking soda
1/2 cup butter
1 cup sugar
1 teaspoon vanilla
2 eggs
1 cup plain yogurt

Filling:
2 - 8 oz. pkgs. cream cheese, softened
1/2 cup sugar
1 teaspoon lemon extract

Streusel topping:
1/2 cup brown sugar
1/2 cup flour
3 tablespoons butter

Mix flour, baking powder and baking soda together. Cream butter, sugar, vanilla, and eggs well. Add dry ingredients alternately with yogurt. Spread half of cake batter into greased and floured 9" x 13" pan. Mix all filling ingredients together. Pour filling over cake batter in pan. Cover with remaining half of batter. Mix streusel ingredients until crumbly. Cover top of cake with streusel topping. Bake at 350° for 40 - 45 minutes. Serves 12.

Submitted by:

Abriendo Inn
300 W. Abriendo Avenue
Pueblo, Colorado 81004
(719) 544-2703
Kerrelyn M. Trent

Full breakfast
7 rooms, 7 private baths
Children, over 7
No pets
No smoking
Mastercard, Visa, Am Ex

Outstanding estate home in park-like setting. Unobtrusive antiques abound, and add to the enchanting atmosphere. In-room phones and TV. Walking distance to restaurants, shops & galleries. Minutes from mountains, fishing, rafting, golf, and many other attractions.

CRUMB CAKE

4 cups flour
2 cups sugar
1 teaspoon baking soda
1 teaspoon baking
  powder

1/2 cup margarine or
  lard
Enough milk or juice to
  make correct batter
  consistency

In large bowl mix all ingredients except milk or juice. Add small amount of liquid to enough dry mix to make 2/3 cup of crumbs. Reserve for topping. Mix remainder of liquid into dry ingredients for batter. It should be stiff, but not too dry. Variations: Add your favorite berries, crushed pineapple, etc. Top with crumbs. Bake at 350° for 25 - 30 minutes. Makes 24 muffins or 2 sheet cakes.

Submitted by:

Lamplighter Inn
26 Bradford St.
Provincetown, Mass. 02657
(508) 487-2529
Michael R. Novik
$45.00 - $130.00 (seasonal)

Continental plus breakfast
10 rooms, 8 private baths
Children, over 10
No pets
Smoking allowed
Mastercard, Visa, Am Ex

Charming Greek Revival sea captain's house, commanding spectacular views of Cape Cod Bay and harbor from our choice hilltop location. Stunning gardens, parking, and daily maid service. Walking distance to everything.

DUTCH CHERRY COFFEE CAKE

2 cups canned cherries	3/4 cup sugar
1 1/2 cups sifted flour	2 eggs
1/2 teaspoon salt	1/2 cup milk
3 teaspoons baking powder	1 teaspoon vanilla
	1/2 cup liquid shortening

Drain cherries. Sift flour, salt, baking powder and sugar together. In a blender mix egg, milk, vanilla and shortening. Add to flour mixture and beat until smooth. Fold in cherries. Bake in greased 7" x 11 " x 11 1/2" pan at 350° for 50 minutes.

Submitted by:

Katie's Wild Rose Inn   Full breakfast
E. 5150 Coeur d'Alene   4 rooms, 2 private baths
  Lake Drive   No children
Coeur d'Alene, Idaho 83814   No pets
(208) 765-9474   No smoking
Lee & Joisse Knowles   Mastercard & Visa
$65.00 to $85.00

Coeur d'Alene is the Las Vegas of the north, and many people come here to be married. We cater to newlyweds. Cozy rooms, near swimming, tennis courts, hiking trails, and downtown shopping.

EARLY BIRD COFFEE CAKE

1 1/4 cups flour	1/4 teaspoon cinnamon
1/4 teaspoon salt	1/4 teaspoon nutmeg
1 teaspoon baking powder	1 cup brown sugar
	1/3 cup shortening
1/4 teaspoon baking soda	1/2 cup sour milk
	1 egg

Sift dry ingredients together, cut in brown sugar and shortening. Reserve 1/2 cup. Add milk and egg, mix well. Pour into greased 8" pan. Sprinkle on reserved topping. Bake at 350° for about 25 minutes, until golden, and toothpick inserted in center comes out clean.

Submitted by:

Battle Island Inn   Full breakfast
R.D. #1, Box 176   6 rooms, 6 private baths
Fulton, New York 13069   Children allowed
(315) 593-3699   No pets
Richard & Joyce Rice   No smoking
$50.00 to $80.00   Mastercard, Visa, Am Ex, Disc.

Battle Island Inn, circa 1840, is located across from the Oswego River just 7 miles from historic Oswego on Lake Ontario. The inn is furnished with period antiques throughout and a full breakfast is served in our elegant Empire dining room.

EASY MORNING COFFEE KUCHEN

1 egg	1 can pie filling (any
Milk	flavor)
2 cups flour	
1 stick margarine,	Topping:
softened	1 cup flour
2 teaspoons baking	1 stick margarine,
powder	softened
1/2 cup sugar	1/2 cup sugar

Beat egg well, add enough milk to egg to make 1 cup liquid. Add flour, margarine, baking powder and sugar to egg, and mix well. Spread in greased and floured 9" x 13" pan. Spread pie filling on top of batter. Mix topping until it forms small balls. It's best to swirl mixture in the bottom of a large pan. These balls are called "rivels" by our German ancestors. Spread the "rivels" on top of the pie filling and bake for 30 minutes at 400°. Makes 12 servings.

Submitted by:

Thistle Hill Bed & Breakfast   Full breakfast
Route 1, Box 93   4 rooms, 2 private baths
WaKeeney, Kansas 67672   Children allowed
(913) 743-2644   No pets
Dave & Mary Hendricks   Restricted smoking
$40.00 to $50.00

Comfortable, secluded, cedar farm home halfway between Kansas City & Denver along I-70. Experience farm life & visit Castle Rock. Self-guided prairie wildflower walks in our 60 acre prairie restoration project. Hearty country breakfast by the fireplace or on the summer porch overlooking the herb garden.

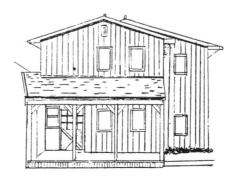

GINA'S ITALIAN CAKE

5 eggs
2 cups sugar
1 cup milk
1/2 cup oil
1/4 cup lemon juice
  (1 small lemon)

4 teaspoons baking
  powder
4 1/2 cups flour
1/2 cup raisins
1/2 cup chopped nuts
1/2 cup chocolate chips

Butter and flour large bundt pan. Mix eggs and sugar. Add milk, oil, lemon juice. In separate dish, add baking powder to flour and mix well. Add to liquid ingredients. Mix well. Add raisins, nuts, and optional chocolate chips and mix again. Bake at 350° for 20 minutes. Reduce heat to 300° and continue baking for another 30 minutes.

Submitted by:

The Arroyo Village Inn
407 El Camino Real
Arroyo Grande, California
  93420
(805) 489-5926
John & Gina Glass
$95.00 to $165.00

Full breakfast
7 rooms, 7 private baths
Children, over 10
No pets
No smoking
Mastercard, Visa, Am Ex,
  Discover

We offer a delightful blend of yesterday's charm & hospitality with today's comforts & conveniences. Country Victorian is furnished with Laura Ashley prints and special touches making each guest feel at home: beautiful antiques, window seats, balconies & skylights. Near Hearst Castle, San Luis Obispo, spas, wineries and beaches.

HEATH BRUNCH COFFEE CAKE

1/4 lb. butter
2 cups flour
1 cup brown sugar
1/2 cup white sugar

1 cup buttermilk
1 teaspoon baking soda
1 egg
1 teaspoon vanilla

Topping:
1 1/2 cups crushed
Heath English Toffee
candy bars

1/4 cup chopped pecans
or almonds

Blend butter, flour, and sugars until crumbly. Reserve 1/2 cup of mixture for topping. Add buttermilk, soda, egg and vanilla to remainder of dry ingredients. Blend well. Pour into greased and floured 10" x 10" x 2" cake pan. Mix candy bar and nuts with 1/2 cup of reserved topping. Sprinkle over the top of batter and bake at 350° for 30 - 40 minutes. Enjoy! Makes 16 pieces.

Submitted by:

The Chichester-McKee House
800 Spring St.
Placerville, Calif. 95667-4424
(916) 626-1882
(800) 831-4008
Doreen & Bill Thornhill
$75.00 to $80.00 (double)

Full breakfast
3 rooms, 3 private half baths
Children allowed
No pets
Restricted smoking
Mastercard, Visa,
Discover

Elegant Victorian built by lumber baron D.W. Chichester. Fireplaces, fretwork, stained glass, antiques and relaxing hospitality. Robes, a/c, near Apple Hill & Gold Discovery site. "The Finest" 1892-1992.

MARJE'S QUICK COFFEECAKE

1 box sour cream
   cake mix

2 teaspoons cinnamon

Topping:
1/2 cup flour
1/3 cup sugar

Cinnamon to taste
1/3 stick butter

Add 2 teaspoons cinnamon to dry cake mix. Follow directions for making mix on box. Put in well-greased 9" x 13" pan. Mix flour, sugar and cinnamon. Cut in butter until consistency of large peas. Sprinkle on top of batter, and bake at 350° for 25 - 30 minutes. Makes 12 - 15 servings.

Submitted by:

Harding House
  Bed & Breakfast
219 North 20th Street
St. Joseph, Missouri 64501
(816) 232-7020
Glen & Mary Harding
$30.00 to $55.00

Full breakfast
4 rooms, 1 private bath
Children allowed
No pets
Restricted smoking
Mastercard, Visa, Am Ex
  Discover

A renovated turn of the century home, with elegant oak woodwork and pocket doors, beveled glass windows and antiques collected for 40 years. Each bedroom is unique: the Blue Room has an iron baby bed; the Eastlake Room has a romantic working fireplace & queen size bed.

PENNSYLVANIA DUTCH CRUMB COFFEE CAKE

4 cups unsifted flour
1 teaspoon baking powder
2/3 cup shortening
1/2 teaspoon salt
2 1/2 cups granulated sugar

2 eggs, prebeaten
1 1/2 cups buttermilk
1 teaspoon baking soda
1 cup brown sugar
1/2 cup coconut
1 teaspoon cinnamon

Blend first five ingredients together, and set aside one cup of this mixture as a topping base for use later. In separate bowl, mix the eggs, buttermilk and baking soda together. Then blend the remaining portion of the original crumb mixture, stirring thoroughly. There will be some small lumps in batter. Add 1 cup brown sugar, 1/2 cup coconut and 1 teaspoon cinnamon to the cup of original crumb topping mixture set aside earlier. Pour coffee cake batter mixture into 3 greased and floured 8" cake pans. Sprinkle topping equally on top of batter in all 3 pans. Bake at 350° for 35 minutes.

Submitted by:

Bechtel Mansion Inn
400 W. King Street
East Berlin, Penn. 17316
(800) 331-1108
Ruth Spangler, Charles &
  Mariam Bechtel
$80.00 to $130.00

Full breakfast
8 rooms, 8 private baths
Children allowed
No pets
Restricted smoking
Mastercard, Visa, Am Ex,
  Discover

Romantic, restored Queen Anne style mansion in Pennsylvania Dutch country, on the National Register. Air-conditioned & tastefully furnished with quality antiques, porcelains, oriental carpets & lace curtains. Popular with history & architecture buffs & honeymooners.

PINEAPPLE CAKE

1 1/2 cups sugar
2 eggs
2 cups flour
1 teaspoon soda
1/2 teaspoon salt
20 oz. can crushed
   pineapple, undrained

Topping:

1/2 cup brown sugar
1/2 cup crushed
   pecans

Mix all ingredients together. Pour into greased 9" x 13" pan. Sprinkle brown sugar and pecans on top. Bake 25 - 35 minutes in 350° oven. It's simple, but so tasty! Makes 10 - 12 large servings.

Submitted by:

Cliff House B&B
122 Fairmount Drive
Madison, Indiana 47250
(812) 265-5272
Jae Breitweiser
$50.00 to $75.00

Continental plus breakfast
6 rooms, 6 private baths
Children allowed
No pets
Restricted smoking
Mastercard & Visa

1885 Victorian overlooking Ohio River, candlelight breakfast on Haviland china. Rooms decorated with authentic antiques, including canopy beds. Near historic museums, antique shops, specialty shops, state parks, tennis, golfing, fishing, and swimming. Handicapped facilities.

SHOO FLY COFFEE CAKE

4 cups flour	1 tablespoon baking
2 cups sugar	soda
1 teaspoon salt	1/2 cup flour
1 cup Crisco shortening	1/2 cup sugar
2 cups warm water	1/2 stick margarine
1 cup baking molasses	1 teaspoon cinnamon

Blend first four ingredients until crumbly. Take out one cup of crumbs and set aside. In large bowl mix water, molasses and baking soda. Pour over flour mixture. Stir until blended. Pour into greased and floured 9" x 15" cake pan. Mix the cup of crumbs with flour, sugar, margarine, and cinnamon. Sprinkle atop batter. Bake at 350° for 50 - 60 minutes. Test by inserting toothpick in center, it should come out clean when cake is done. Makes 15 servings.

Submitted by:

National Pike Inn	Full breakfast
9 W. Main St., P.O. Box 299	4 rooms, 2 private baths
New Market, Maryland 21774	Children, over 10
(301) 865-5055	No pets
Tom & Terry Rimel	No smoking
$55.00 to $125.00	Mastercard & Visa

Federal 1796 - 1804, a/c, guest rooms each decorated in different theme. Large Federal sitting room, private enclosed courtyard, Colonial dining room. Historic area with antique shops and fine dining a few steps away. Create your "New Market Memory!"

STRAWBERRY BUNDT CAKE

3 cups flour
3 teaspoons baking powder
1 teaspoon salt
4 eggs
2 cups sugar
1 cup oil

1/2 cup orange juice
1 teaspoon almond extract
2 cups sliced strawberries
Cinnamon-sugar mixture

Preheat oven to 350°. Beat all ingredients except strawberries and cinnamon-sugar together in bowl. Place half of batter in well-greased and floured bundt pan. Sprinkle strawberries on batter. Top with other half of batter. Place a sprinkle of cinnamon-sugar on top. Bake for approximately 1 hour until toothpick tester comes out clean.

Submitted by:

Greenbriar Inn
315 Wallace
Coeur d'Alene, Idaho 83814
(208) 667-9660
Kris McIlvenna
$55.00 to $85.00

Full breakfast (gourmet)
9 rooms, 7 private baths
Children, over 3
No pets
No smoking
Mastercard, Visa, Am Ex, Disc.

Built in 1908, the city's only nationally registered inn. 4 blocks from downtown and 5 blocks from the lake, the inn reflects the residential charm of years gone by. 40' high maples, outdoor spa, afternoon refreshments, and a famous 4-course breakfast in the morning!

STRAWBERRY RHUBARB COFFEE CAKE

Filling:
4 1/2 cups chopped
  rhubarb
24 oz. frozen, sliced
  strawberries, thawed
3 tablespoons lemon
  juice
1 1/2 cups sugar
1/2 cup cornstarch

Topping:
3/4 cup sugar
1/2 cup flour

Cake:
3 cups flour
1 cup sugar
1 teaspoon baking
  powder
1 teaspoon salt
1 cup softened butter
1 cup buttermilk
2 eggs, slightly beaten
1 teaspoon vanilla

1/4 cup softened
  butter

For filling: Combine rhubarb and strawberries in saucepan and cook, covered, over medium heat 5 minutes, stirring occasionally. Add lemon juice, sugar and cornstarch. Cook, stirring, for 5 minutes or until thickened. Cool. For cake batter: Combine dry ingredients in large bowl. Cut butter into flour mixture until crumbly. Beat together buttermilk, eggs, and vanilla, add to flour mixture. Spread half of batter in greased 9" x 13" baking pan. Spread fruit over batter. Spoon remaining batter in small mounds on top of filling. Mix topping ingredients until crumbly. Sprinkle over top of cake. Bake at 375° for 45 minutes. Serve slightly warm. Yields 12 - 16 servings.

Submitted by:

Swiss Woods B&B
500 Blantz Road
Lititz, Pennsylvania 17543
(717) 627-3358 or
(800) 594-8018
Debrah & Werner Mosimann
$66.00 to $105.00

Full breakfast
7 rooms, 7 private baths
Children allowed
No pets
No smoking
Mastercard & Visa

Overlooks Speedwell Fordge Lake, in Pennsylvania Dutch country. Flowering perennials and annuals, sandstone fireplace in living room, with natural woodwork, and sunny windows. Queen beds, patios or balconies. Great view, refreshing quiet, and a touch of the continent.

SUEÑOS PEAR GINGER UPSIDE DOWN CAKE

1/2 cup butter	1 cup boiling coffee
1 cup brown sugar	2 cups sifted flour
4 - 5 sliced or halved	3/4 teaspoon ginger
pears (fresh or canned)	1/4 teaspoon nutmeg
1 cup molasses	1/4 teaspoon
1/2 cup sugar	allspice
1/2 cup shortening	1 teaspoon salt
1 teaspoon soda	1 egg

In 10" iron skillet, melt butter and add brown sugar, stirring until well blended. Turn off heat and arrange the pears in the skillet. In bowl combine molasses, sugar and shortening. Mix well. Dissolve the soda in boiling coffee. Add to molasses mixture. Add flour, ginger, nutmeg, allspice, and salt. Mix well. Add egg, blend well. Pour over pears in skillet. Bake 35 minutes at 350°. Turn out of pan immediately. Serves 6 - 8.

Submitted by:

Casas de Sueños Old Town	Full breakfast (gourmet)
B&B Inn	12 rooms, 12 private baths
310 Rio Grande Southwest	Children, over 12
Albuquerque, N.M. 87104	No pets
(505) 247-4560	Restricted smoking
Mari Penshurst-Gersten	Mastercard, Visa, Am Ex
$85.00 to $250.00	

World famous architecture combined with Mexican hacienda atmosphere: country gardens, private courtyards, within walking distance of historic Old Town, museums, theatre, zoo, shops, galleries & fine dining. Private casitas were originally occupied by Southwestern artists. Overlooks ACC Golf Course.

"THE SPRINGS" OVERNIGHT COFFEE CAKE

3/4 cup margarine, softened
2 eggs
8 oz. carton sour cream
2 cups plain flour

Topping:
3/4 cup brown sugar, packed
1/2 cup chopped pecans

1 teaspoon baking powder
1 teaspoon baking soda
1/2 teaspoon salt
1 teaspoon ground nutmeg

1 teaspoon ground cinnamon

Combine margarine and sugar, and cream until light and fluffy. Add eggs and sour cream, mixing well. Combine next 5 ingredients. Add to batter & mix well. Pour into greased & floured 9" x 13" x 2" baking pan. For topping: Combine brown sugar, pecans and cinnamon, mixing well. Sprinkle over batter. Cover and chill overnight. Uncover and bake at 350° for 35 minutes. Makes 6 - 8 servings.

Submitted by:

Shenandoah Springs
HC 6, Box 122
Madison, Virginia 22727
(703) 923-4300
Anne & Douglas Farmer
$65.00 to $120.00

Full breakfast
6 rooms, 3 1/2 private baths
Children allowed
No pets
Restricted smoking

Relax on 1,000 acres of forest land, meadows, shady lanes, bridle trails and scenic views. Fishing, canoeing, ice skating on Shenandoah Springs Lake, and cross-country skiing on our trails. Fireplaces, cozy bedrooms, cabins available. Wilderness hideaway!

TRAILBLAZER COFFEE CAKE

1 cup flour
2 teaspoons baking
powder
2 eggs
1/4 teaspoon orange
extract
1 cup sugar

1/2 cup chopped,
toasted pecans
1 cup chopped, peeled
apples
1 cup trail mix (prefer-
ably soft, with coconut,
apricots, banana, etc.)

Combine flour and baking powder. In a separate bowl, beat eggs and orange extract until foamy. Stir in sugar. Add flour mixture, stir until well combined. Stir in nuts, apples, and trail mix. Spread in greased 9" pie or cake pan. Bake at 350° for 40 minutes or until golden and center is firm. Serve warm or cold. Makes 8 servings.

Submitted by:

COLVMNS By the SEA
1513 Beach Drive
Cape May, New Jersey 08204
(609) 884-2228
Barry & Cathy Rein
$105.00 to $165.00

Full breakfast
11 rooms, 11 private baths
Children, over 12
No pets
Restricted smoking

Elegant Victorian mansion on the ocean in landmark village. Large, airy, antique-filled rooms, gourmet breakfast, high tea and evening snacks. Complimentary bikes, beach badges and hot tub. Great for history buffs, birders or just to relax.

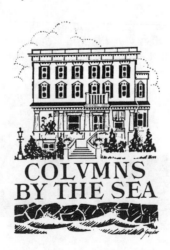

COLVMNS
BY THE SEA

YELLOW COFFEE CAKE

1 Duncan Hines yellow
  cake mix
2 eggs
8 oz. carton sour cream
1/2 cup oil

1/2 cup ginger ale
1/2 cup sugar
2 teaspoons cinnamon
1 cup nuts,
  chopped

Preheat oven to 350°. Place cake mix, eggs, sour cream, oil, and ginger ale in bowl, beat 2 minutes. Fold in sugar, cinnamon, and nuts. Pour into well-greased and floured bundt pan. Bake for 45 minutes - 1 hour. Let cool 20 minutes. Remove from pan.

Submitted by:

Pine Ridge Inn
2893 West Pine St., Hwy. 89
Mount Airy, N.C. 27030
(919) 789-5034
Ellen & Manford Haxton
$60.00 to $100.00

Full/Continental plus breakfast
6 rooms, 6 private baths
Children allowed
No pets
Restricted smoking
Mastercard, Visa, Am Ex

Luxurious living, from picturesque, antique-filled living room to simple comforts of conference nook, original works of art, and fresh flowers or potted plants. Library, indoor hot tub, exercise room with Nautilus equipment, backyard swimming pool, nearby golf course, or stroll 8 acres of rolling hills. Pilot Mtn. views. Gracious hospitality.

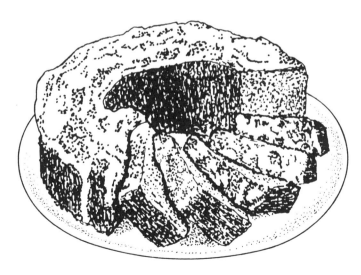

QUICK & YEAST BREADS

APPLE LOAVES

1 stick butter, room
temperature
1/2 cup sugar
4 eggs
1 1/2 - 2 teaspoons
cinnamon
1 teaspoon vanilla

1 box Jello French
Vanilla instant pudding
1 box yellow cake mix
1 cup milk
2 Granny Smith apples,
grated

Preheat oven to 350°. Cream butter and sugar. Add eggs, one at a time, beating after each addition. Add flavorings and pudding. Mix well. Add cake mix, alternating with milk. Mix all ingredients about 1 1/2 minutes. Fold in grated apple very carefully. Pour into 6 greased and floured 3 1/4" x 6 1/4" pans. Or can be baked in greased and floured tube pan. Check loaf pans after 30 minutes. Check tube pan after 50 - 55 minutes. Serve with sour cream. Makes 12 servings.

Submitted by:

The Phoenix' Nest on Amelia
619 S. Fletcher Avenue
Amelia Island, FL 32034
(904) 277-2129
Harriett J. Fortenberry
$65.00 to $85.00

Continental breakfast
4 suites, 4 private baths
Children allowed
No pets
Smoking allowed
Mastercard & Visa

Private, restful, gracious suites that are romantic, interesting and fun. Bedrooms have ocean views ranging from "good" to "grand". 250 year old magazine collection, videos/VCR, surf fishing gear, bikes and boogie boards. Private club tennis, golf and beachfront pool within 5 miles. 45 minutes from Jacksonville.

BANANA NUT BREAD

1/2 cup shortening	1 teaspoon banana
1 cup sugar	extract
2 eggs	1 1/4 cups sifted flour
8 ripe bananas	1/2 teaspoon salt
	1/2 cup walnut pieces

Blend all ingredients in order they are listed. Bake in loaf pan at 350° for 30 - 40 minutes. Test with knife or toothpick. Makes 12 slices.

Submitted by:

The Gables Inn
103 Walker Street
Lenox, Mass. 01240
(413) 637-3416
Mary & Frank Newton
$60.00 to $195.00

Continental plus breakfast
19 rooms, 17 private baths
Children, over 12
No pets
Restricted smoking
Mastercard, Visa, Am Ex

Authoress Edith Wharton's home at turn of the century, built in 1885. Antique period furnishings. Theme rooms and 3 suites, in addition to library and garden. Woodburning fireplaces in 9 of the bedrooms. Breakfast served in warmly appointed dining room overlooking tennis court & pool. Open year round. Low off-season rates.

CARROT-APPLE-PRUNE BREAD

12 eggs, beaten
1 cup oil
5 - 6 cups buttermilk
4 cups applesauce (best if unsweetened)
1 cup sugar
12 - 13 cups whole wheat flour (or your choice)

7 teaspoons baking soda, sifted
6 teaspoons baking powder
6 - 8 cups grated carrot
2 - 3 cups soft prunes (chopped, no pits, best if soaked)
2 cups walnuts (opt.)
Peel of 1 lemon, grated

Mix 12 eggs in 2 gallon size bowl or wok. Add 1 cup oil. Add buttermilk. Add applesauce. Mix well. Add sugar. Gradually mix in flour, baking soda and baking powder. Batter will be thick. Add grated carrot, prunes and walnuts. Add grated lemon peel. Divide into 5 - 6 well buttered and floured medium bread tins. Bake 1 hour at 350°, or until knife comes out clean. Makes 5 - 6 medium size loaves of moist, delicious, not-too-sweet bread!

Submitted by:

Acorn Inn, Inc.
P.O. Box 431
Nellysford, Virginia 22958
(804) 361-9357
Kathy & Martin Versluys
$39.00 to $85.00

Continental plus breakfast
Children allowed
No pets
Restricted smoking
Visa

3 charming options in lodging: cottage with kitchen & bath; renovated horse stable with 10 bedrooms, 4 baths (handicapped accessible), kitchenette, common lounge, Scandinavian soapstone bakeoven & skylights; & 2 bedrooms in farmhouse. Cozy international atmosphere & environmentally friendly approach to life.

CHEDDAR CHEESE & BUTTERMILK BREAD

1 pkg. yeast	1 teaspoon baking
1/4 cup warm (90° - 100°) water	powder
3 1/2 cups bread flour (divided)	1 tablespoon sugar
1 teaspoon salt	1 cup buttermilk
	1 cup grated Cheddar cheese

Dissolve yeast in the water. Add remainder of ingredients except 1/2 cup flour. Mix well. Turn onto surface floured with remaining 1/2 cup flour. Knead 5 minutes. Place into greased bowl. Turn to coat all sides. Let rise approximately 1 hour in a warm place. Punch down. Knead lightly a second time and divide into 2 pieces: one equal to 2/3 of dough and one equal to 1/3 of dough. Grease 1 regular bread pan (9 1/2" x 5") and 1 small bread pan (7 1/2" x 4"). Place dough in pans and let rise to double. Bake in preheated oven at 375°, small loaf for 25 minutes, large loaf for 35 minutes. Note: May brush top of loaves with milk or egg white before baking for a shiny crust.

Submitted by:

The Park House
888 Holland St.
Saugatuck, Michigan 49453
(616) 857-4535 or
(800) 321-4535
Joe & Lynda Petty
$75.00 to $160.00

Continental plus breakfast
9 rooms, 9 private baths
Children allowed
No pets
Restricted smoking
Mastercard, Visa, Discover

City's oldest residence (1857) once hosted Susan B. Anthony. Wide plank pine floors & wraparound porch speak of original owner's VT heritage. Cozy to elegant rooms. Family Loft sleeps 5, Master Suites offer f/p, jet tubs, TV/VCR, breakfast in bed. 4 rooms with balconies & a luxury cottage provide the ultimate in privacy.

CHOCOLATE ZUCCHINI BREAD

3 eggs
3/4 cup vegetable oil
2 cups sugar
2 teaspoons vanilla
2 1/2 cups flour
1 teaspoon salt
1 1/2 teaspoons baking
  soda

1 teaspoon cinnamon
1/2 cup cocoa
1/2 cup milk
2 teaspoons grated
  orange peel
2 cups zucchini
1 cup chopped
  walnuts

Preheat oven to 350°. Beat eggs, oil, sugar and vanilla. Combine dry ingredients. Add milk, fold in orange peel, zucchini and nuts. Bake in 2 greased and floured 5" x 9" loaf pans for 50 minutes. Cool before removing from pans. Makes 8 - 10 servings per loaf.

Submitted by:

The Inn at Blue Stores
Box 99, Star Route
Hudson, New York 12534
(518) 537-4277
Linda Saulpaugh
$95.00 to $150.00

Full breakfast
4 rooms, 4 private baths
Children, over 10
Restricted smoking
Mastercard, Visa, Am Ex

Arts & Craft Mission-style home on 100 acre working farm in the heart of historic Hudson Valley. A relaxing country experience: lounge by the pool, walk through the gardens, or feed the ducks. Afternoon tea and cookies served by the pool or on the expansive porches.

CINNAMON SUGAR BREAD

3/4 cup milk	2 pkgs. yeast
1/4 cup sugar	3 egg yolks, well-beaten
1 1/2 teaspoons salt	4 1/4 cups flour
1 cup margarine	1/2 cup sugar
1/2 cup warm water	2 teaspoons cinnamon
(105° - 115°)	1/4 cup butter, melted

Scald milk. Stir in sugar, salt and 1 cup margarine. Cool to warm. Pour warm water in large bowl. Sprinkle or crumple yeast into water. Stir until dissolved. Add lukewarm milk mixture and beaten egg yolks. Stir until blended. Add flour and beat until well mixed. Cover tightly with foil and refrigerate at least 4 hours or overnight. Combine sugar & cinnamon until well blended. Divide dough in half. Again divide each half into 3 equal pieces. Roll each piece into 18" strand. Braid 3 pieces together and seal ends well. Place on greased baking sheet. Brush with half of melted butter and half of cinnamon-sugar. Repeat with remaining 3 pieces of dough. Cover & let rise in warm place for about an hour, until doubled in size. Bake in 400° oven for 25 - 35 minutes until top is honey brown. Makes 4 - 6 servings per loaf.

Submitted by:

Upper Byrd Farm B&B
6452 River Road West
Columbia, VA 23038
(804) 842-2240
Ivona Kaz-Jepsen &
Maya Laurinaitis
$60.00 to $70.00

Full breakfast
4 rooms, 2 semi-private baths
Children, over 12
No pets
Restricted smoking

Turn-of-the-century farmhouse nestled in the Virginia countryside on 26 acres, overlooking the James River. Visit Ashlawn and Monticello. See the State's capitol, or simply relax by the fire, surrounded by antiques and original art.

DATE NUT BREAD

1 - 8 oz. pkg. dates	2 teaspoons baking
1 cup hot water	powder
3 eggs	1 teaspoon ground
2 cups sugar	cloves
3/4 cup vegetable oil	1 teaspoon allspice
2 cups plain flour	1 teaspoon cinnamon
1/2 teaspoon salt	1 cup chopped nuts

Soak dates in hot water. Meanwhile, beat eggs and add sugar and oil. Stir in dry ingredients and mix lightly. Add nuts, and dates in their soaking water, and mix just to combine. Pour batter into a greased and lined loaf pan. Bake at 325° for one hour, or until toothpick inserted in the center comes out clean.

Submitted by:

Cedar Grove Mansion	Full breakfast
2200 Oak Street	22 rooms, 22 private baths
Vicksburg, Mississippi 39180	Children, over 6
(800) 862-1300	No pets
Ted Mackey	Restricted smoking
$85.00 to $160.00	Mastercard, Visa, Am Ex

1840's mansion, with gaslit chandeliers, Italian marble mantels & gold leaf mirrors. Union cannonball is lodged in parlor wall. Mississippi's finest inn, 4 acres of formal gardens, fountains, gazebos, courtyards, pool, tennis, croquet and spa. Magnificent views, and AAA 4-Diamond rating.

HEART HEALTHY
STRAWBERRY/BLUEBERRY BREAD

1 pint blueberries/
  strawberries combined
1 tablespoon sugar
1 1/2 cups all-purpose
  flour
1 cup packed brown
  sugar
1 1/2 teaspoons
  cinnamon

1/2 teaspoon salt
1 teaspoon baking
  soda
3/4 cup canola oil
4 oz. Egg Beaters or
  egg substitute
3/4 cup chopped
  pecans

Preheat oven to 350°. Grease and flour one 9" x 5" loaf pan. Wash, hull and slice strawberries, mix with blueberries and tablespoon of sugar and set aside. Combine flour, brown sugar, cinnamon, salt and baking soda in large bowl. Stir oil and egg beaters into berry mixture. Mix well. Pour wet into dry ingredients. Stir briefly, add pecans and blend just until moistened. Smooth into prepared pan and bake approximately 45 minutes, or until tester comes out clean. Cool in pan 10 minutes, then turn onto rack and cool completely. Bake the day before for better flavor. Can be prepared and frozen for 1 month.

Submitted by:

Henry Ludlam Inn
Cape May County
1336 Route 47
Woodbine, New Jersey 08270
(609) 861-5847
Ann & Marty Thurlow
$65.00 to $90.00

Full breakfast
5 rooms, 3 private baths
Children, over 12
No pets
No smoking
Mastercard, Visa, Am Ex

Romantic, historic lakeside inn, featuring bedroom fireplaces, featherbeds, and creative breakfasts. Voted "Best of Shore for 1991", AC Magazine.

"HEART-SMART" BANANA BREAD

1 1/2 cups flour	1 teaspoon vanilla
1 teaspoon baking soda	1/2 cup safflower oil
1 cup sugar	1 cup plain nonfat
1/2 teaspoon salt	yogurt
(or less)	1/2 cup raisins
1 1/2 cups mashed	
bananas	(Safflower margarine to
1/2 cup egg substitute	grease baking pan)

Sift together all dry ingredients. Beat bananas, egg substitute, vanilla and oil together and add yogurt. Add raisins to moist ingredients. Pour over dry ingredients, and then use a wire whisk until very smooth. Place in loaf pan greased with safflower margarine. Bake at 350° for one hour. Makes 1 loaf.

Submitted by:

Woodstock Inn B&B
1212 W. Lexington
Independence, Missouri
 64050
(816) 833-2233
Ben & Mona Crosby
$40.00 to $65.00

Full breakfast
11 rooms, 11 private baths
Children allowed
No pets
No smoking
Mastercard, Visa, Am Ex

Renovated 1900's home in the heart of historic city. Near religious and historical sights. All sizes of beds are available.

JOHN'S ZUCCHINI BREAD

3 eggs	1 teaspoon salt
2 cups sugar	1 1/2 teaspoons
2 teaspoons vanilla	cinnamon
2 cups grated zucchini	1/4 teaspoon baking
3 cups flour	powder
2 teaspoons baking	1 cup raisins
soda	1 cup chopped walnuts

Beat first four items until mixed very well. Blend in remaining ingredients. Bake at 325° in 9" x 5" x 3" greased loaf pan for 60 minutes. Makes 2 loaves.

Submitted by:

Camino Hotel B&B	Full breakfast
P.O. Box 1197	10 rooms, 4 private baths
4103 Carson Rd.	Children allowed
Camino, California 95709	No pets
(916) 644-7740	No smoking
Paula Nobert, John Eddy	Mastercard, Visa, Am Ex,
$55.00 to $85.00	Discover

Artfully restored turn of the century loggers barracks in Apple Hill and grape growing region of CA's Gold Country. 45 apple orchards, 13 wineries & 12 Christmas tree farms minutes from Hotel. Restaurant and general store across the street. Gift shoppe. Senior, group & business rates.

LEMON PECAN BREAD

1/3 cup melted & cooled sweet butter
1 cup sugar
3 tablespoons lemon extract
2 extra large eggs
Grated rind of 1 large lemon (reserve juice)

1 1/2 cups sifted all-purpose unbleached flour
1 teaspoon salt
1 teaspoon baking powder
1/2 cup whole milk
1/2 cup chopped pecans

Topping:
Reserved lemon juice from 1 large lemon

1/2 cup+ powdered sugar

Preheat oven to 350°. Butter standard loaf pan, and line bottom only with waxed paper. Mix together first five ingredients. Stir together dry ingredients, then add to sugar/butter mixture, with milk. Carefully fold in pecans. Do not overmix. Pour into pan. Bake 50 - 55 minutes. Combine juice from lemon and approximately 1/2 cup powdered sugar. After removing loaf from pan, pour this mixture slowly over bread until all of the liquid is soaked into bread. Wrap overnight in plastic wrap. Makes 12 - 15 servings.

Submitted by:

Victorian Inn on the Park
301 Lyon Street
San Francisco, Calif. 94117
(415) 931-1830 or
(800) 435-1967
Lisa & William Benau
$88.00 to $144.00

Continental plus breakfast
12 rooms, 12 private baths
Children allowed
No pets
Restricted smoking
Mastercard, Visa, Am Ex
Discover, Diners

1897 Queen Anne Victorian restored to original splendor, adjacent to Golden Gate Park, a jogger's paradise. Belvedere Room has marble fireplace, balcony overlooking the park, and antique stained glass French doors leading to Roman tub for two. Family-owned and operated; each guest is personally welcomed.

LEMON YOGURT BREAD

3 cups flour	3 eggs
1 teaspoon salt	1 cup oil
1 teaspoon baking soda	1 cup sugar
1/2 teaspoon baking powder	2 cups lemon yogurt
1 cup poppy seeds	2 tablespoons fresh lemon juice

Sift first four ingredients, stir in seeds. Beat eggs in large bowl, add oil, sugar, lemon yogurt and lemon juice, and mix well. Add to dry ingredients. Spoon into 2 greased loaf pans, or 1 large bundt pan. Bake at 325° for one hour.

Submitted by:

The Wedgwood House
111 W. Bridge Street
New Hope, Penn. 18938
(215) 862-2570
Nadine Silnutzer &
  Carl Glassman
$60.00 to $150.00

Continental plus breakfast
6 rooms, 4 private baths
Children allowed
No pets
No smoking
Am Ex

Vintage village Victorian, circa 1870, is a "Painted Lady" with 5 shades of blue and white exterior paints. 3 Diamond, AAA approved and rated "Excellent" by the AB&BA, inn features wraparound verandah, and 2 gazebos on 2 tree-shaded acres of grounds. Yet only 2 blocks from thriving art colony of New Hope.

MOM'S CARROT TEA BREAD

2 cups sugar
3/4 cup vegetable oil
4 eggs, unbeaten
2 cups flour
2 teaspoons baking powder

1 1/2 teaspoons baking soda
1 teaspoon salt
2 teaspoons cinnamon
3 cups raw grated carrot

Carrot Bread Icing:
1/2 cup soft butter
8 oz. soft cream cheese

1 lb. box confectioners sugar
1 teaspoon vanilla
1 cup chopped pecans

Cream sugar and oil until fluffy. Add eggs and beat well. Sift together flour, baking powder, baking soda, salt and cinnamon. Add dry ingredients to creamed mixture. Fold in grated carrots. Bake in large oiled and floured loaf pan at 300° for 50 - 55 minutes. Cool bread. Icing: Beat butter and cream cheese together until light (soft). Gradually add sugar, mix well. Add vanilla and nuts. Frost the cooled bread loaf.

Submitted by:

Century House
10 Cliff Road
Nantucket Island, Mass.
  02554
(508) 228-0530
Gerry Connick &
  Jean E. Heron
$65.00 to $145.00

Continental plus breakfast
10 rooms, 8 private baths
Children allowed
No pets
Restricted smoking

Originally opened in 1833, we offer authentically restored, beautifully appointed rooms. In the residential Historic District, near beaches, restaurants, galleries, theatre, bicycle rentals and tennis facilities.

ORANGE BREAD

2 oranges	2 tablespoons melted
1/3 cup water	butter
1 cup sugar	1/2 teaspoon salt
1 cup milk	4 teaspoons baking
1 beaten egg	powder
	2 1/2 scant cups flour

Cook peel of 2 oranges until tender. Pour off water, cut into thin slices, add water and sugar. Cook until it becomes a thick syrup. Cool. Add milk, egg, and butter. Mix and add salt, baking powder and flour. Stir gently until mixed. Put in loaf pan and bake at 325° for one hour. Makes 1 loaf.

Submitted by:

Log Castle Bed & Breakfast	Full breakfast
3273 E. Saratoga Road	4 rooms, 4 private baths
Langley, Washington 98260	Children, over 10
(206) 221-5483	No pets
Senator Jack & Norma Metcalf	No smoking
$80.00 to $100.00	Mastercard, Visa, Discover

Log lodge on a private secluded beach on Whidbey Island. Turret bedrooms, wood stoves, magnificent view. Peaceful and serene with sounds of gulls and the sea.

ORANGE NUT BREAD

3/4 cup sugar
2 tablespoons soft
  shortening
1 egg
3/4 cup milk

3/4 cup strong orange
  juice (use frozen)
3 cups flour
3 1/2 teaspoons baking
  powder
3/4 cup chopped nuts

Mix sugar, shortening and egg thoroughly. Dilute frozen orange juice with only one can of water, so that juice is very strong. Stir in milk and orange juice. Blend dry ingredients, stir in. Add nuts. Bake at 350° in 9" x 5" x 3" greased loaf pan for 60 - 70 minutes.

Submitted by:

Harrison House
124 W. Harrison
Guthrie, Oklahoma 73044
(405) 282-1000
Phyllis Murray/Claude & Jane
  Thomas, owners
$52.00 to $102.00

Continental plus breakfast
35 rooms, 35 private baths
Children allowed
Restricted smoking
Mastercard, Visa, Am Ex,
  Discover

5 buildings, all on National Register of Historic Places, with 6 retail shops, an elegant restaurant, and conference rooms for up to 425 persons. The complex has elevators and some rooms which are fully physically challenging. Easy access to live theatre, museums and historic touring.

PEAR-PECAN BREAD

1 cup sugar	1/2 teaspoon cinnamon
1/2 cup Crisco oil	1/2 teaspoon freshly
2 eggs	grated nutmeg
1/4 cup sour cream	1 1/2 cups chopped,
1 teaspoon vanilla	peeled pears
2 cups all-purpose flour	1/2 cup chopped pecans
1 teaspoon baking soda	1/2 teaspoon grated
1/2 teaspoon salt	lemon peel

Grease and flour 9" x 5" loaf pan. Combine sugar and oil in large bowl, and beat with electric mixer at medium speed well for 3 minutes. Add eggs, one at a time, beating well after each addition. Mix in sour cream and vanilla. Sift dry ingredients and add to sour cream mixture. Stir in pears, nuts and peel. Spoon into prepared pan. Bake at 350° for 1 hour and 5 - 10 minutes or until tester inserted in center comes out clean. Cool in pan 10 - 15 minutes. Turn out on rack to cool completely. Freezes well. Makes 1 loaf.

Submitted by:

Applewood Manor	Full breakfast (gourmet)
62 Cumberland Circle	5 rooms, 5 private baths
Asheville, N.C. 28801	Children, over 12
(704) 254-2244	No pets
Susan Poole &	No smoking
Maryanne Young	Mastercard, Visa,
$75.00 to $100.00	Discover

Fine Colonial Revival style home on 2 secluded acres in Historic District. Antiques & collectibles, queen size beds, fireplaces, & balconies. Afternoon tea served on side porch in spring & summer, or by fireside in autumn & winter. Badminton, bicycles, and croquet.

PISTACHIO BREAD

1 Duncan Hines butter
cake mix
4 oz. pkg. instant
pistachio pudding
8 oz. sour cream
4 eggs

1/4 cup water
1/4 cup oil

Topping:
4 tablespoons sugar
2 tablespoons cinnamon

Mix all ingredients together. Pour half of batter into 2 greased loaf pans. Sprinkle with half of the topping, then spread remainder of batter. Finish with remainder of topping. Bake at 350° about 1 hour. Makes 2 loaves.

Submitted by:

Stonewood Haus
Box 10201
Green Bay, Wisconsin 54155
(414) 499-3786
JoAnn Naumann King
$59.00 to $89.00

Full/Continental plus breakfast
5 rooms, 2 private baths
Children, over 12
No pets
No smoking
Mastercard, Visa, Discover

Tranquility nestled on a hillside in 9 wooded acres. Spectacular views, creek, rock garden, decks, patio, wild animals to entertain you, fireplaces, a/c, cozy rooms, modern features with Old World charm. Hospitality - your comfort is my priority. Many sports adjacent to inn.

PORTUGUESE SWEETBREAD

2 pkgs. active dry yeast	2 teaspoons salt
3/4 cup warm water	6 eggs
1 cup warm milk	2 cups sugar
1/2 cup butter or	8 cups all-purpose
margarine	flour

Sprinkle yeast into water in large bowl. Mix milk, butter and salt; add to yeast mixture. Beat eggs and sugar until light and add to mixture. Gradually add 3 cups flour (enough so dough is workable). Place dough on lightly floured board and knead about 10 minutes or until dough is smooth and elastic. Place in lightly greased bowl and let rise for about 1 hour (until doubled in size). Punch down and let rest for 10 minutes. Divide dough into 4 greased loaf pans. Cover and let rise in warm place for another hour. Preheat oven to 375°. Bake for approximately 30 minutes or until well-browned. Brush with butter while still hot. Let cool. Makes 4 loaves.

Submitted by:

Kilauea Lodge	Full breakfast
P.O. Box 116	12 rooms, 12 private baths
Volcano, Hawaii 96785	Children allowed
(808) 967-7366	No pets
Albert & Lorna Jeyte	Restricted smoking
$85.00 to $105.00	Mastercard & Visa

Mountain lodge nestled among giant pines in Volcano Village. 1 mile from Volcanoes National Park. Fireplaces, hearty breakfast. Full-service restaurant features continental cuisine. Dinners alongside historic fireplace of friendship. Perfect base to explore volcano area.

PUMPKIN BREAD

3 1/3 cups flour	1 teaspoon nutmeg
3 cups sugar	4 eggs
1 1/2 teaspoons baking soda	14 oz. can pumpkin
1 teaspoon cinnamon	1 cup salad oil

Mix all dry ingredients with liquid. Pour into 2 greased and floured loaf pans. Bake at 350° for 1 1/2 hours. Makes 2 delicious loaves!

Submitted by:

Ski Inn
Route 108
Stowe, Vermont 05672
(802) 253-4050
Mrs. Larry Heyer
$40.00 to $50.00

Continental breakfast   (Full
 breakfast & dinner/ski seas.)
10 rooms, 5 private baths
Children allowed
No pets
Smoking allowed
Am Ex

Traditionally old New England inn in appearance, but comfortably modern. Located back from the highway among the evergreens, it's a quiet place to relax and enjoy. In winter, a skier's delight, close to Mt. Mansfield's downhill trails. Miles of cross country trails at our back door.

SALLY'S HAWAIIAN BREAD

1 cup vegetable oil	1 teaspoon cinnamon
2 cups sugar	2 teaspoons vanilla
3 eggs	1 cup crushed pine-
2 1/2 cups flour	apple, drained
1 teaspoon salt	1 cup grated coconut
1 teaspoon baking soda	2 cups raw grated carrots

Cream oil, sugar and eggs until light. Sift together flour, salt, soda and cinnamon. Add to creamed mixture. Gently fold in vanilla, pineapple, coconut, and carrots. Divide batter between 2 well-greased 9" x 5" x 3" loaf pans. Let batter rest 20 minutes. Then bake in 350° oven for 60 minutes. It's a winner!

Submitted by:

Silver Rose Inn	Continental plus,
351 Rosedale Rd.	California breakfast
Calistoga, California 94515	No children
(707) 942-9581	No pets
Sally & J-Paul Dumont	No smoking
$110.00 to $185.00	Mastercard, Visa, Discover

Experience quiet elegance on country estate situated on beautifully landscaped knoll in Napa Valley with outstanding views. Spacious home on 23 acres. Explore our different environments, terrace, patio, pool & deck areas, outside jacuzzi, rose gardens and gazebo.

SUNFLOWER SEED BREAD

1 1/4 cups lukewarm
  water
1 pkg. active dry yeast
2 tablespoons sugar
1/4 cup maple syrup
  or honey
1/2 cup buttermilk
1/4 cup vegetable oil

1 teaspoon salt
2 cups whole wheat
  flour
2 cups unbleached all-
  purpose flour
1 cup toasted sunflower
  seeds

Preheat oven to 375°. In large mixer bowl, combine water, yeast, and sugar; let stand for 10 minutes. Stir in maple syrup, buttermilk, oil, and salt. Add flours and sunflower seeds, combine well. Mixture will be sticky & moist. Cover with tea towel and let rise in warm place for 1 hour. Punch down and turn dough onto floured surface. Knead for 10 minutes. Form into ball. Oil bowl and the top of dough. Return dough to bowl, cover with a tea towel, and let rise again for 30 - 45 minutes. Punch down and divide dough into 2 equal parts, form into loaves, place in 2 - 8 3/4" x 4 3/4" greased bread pans. Cover with tea towel and let rise for 45 minutes. Bake for about 30 minutes, or until they sound hollow when tapped and crusts are a deep golden brown. Let stand for 5 minutes, then tip onto a rack to cool.

Submitted by:

The Columbus Inn
445 Fifth Street
Columbus, Indiana 47201
(812) 378-4289
Paul A. Staublin
$79.00 to $225.00

Full breakfast
34 rooms, 35 private baths
Children allowed
No pets (can be arranged)
Restricted smoking
Mastercard, Visa, Am Ex, Disc.

History, hospitality & comfort in former 1895 city hall. Victorian elegance with ornate woodwork, elaborate tin ceilings & ornamental tile. Attention to detail expected in a premier hotel, with intimate atmosphere - feel like a V.I.P. Only AAA 4-Diamond B&B in the Midwest.

SWEDISH RYE BREAD

4 cups rye flour	1 cup sugar
1 cup all-purpose flour	1 cup molasses
2 tablespoons salt	1/2 cup shortening
1 quart buttermilk	1 tablespoon caraway
(or water)	seed (opt.)
1 pint potato water	1/2 cup orange peel,
2 mashed potatoes	cut finely (opt.)
2 cakes of yeast	11 - 12 cups flour

Mix first 2 flours, salt, buttermilk or water, potato water, potatoes, and yeast. Let rise to double in size. Boil together sugar, molasses, shortening, caraway seed and orange peel. Cool and put into bread mixture. Work in 11 or 12 cups white flour to make a dough that does not stick to board or hands. Form into 4 large or 6 medium size loaves. Let rise to double in size. Bake at 375° for one hour. Makes 4 - 6 loaves.

Submitted by:

Swedish Country Inn
112 W. Lincoln
Lindsborg, Kansas 67456
(913) 227-2985
Virginia Brunsell
$45.00 to $70.00

Full breakfast
19 rooms, 19 private baths
Children allowed
No pets
No smoking
Mastercard & Visa

Inn is furnished with Swedish pine furniture. All but four beds have handmade quilts. Each room has TV and telephone. Sauna for guests, as well as tandem and regular bicycles. Buffet Scandinavian breakfast. Walking distance to shops and galleries.

UMPLEBY HOUSE DATE NUT BREAD

1 cup chopped dates	2 eggs
2 teaspoons baking soda	4 cups sifted flour
2 cups boiling water	1 teaspoon salt
2 tablespoons butter	2 teaspoons vanilla
1 cup brown sugar,	extract
packed	1 1/2 cups chopped
1 cup granulated sugar	nuts

Combine dates, baking soda and boiling water, let cool. In large bowl cream together butter, sugars, and eggs. Add flour and salt. Add date mixture, vanilla and nuts. Bake in 350° oven for one hour. Makes 3 - 3" x 7" loaves. This bread is wonderful served with whipped cream cheese!

Submitted by:

Umpleby House
117 W. Bridge Street
New Hope, Pennsylvania
 18938
(215) 862-3936
Tracey Wentzel/Kirk
 Fredendall
$70.00 to $150.00

Continental plus breakfast
6 rooms, 6 private baths
Children allowed
No pets
No smoking
Am Ex
Owners: Carl Glassman/
 Nadine Silnutzer

Handsome Classic Revival stone manor house, circa 1833, offering lodging since 1985. In Historic District, 3-Diamond AAA rated, 26" thick stone walls, wide pine floors and brick paths through flowering gardens. Member: Wedgwood Collection of Inns.

WHOLE WHEAT WILD MAINE BLUEBERRY BREAD

3/4 cup butter
1 1/2 cups sugar
3 eggs
1 1/2 teaspoons vanilla
2 cups unbleached white flour
1 cup whole wheat flour
1 1/2 teaspoons baking powder
1 1/2 teaspoons baking soda
1/4 teaspoon salt
1 1/2 cups sour cream
15 oz. can wild Maine blueberries (drained)

Combine butter, sugar, eggs, and vanilla. Beat with electric mixer at medium speed for 2 minutes. Separately combine dry ingredients. Add flour mixture and sour cream alternately to butter mixture. Stir in blueberries. Grease 2 - 8 1/2" x 4 1/2" x 2 3/4" pans. Bake at 350° for 55 - 60 minutes or until cake tester comes out clean. Cool 5 minutes before removing from pan. Makes 2 loaves.

Submitted by:

Silver Maple Lodge/Cottages
S. Main St., R.R. #1, Box 8
Fairlee, Vermont 05045
(802) 333-4326 or
(800) 666-1946
Scott & Sharon Wright
$44.00 to $64.00

Continental breakfast
14 rooms, 12 private baths
Children allowed
Pets allowed
Restricted smoking
Mastercard, Visa, Am Ex, Discover

Historic B&B country inn located in scenic 4-season recreational area. Enjoy boating, fishing, bicycling, golfing, canoeing, hiking, tennis & hot air balloon flights nearby. Cozy rooms in an antique farmhouse or handsome knotty pine cottages.

WILD BLUEBERRY-BANANA BREAD

2/3 cup sugar
1 1/2 cups flour
1/4 teaspoon salt
2 teaspoons baking
powder
3/4 cup quick-cooking
Quaker oats

1/3 cup Wesson oil
2 eggs, slightly
beaten
2 large bananas,
mashed
3/4 cup wild blueberries
(fresh or frozen)

Sift together sugar, flour, salt, and baking powder in mixing bowl. Stir in oats. Add oil, eggs, bananas and blueberries, and stir just until all ingredients are mixed and moist. Pour into greased and floured 9" x 5" loaf pan. Bake in preheated 350° oven for 60 - 65 minutes. Cool in pan 10 minutes, remove from pan and let cool on wire rack. Wrap and store in refrigerator several hours before slicing. (Variation: Substitute 3/4 cup wild raspberries or strawberries for blueberries.)

Submitted by:

Lindgren's Bed & Breakfast
CR 35 - W 191
P.O. Box 56
Lutsen, Minn. 55612-0056
(218) 663-7450
Bob & Shirley Lindgren
$80.00 to $110.00

Full breakfast
4 rooms, 4 private baths
Children, over 12
No pets
Restricted smoking
Mastercard & Visa

1920's log home in Superior National Forest on walkable shoreline of Lake Superior. Knotty cedar interior decorated with hunting trophies. Massive stone fireplaces, Finnish sauna, whirlpool, baby grand piano, color TV/VCR. Near skiing, golfing, mountain biking, skyride, hiking trails, and alpine slide. Spacious manicured grounds.

ASSORTED
BAKED GOODS

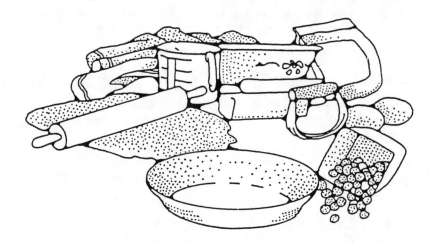

ALMOND SCONES

2 - 2 1/4 cups biscuit mix
4 tablespoons sugar
1/2 cup chopped
  almonds
1/3 cup whipping cream
  (or half & half)
1/2 teaspoon almond
  extract

1 egg, slightly beaten

For tops of scones:
Additional whipping
  cream
Slivered blanched
  almonds
Sugar

Mix biscuit mix, sugar, and almonds. Add whipping cream, extract, and egg. Mix gently until soft dough forms. Gently pat into 8" - 9" circle on lightly buttered cookie sheet, with floured fingers. Brush tops of scones with whipping cream, and sprinkle with slivered almonds and sugar. Cut into 8 wedges so inside bakes evenly. Bake at 425° approximately 12 minutes until top is light brown. Separate carefully. Serve hot with real butter, jam, and unsweetened whipped cream. Do not bake ahead of time! Makes 8 scones.

Submitted by:

Farmstead B&B Ltd.
13501 Highland Road
Hartland, Michigan 48353
(313) 887-6086
Mac & Marlene Lipon
$55.00 to $65.00

Full breakfast
4 rooms, 2 private baths
No children
No pets
No smoking
Mastercard, Visa, Am Ex

Nearly 100 year old farmhouse with flower and herb gardens on 10 acres. Near golf, shopping, antiques, skiing, you-pick farms. Country teatime offered by reservation 2 - 5 P.M. Indoor & outdoor Christmas fantasy light display attracts the young at heart. Country breakfast.

ALPENHAUS CORNBREAD

1 1/2 cups yellow
  cornmeal
1 cup all-purpose flour
1/3 cup sugar
1 teaspoon salt
1 tablespoon baking
  powder

2 eggs
6 tablespoons butter
  (melted & cooled)
6 tablespoons
  shortening
1 1/2 cups whole milk

Preheat oven to 400°. Sift cornmeal, flour, sugar, salt and baking powder into mixing bowl. To the slightly beaten eggs add the butter and shortening and stir in the milk. Add to dry ingredients and beat together for one minute. Do not overbeat. Pour into lightly buttered shallow 8" x 12" pan and bake in the center of the oven until golden brown or until the bread comes away from the edges slightly. Serve hot. Makes 1 - 9" loaf.

Submitted by:

The Captain's Alpenhaus
6941 West Lake Boulevard
Tahoma, California 96142
(916) 525-5000
Captain Joel Butler
$60.00 to $90.00

Full breakfast
13 rooms, 12 private baths
Children allowed
No pets
Restricted smoking
Mastercard, Visa, Am Ex

Cozy, quaint, European-style country inn, with gourmet quality restaurant, stone fireplace, cottages nestled in the pine trees, and bed & breakfast rooms in the inn. On Lake Tahoe's unspoiled, scenic and quiet West Shore.

APPLE ALMOND CRISP

10 - 12 peeled, sliced green apples	1 cup flour
1/2 cup sugar	1 cup brown sugar
1 teaspoon cinnamon	Dash of salt
Dash of salt	1/2 teaspoon baking powder
1/4 cup chopped almonds	1 teaspoon cinnamon
1 1/2 cups oatmeal	1/4 teaspoon allspice
	1/2 cup melted butter

Toss apple slices with sugar, cinnamon and salt. Place mixture in 9" x 13" glass baking dish. Mix dry ingredients for crisp topping. Toss dry mixture with butter until crumbly. Sprinkle topping over apple mixture. Bake at 350° for 45 minutes. Serve for breakfast topped with a small amount of fresh whipped cream. Makes 10 - 12 servings.

Submitted by:

Blue Violet Mansion	Full breakfast
443 Brown St.	6 rooms, 6 private baths
Napa, California 94559	Children allowed
(707) 253-BLUE	No pets
Bob & Kathy Morris	No smoking
$90.00 to $195.00	Mastercard & Visa

1886 Queen Anne Victorian mansion on 1 acre in historic town. Gazebo with swing. Deck with seating & hammock. Outdoor spa. Antiques. 2 parlors & sunroom for guests. In-room spas, fireplaces, & balconies available. Evening dessert. Candlelight dinner available.

APPLE-OATMEAL CRISP

1 1/2 lbs. (4 - 5) cooking apples (MacIntosh are best)
1/2 cup (1 stick) margarine
3/4 cup brown sugar, packed

3/4 cup quick cooking oatmeal
1/2 cup flour
1 teaspoon ground cinnamon

Pare and slice apples; arrange in buttered 6-cup baking dish. Melt margarine in medium saucepan or in microwave in a large bowl. Remove from heat and add remaining ingredients. Sprinkle mixture over apples. Bake at 350° until crumbs are golden and apples are tender, about 30 minutes. Serve hot. Can be prepared the night before, covered with plastic wrap and refrigerated. Bake in the morning so it's fresh and hot at breakfast! Makes 6 - 8 servings.

Submitted by:

The Inn at Narrow Passage
U.S. 11 South, P.O. Box 608
Woodstock, Virginia 22664
(703) 459-8000
Ellen & Ed Markel
$55.00 to $95.00

Full breakfast
12 rooms, 10 private baths
Children allowed
No pets
Restricted smoking
Mastercard & Visa

Historic log inn on 5 acres on the Shenandoah River has welcomed travelers for over 250 years. The inn features comfortable guest rooms, a lovely Colonial dining room for breakfast by the fire, and executive conference facilities. Near fishing, hiking, rafting, historic sites, caverns, restaurants, and antiquing. 2 miles from I-81, Exit 283.

APRICOT CASSEROLE

1 1/2 cups butter, melted (divided)	29 oz. can apricot halves, drained
16 oz. box Ritz crackers	16 oz. light brown sugar

Cut apricot halves into 4 sections each. Crush Ritz crackers. Pour 1/2 cup of melted butter evenly in bottom of 2 or 3 qt. casserole dish. Layer bottom sparingly with crushed crackers. Put 1/3 of quartered apricot halves on top of crackers. Sprinkle half of the brown sugar over apricots, then put on another layer of crackers. Pour 1/2 cup butter over that. Then layer apricots, remainder of brown sugar, the rest of the crackers, and final 1/2 cup of melted butter. Bake at 300° for 1 hour uncovered.

Submitted by:

Country Sunshine
R.R. #2, Box 275
Leeds, Alabama 35094
(205) 699-9841
Kay Red Horse
$55.00 to $65.00

Full breakfast
4 rooms, 3 private baths
Children, over 14
No pets
No smoking

Ranch type setting, horses, 4 1/2 acres, and barn. 5 minutes off I-20. Homemade sawmill gravy, biscuits, and pear preserves.

BASIL OAT SCONES

1/2 cup + 2 tablespoons oatmeal (divided)	1 tablespoon dried basil
2 cups flour	1 tablespoon dried parsley
2 1/2 teaspoons baking powder	1/4 cup softened butter
1 tablespoon sugar	1/2 cup cream
1/2 teaspoon salt	1 egg, slightly beaten
	Water

Preheat oven to 450°. Combine 1/2 cup oats, remainder of dry ingredients, and herbs in bowl. Stir well with fork. Add butter in pieces to dry mixture and cut in with pastry blender or use fingertips until mixture looks like crumbs. Stir in cream and egg. Mix until moistened. Gather dough into a ball and press until it stays together. Turn dough out onto floured board. Knead lightly about 15 seconds, 8 - 10 times. Pat dough into circle 8" across. Brush with water and sprinkle with 2 tablespoons oats. Cut into 8 wedges. Place scones about 1" apart on ungreased baking sheet. Bake 10 - 12 minutes or until tops are lightly browned. Wonderful served with apricot jam!

Submitted by:

Sweet Basil Hill Farm B&B Inn
15937 W. Washington St.
Gurnee, IL 60031
(708) 244-3333
Bob & Teri Jones
$65.00 to $105.00

Continental plus breakfast
3 suites, 3 private baths
Children allowed
No pets
No smoking
Mastercard & Visa

Country getaway atop a hill on 7 acres, has sheep, llamas, & gardens. Common Room, decorated with English Pine antiques, beckons with cozy fireplace. Featured in Country Home & Innsider Magazines, the Chicago Tribune & Sun-Times. ABBA rated with 3 crowns. Our first concern is your comfort & privacy!

BLACKBERRY COBBLER

1 qt. fresh or frozen blackberries	1/4 cup butter or margarine
1/2 cup water	1 cup self-rising flour *
1 1/2 - 2 cups sugar, divided	1 cup milk
1 teaspoon lemon juice	1/2 teaspoon ground cinnamon

In large saucepan combine berries, water and 1/2 - 1 cup sugar. Cook until mixture is hot and sugar is dissolved. Remove from heat and add lemon juice. Melt butter in 2 qt. baking pan. Combine 1 cup sugar and flour in medium mixing bowl. Stir in milk. Add cinnamon. Pour batter over melted butter in pan, but do not stir. Spoon berries over batter, but do not stir. Batter will rise to the top to form a crust. Bake in 350° oven for 40 - 45 minutes. Serve with a spoonful of whipped cream. Makes 6 - 8 servings. * Note: Use 1 cup all-purpose flour with 2 teaspoons baking powder and a dash of salt in place of self-rising flour.

Submitted by:

The Barrington Inn	Continental plus breakfast
Beach Avenue, P.O. Box 397	6 rooms, 6 private baths
Block Island, R.I. 02807	Children, over 12
(401) 466-5510	No pets
Joan & Howard Ballard	No smoking
$45.00 to $140.00	Mastercard & Visa

Century-old, completely renovated Victorian farmhouse, designated 1 of 12 "last great places in the Western Hemisphere" by the Nature Conservancy. Bright, cheerful corner rooms with spectacular water views. Walk to beach, restaurants and shops. Reasonable off-season rates. Brochure available.

BLUEBERRY PEACH PASTRY PIZZA

1 loaf frozen white
    bread dough
3 oz. cream cheese,
    softened
1/2 cup powdered
    sugar
3/4 cup blueberry pie
    filling

2 fresh peaches, peeled
    & sliced (or frozen
    slices, thawed &
    patted dry)
1/2 cup fresh blueber-
    ries (or frozen, thawed
    & patted dry)
2 tablespoons cinnamon/
    sugar mix

Thaw bread dough in bag in refrigerator overnight. Preheat oven to 350° (375° high altitude). Mix together softened cream cheese and powdered sugar. Roll and pat out dough on a greased round pizza pan. Spread with cream cheese mix. Spread with blueberry pie filling. Lay peach slices and blueberries around dough. Sprinkle with cinnamon/sugar mixture. Bake 25 - 30 minutes until edges of crust are golden and fruit is bubbly. Cool on rack 5 minutes. Slice into wedges and serve warm. Makes 8 - 10 servings.

Submitted by:

Meadow Creek B&B Inn
13438 Highway 285 @
    Douglass' Ranch
Pine, CO   80470
(303) 838-4167
Pat & Dennis Carnahan;
Judy & Don Otis
$69.00 to $120.00

Full breakfast
7 rooms, 7 private baths
(2 have jacuzzi & gas log f.p.)
Children, over 10
No pets
Restricted smoking
Mastercard & Visa

Romantic country inn in Rocky Mountains, one hour S.W. of metro Denver. On 35 acres of pine and aspen trees with meadow, and rock outcroppings. Outside jacuzzi & sauna room. Family owned and operated. Renovated in 1988, with deluxe bedroom added in 1992.

BLUEBERRY PULL-APART

4 cans large-size biscuits
Cinnamon-sugar mixture
1/3 - 1/2 cup melted
 butter

2 tablespoons honey
1 1/2 - 2 cups fresh
 or frozen blueberries

In greased bundt pan, arrange 2 cans of biscuits that have been separated, quartered, and rolled in cinnamon-sugar mix. Combine melted butter and honey. Pour half over biscuits. Add half of berries evenly over biscuits. Repeat with remaining ingredients. Bake at 325° approximately 35 - 45 minutes until raised and brown. Invert onto plate and allow to cool slightly before serving. Serves 10 - 12.

Submitted by:

Stillmeadow B&B at
 Hampstead
P.O. Box 565, 545 Main St.
Hampstead, N.H. 03841
(603) 329-8381
Lori Offord
$50.00 to $90.00

Continental plus breakfast
4 1/2 rooms, 4 private baths
Children allowed
Pets allowed, with advance
 approval
No smoking
Am Ex

Greek Renaissance Colonial built in 1850, resting on gentle acres of meadow. 5 chimneys, 3 staircases, honeymoon suite with brass bed & sitting room, family suite with crib and access to fenced-in playyard. Private parlor with woodstove & formal dining room. Sports nearby.

BREAKFAST FLAN

1/4 cup unsalted butter	3/4 cup flour
4 eggs	Thinly sliced fruit such
1/2 teaspoon almond or	as peaches
vanilla extract	Sugar & chopped
3/4 cup skim milk	almonds to taste

Preheat oven to 400°, and melt butter in baking dish in oven. Using a blender, mix 4 eggs and extract for about two minutes. Add milk and mix for another minute. Add flour and mix for one more minute. Pour into hot, sizzling buttered baking dish. Top with sliced fruit. Sprinkle on sugar and chopped almonds. Bake for 15 minutes. Serves 6 - 8.

Submitted by:

The Woodstocker
  Bed & Breakfast
Route #4, 61 River Street
Woodstock, Vermont 05091
(802) 457-3896
Liza Deignan &
  Romano Formichella
$65.00 to $115.00

Full breakfast
9 rooms, 9 private baths
  (includes 3 suites)
Children allowed
No pets
No smoking
Mastercard & Visa

Located in historic Woodstock village. We offer nine lovely rooms, three of which are suites with living room and kitchen. Relax in our luxurious whirlpool and enjoy our bountiful buffet breakfast.

BREAKFAST TREATS

2 - 8 oz. pkgs. Philadel- phia cream cheese 1/2 cup sugar 2 egg yolks 2 loaves white or wheat sandwich bread	2 sticks margarine, melted 1/2 cup sugar mixed with cinnamon to taste

Cut crusts from bread. Flatten each slice with rolling pin, set aside. Mix cream cheese, sugar & egg yolks. Spread on flattened bread slices. Roll diagonally into crescent shape. Brush melted margarine on crescents, roll in sugar-cinnamon mixture. Freeze in single layer on cookie sheet, then bag for storage in freezer. When ready to use bake at 350° for 8 - 10 minutes and lightly browned. Makes 20 treats per loaf of bread.

Submitted by:

Upper Feather B&B
256 Commercial Street
Portola, California 96122
(916) 832-0107
Jon & Lynne Haman
$40.00 - $60.00 + tax

Full breakfast
6 rooms
Children allowed
Pets allowed
No smoking

Old-fashioned simple comfort, no TV, room phones or radios. Lots of board games, jigsaw puzzles, popcorn and conversation. Walk to restaurants, wild and scenic river, railroad museum (even drive a locomotive!), only 1 hour from Reno, Nevada.

CARAMEL PECAN ROLLS

Dough:
1 env. active dry yeast
1 cup warm (110°)
   water, divided
2 teaspoons sugar
1 teaspoon salt
2 cups all-purpose flour

Topping:
6 tablespoons light
   brown sugar
6 tablespoons butter,
   melted

Filling:
3 tablespoons butter,
   melted
3 tablespoons brown
   sugar
1/8 teaspoon cinnamon
1/4 cup chopped pecans

Ground cinnamon
18 pecan halves,
   broken

Dough: Dissolve yeast in 1/4 cup warm water in large bowl. Stir in remaining 3/4 cup water. Stir in sugar, salt, then flour. Mix well. Cover bowl with cloth and let rest 20 minutes. Turn out onto floured board and turn dough twice to coat with flour. Pat or roll into 10" x 4" rectangle pan. Spread top with filling. Brush with melted butter, then sprinkle evenly with brown sugar, cinnamon and pecans. Roll up like jelly roll starting at long side. Using sharp knife, cut crosswise into 6 thick slices about 1 1/2". Place 1 tablespoon brown sugar, 1 tablespoon melted butter, 3 broken pecan halves and a sprinkle of cinnamon in each of six muffin cups. Place slice of dough, cut side down, in pan. Place on middle shelf of cold oven. Turn oven to 350°. Bake 30 minutes or until golden brown. Makes 6 rolls.

Submitted by:

Teetor House
300 W. Main
Hagerstown, Indiana 47346
(317) 489-4422
Jack & JoAnn Warmoth
$70.00 to $85.00

Full breakfast
4 rooms, 4 private baths
Children allowed
No pets
Restricted smoking
Mastercard & Visa

Historical inn, historical tour. Convenient drive, 5 miles from I-70, fully air-conditioned. Player-Grand Steinway piano in large living room for guests' use. Walking distance to excellent restaurants. Fitness center with Olympic-size indoor pool for guests.

CINNAMON-ORANGE ROLLS

2 pkgs. dry yeast
1/3 cup warm water
1 cup milk, scalded
1 stick oleo or butter

1/2 cup sugar
3 eggs
1 teaspoon salt
4 3/4 cups flour

Filling:
1 stick oleo
1 1/2 teaspoons
  cinnamon

1/4 cup grated orange
  rind
1/2 cup sugar

Dissolve yeast in warm water. Scald milk, add oleo while hot. Beat eggs and add sugar gradually while beating. Add milk and oleo mixture to eggs and sugar. Add salt and yeast. Stir in 2 cups flour and beat well. Add remainder of flour. Let rise until doubled. Roll 1/4 of dough at a time on floured board. Combine filling ingredients and spread on top of dough. Roll as if making a jelly roll. Cut into 1 1/2" pieces and place cut side up in greased muffin pans. Let rise and bake in 350° oven for 12 minutes. Frost rolls with powdered sugar frosting if desired. Makes a bunch!

Submitted by:

The Cinnamon Inn
426 Gunnison Ave.
P.O. Box 533
Lake City, Colorado 81235
(303) 944-2641
Mel & Gwendolyn Faber
$60.00 to $85.00

Full breakfast
5 rooms, 1 private & 2
  shared baths
Children allowed
Pets allowed outside only
No smoking
Mastercard & Discover

Near 5 - 14,000' peaks for hiking, alpine meadows, fishing at Lake San Cristobal, fly-fishing, biking or rock-hunting. Next to the inn, Gwendolyn has a lovely gallery - watercolour classes are offered.

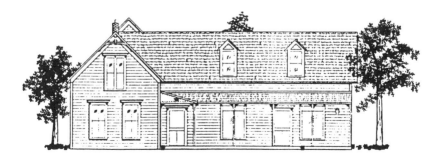

CINNAMON ROLLS

Dough:

1 pkg. (2 1/2 teaspoons) yeast
1/2 cup warm water
1/2 cup lukewarm milk
1/3 cup sugar

1/3 cup softened butter
1 teaspoon salt
1 egg
3 1/2 - 4 cups all-purpose flour

Filling:

3/4 cup sugar
4 tablespoons cinnamon
1/3 cup melted butter

Glaze:

1 cup powdered sugar
1 tablespoon milk
1/2 teaspoon vanilla

Dissolve yeast in warm water in a 2 1/2 quart bowl. Stir in milk, sugar, butter, salt, egg and 2 cups of flour. Beat until smooth. Then add enough remaining flour to make it easy to handle, so you can knead it to be smooth. This should pull like elastic. Grease the bowl and put dough in. Cover and let rise for about 1 1/2 hours. On a well-floured surface, roll out dough with a rolling pin to 15" x 9". Brush melted butter all over top surface. Sprinkle cinnamon and sugar on top of butter. Roll up tight starting on long side. Pinch seam tight. Cut slices 1 1/4", lay flat in greased round average size cake pan. Let rise 30 minutes (covered). Bake at 375° for about 20 - 30 minutes. Should be golden brown. Cool. Beat glaze ingredients together until smooth. Spread on rolls and enjoy. Makes 1 dozen rolls.

Submitted by:

Wildflower Inn
Darling Hill Road
Lyndonville, Vermont 05851
(802) 626-8310
Jim & Mary O'Reilly
$80.00 to $125.00

Full breakfast
21 rooms, 17 private baths
Children allowed
No pets
No smoking
Mastercard & Visa

Scenic views: sunning beside heated inground pool or watching our farm animals feed in the beautiful fields & barn. Sleigh & hay rides will take you through the beauty of all 4 seasons. Dine at night in relaxing country atmosphere, minutes from skiing, skating and shopping.

CLAFOUTI

1 1/4 cups 1% milk	2/3 cup all-purpose flour
3 eggs	flour
1/4 cup granulated	2 cups Washington bing
sugar	cherries, pitted
2 teaspoons vanilla	1/3 cup granulated
extract	sugar

In food processor, place milk, eggs, and vanilla. Cover and blend 1 minute. Add 1/4 cup sugar and blend. Add flour and beat 1 more minute. Pour 1/4" layer of batter in Pyrex pie pan. Set over moderate heat for a minute or two until a film of batter has set in bottom of dish. Remove from heat. Spread cherries over batter. Sprinkle on 1/3 cup sugar. Pour on the remainder of batter and smooth the surface. Place in preheated 350° oven and bake for 1 hour. Clafouti is done when it has puffed and browned and a knife plunged into center comes out clean. Sprinkle with powdered sugar. Do not serve hot, but it should be warm. Serves 6 - 8.

Submitted by:

Moon & Sixpence Inn   Full breakfast
3021 Beaverton Valley Road   5 rooms, some private baths
Friday Harbor, Wash. 98250   Children, over 12
(206) 378-4138   No pets
Evelyn & Charles Tuller   Restricted smoking
$65.00 to $95.00   Personal checks

Early 1900 farmhouse, fully restored and furnished with well used & much loved family antiques. Comfortable rooms, a weaving studio, breakfast in sunny dining room with various German/Dutch delights, and classic country service.

CLAFOUTIS (FRENCH FLAN)

2 oz. plain flour	**Pinch of salt**
3 oz. sugar	**2/3 cup warm milk**
2 eggs	**1 can dark bing cherries**

Mix in bowl flour, sugar, eggs, and salt, and add warm milk. Pour mixture into greased 8" diameter pie dish. Drain cherries and spread evenly on mixture in pie dish. Cook in 375° oven for approximately 45 minutes or until brown. Makes 8 servings.

Submitted by:

Old Thyme Inn
779 Main St.
Half Moon Bay, Calif. 94019
(415) 726-1616
George & Marcia Dempsey
$65.00 to $210.00/2 people

Full breakfast
7 rooms, 7 private baths
Children, over 6
No smoking
Mastercard & Visa

A B&B with an herbal theme. All rooms named after an herb. Guests are invited to walk in George's herb garden and take cuttings. Some rooms have double-size whirlpool tubs and fireplaces. Rates are reasonable, especially during the week.

CRANBERRY-APPLE BAKE

3 cups unpeeled apples, chopped to bite-size, & sprinkled with lemon juice
2 cups whole raw cranberries
1 cup sugar
1 1/2 cups uncooked quick-cooking oats

1/2 cup firmly packed brown sugar
1/3 cup flour
1/3 cup chopped pecans
1/2 cup melted margarine

Combine apples, cranberries and sugar. Mix well and put into a 2 quart casserole. Mix remaining ingredients and spread on top of apple mixture. Bake uncovered in 300° oven for one hour, until bubbly and lightly browned. Serve warm with cream if desired. Makes 8 - 10 servings.

Submitted by:

Hacienda del Sol
P.O. Box 177
Taos, New Mexico 87571
(505) 758-0287
John & Marcine Landon
$55.00 to $115.00

Continental plus breakfast
7 rooms, 5 private baths
Children allowed
No pets
No smoking

One acre & grounds with century old cottonwoods and apple trees. Formerly in Mabel Dodge Lunan estate, parts of this historic inn date back 180 years. Hot tub deck affords unobstructed view of Taos Mtn. Fireplaces, down comforters, antique and handcrafted furniture.

CRANBERRY SCONES

1/4 cup margarine
1 1/3 cups all-purpose
flour
2 tablespoons sugar
2 teaspoons baking
powder
1 egg

1/3 cup halved
cranberries
3 - 4 tablespoons
half & half
Topping:
1 egg, beaten
Sugar

Cut margarine into flour, sugar and baking powder until mixture resembles fine crumbs. Stir in one egg, cranberries, and just enough half & half so dough leaves side of bowl. Turn dough onto floured surface and knead 10 times. Roll 1/2" thick. Cut dough into circles with a glass or floured cutter. Place on greased cookie sheet. Brush with beaten egg and sprinkle with sugar. Bake at 400° for 10 - 12 minutes. Makes 10 - 12 scones.

Submitted by:

Cranberry Inn at Chatham
359 Main St.
Chatham, Mass. 02633
(508) 945-9232
1-800-332-4667 (reserv.)
Richard Morris/Peggy DeHan
$88.00 to $160.00

Continental plus breakfast
18 rooms, 18 private baths
Children, over 12
No pets
Restricted smoking
Mastercard, Visa, Am Ex

Chatham's oldest inn, meticulously restored, historic village location. Individually decorated guest rooms with antique and reproduction furnishings. Televisions, telephones, a/c, fireplaces, and balconies. Walk to fine shops, restaurants and beaches.

CRANBERRY-WALNUT PIE

2 cups cranberries (fresh or frozen)	3/4 cup sugar
1/2 cup chopped walnuts	2 eggs, lightly beaten
1/2 cup sugar	1 teaspoon almond extract
3/4 cup margarine, melted	1 cup flour

Mix cranberries, walnuts, and 1/2 cup sugar together and put into buttered pie plate. Mix remaining ingredients and pour over cranberry mixture. Bake at 325° - 350° for 35 - 40 minutes. For breakfast serve with yogurt sauce; for dessert serve with ice cream. Makes 8 - 12 servings.

Submitted by:

Inn on Carleton	Full breakfast
46 Carleton St.	7 rooms, 3 private baths
Portland, Maine 04102	Children allowed
(207) 775-1910	No pets
Phil & Sue Cox	No smoking
$75.00 to $95.00 (in-season)	Mastercard, Visa & Discover
$60.00 to $80.00 (off-season)	

Graciously restored brick Victorian townhouse, located in the historic Western Promenade area of downtown Portland. Within walking distance of museums, performing art center, Old Port Exchange, restaurants and shopping. Large period rooms decorated with antique furnishings.

INN ON
CARLETON

CROISSANTS Á LA MUSHROOM

1/3 cup chopped onion	3 cups thinly sliced
2 tablespoons butter or	mushrooms (8 oz.)
margarine	1/4 cup sour cream
1/8 - 1/4 teaspoon black	2 - 8 oz. cans
pepper	refrigerator crescent
1/8 teaspoon garlic	dinner rolls
powder	

In large skillet sauté onion in butter until tender. Remove from heat, add pepper, garlic powder and mushrooms. Mix well. Gently fold in sour cream until mushrooms are coated. Separate crescent dough into 16 triangles. Overlap long sides of 2 triangles about 1", pressing edges to seal, & forming 1 large croissant. Spoon 1/4 cup mushroom mixture evenly over each large triangle. Beginning at short point of triangle, roll loosely to opposite point. Place point side down on ungreased baking sheet. Curve edges to create crescent shape. Bake at 375° for 14 - 18 minutes until golden brown. Makes 8.

Submitted by:

Carriage House B&B	Full breakfast
P.O. Box 982-472 Emerald Dr.	3 rooms, 3 private baths
Lake Arrowhead, Calif. 92352	Children, over 12
(909) 336-1400	No pets
Lee & Johan Karstens	No smoking
$90.00 to $120.00	Mastercard, Visa, Discover

New England-style house hidden in the woods has view of Lake Arrowhead. Country decor with featherbeds and down comforters. Fresh ground gourmet coffee at breakfast, in dining area. Beverages and hors d'oeuvres offered in afternoon. Forest & lake walking trails.

DANISH PUFF RECIPE

Dough:
1/2 cup butter

1 cup flour
2 tablespoons water

Topping:
1/2 cup butter
1 cup water

1 teaspoon almond
  extract
1 cup flour
3 eggs

Frost with:
1 can vanilla frosting

Chopped walnuts

For dough: Cut butter into flour until evenly blended. Add water and work with fork to blend evenly. Roll into a ball and divide in half. Pat each half into strip 12" x 3" on ungreased cookie sheet. Strips should be 3" apart. For topping: Bring butter and water to rolling boil. Add extract. Remove from heat. Stir in flour immediately until smooth. Add eggs one at a time, mixing until smooth after each addition. Spread evenly over each of the two strips on cookie sheet. Bake at 350° for one hour or until top is crispy and brown. When cool, frost, and sprinkle with chopped nuts. Makes 8 - 10 servings.

Submitted by:

Anaheim Country Inn
856 South Walnut
Anaheim, California 92802
(714) 778-0150 or
1-(800)-755-7801
Lois Ramont & Marilyn Watson
$55.00 to $80.00

Full breakfast
8 rooms, 6 private baths
Children allowed
No pets
No smoking
Mastercard, Visa, Am Ex,
  Discover

1910 Princess Anne home with beveled, leaded glass windows and turn-of-the-century country furnishings. Relax on airy porches, wander through the garden and under the avocado trees. Near Disneyland, Knott's Berry Farm, Convention Center "Fun Bus" stop.

DRIED FRUIT CREAM SCONES

2 cups all-purpose flour
1 tablespoon baking
  powder
1/2 teaspoon salt
1/4 cup sugar

1/2 cup chopped dried
  fruit (apricots or
  prunes)
1/4 cup raisins
1 1/4 cups heavy cream

Glaze:
3 tablespoons sweet
  butter, melted

2 tablespoons sugar

Preheat oven to 425°. Combine flour, baking powder, salt and sugar. Mix well. Add dried fruit and raisins. Stir in cream, and mix with fork until dough holds together. Transfer dough to lightly floured board. Knead 8 or 9 times. Pat into circle 10" round. Brush with sweet butter and sprinkle top with sugar. Cut circle into 12 wedges. Place each wedge on ungreased baking sheet. Allow 1" between pieces. Bake 15 minutes or until golden brown. Makes 12 pieces.

Submitted by:

Page House Inn
323 Fairfax Avenue
Norfolk, VA 23507
(804) 625-5033
Stephanie & Ezio DiBelardino
$75.00 to $135.00

Continental plus breakfast
6 rooms, 6 private baths
Children, over 12
No pets
Restricted smoking

In-town Georgian Revival mansion, circa 1899, meticulously restored in 1991, with luxury amenities and modern conveniences. Fabulous gourmet breakfasts served with freshly made espresso and capuccino. Walking distance to cultural attractions, downtown financial district and the local medical center. AAA 3-Diamonds.

EASY CARAMEL ORANGE RING

1 tablespoon butter, softened	1 cup firmly packed brown sugar
1/2 cup orange marmalade	1/2 teaspoon cinnamon
2 tablespoons chopped nuts	2 - 10 oz. cans refrigerated buttermilk flaky biscuits
	1/2 cup butter, melted

Preheat oven to 350°. Grease 12-cup bundt pan with 1 tablespoon butter. Place orange marmalade in pan by teaspoonsful. Sprinkle with nuts. In small bowl, combine brown sugar and cinnamon. Mix well, set aside. Separate biscuits. Dip biscuits in melted butter, then sugar mixture. Stand biscuits on edge in pan, spacing evenly. Sprinkle with remaining sugar mixture and drizzle with remaining butter. Bake near center of oven 30 - 40 minutes or until brown. Cool upright in pan for 5 minutes. Invert onto serving plate. Makes 6 - 8 servings.

Submitted by:

The Pittman House	Full breakfast
103 Homer Street	4 rooms, 2 private baths
Commerce, Georgia 30529	Children allowed
(706) 335-3823	No pets
Tom & Dot Tomberlin	No smoking
$50.00 to $65.00	Mastercard & Visa

Two story, four square Colonial house built in 1890. Large front porch with rockers, furnished with antiques throughout. In the foothills of north Georgia, on Highway 441, 2 miles off I-85, about halfway between Atlanta and Greenville, S.C. Large shopping outlet mall at I-85.

EASY "OOHEY-GOOEY" ROLLS

3/4 cup whipping cream, unwhipped	1 teaspoon cinnamon
3/4 cup packed brown sugar	1 loaf frozen bread (Rhodes, Rich, etc.)

Mix together whipping cream, brown sugar and cinnamon. Put in 9" x 13" pan or 2 - 8" round pans. Do not grease pans. Thaw frozen bread so that you can cut it into 15 pieces. Distribute these over whipping cream mixture. Let set at room temperature overnight. Bake at 350° for 15 - 20 minutes or until brown. Makes 8 - 10 servings.

Submitted by:

Queen Anne Inn   Full breakfast
420 W. Washington   5 rooms, 5 private baths
South Bend, Indiana 46601   Children allowed
(219) 234-5959   No pets
Bob & Pauline Medhurst   Restricted smoking
$65.00 to $89.00

1893 Victorian noted for its leaded glass, Frank Lloyd Wright-designed bookcases and Italian imported oak staircase. Furnished in antiques & reproductions. Homemade coffee cakes, omelets or Belgian waffles for breakfast. Near downtown and Notre Dame.

GALISTEO CORNMEAL SCONES

2 cups unbleached flour
1 cup blue or yellow
  cornmeal
1/3 cup sugar
1 tablespoon baking
  powder
1/2 teaspoon baking
  soda

3/4 teaspoon salt
1 teaspoon cinnamon
3/4 cup unsalted butter,
  cut in small pieces
  (1 1/2 sticks)
Currants, nuts, dried
  fruit, etc.
1 cup buttermilk

Combine dry ingredients. Cut in butter with food processor or pastry knife until it resembles small peas. Mix in nuts and fruit. Mix in buttermilk and turn onto board coated lightly with cornmeal. Knead lightly and roll about 1/2" thick. Cut dough into shapes and place on ungreased cookie sheet. Bake at 400° for 12 minutes or until lightly brown. Serve with butter and jam. Makes 16.

Submitted by:

The Galisteo Inn
HC 75, Box 4
Galisteo, New Mexico 87540
(505) 982-1506
Wayne Aarniokoski &
  Joanna Kaufman
$55.00 to $165.00

Continental plus breakfast
12 rooms, 8 private baths
Children, over 12
No pets
Restricted smoking
Mastercard, Visa,
  Discover

Charming, gracious 250 year old adobe hacienda on 8 country acres in the quiet village of Galisteo, only 30 minutes from Santa Fe. 50' lap pool, outdoor spa, sauna, massage, horseback riding, hiking, intimate dinners.

GERMAN SOUR CREAM TWISTS

3 1/2 cups flour	1 teaspoon salt
1 cup shortening	1 teaspoon vanilla
1 pkg. yeast	1 egg
1/4 cup warm water	1+ cups sugar for rolling
3/4 cup sour cream	& sprinkling dough

Dissolve yeast in warm water. Mix flour, shortening, sour cream, salt, vanilla, and egg with yeast mixture well. Refrigerate at least 2 hours. Roll out on sugared board in 2 portions using about 1/2 cup sugar each time. For each portion: Roll out to 4" x 5", fold ends in. Sprinkle with sugar. Repeat this 3 times. Roll to 1/4" thick. Cut into 1" x 4" strips and twist. Press ends to ungreased cookie sheet. Bake 15 minutes at 375°. Makes 3 dozen.

Submitted by:

Landhaus Bed & Breakfast	Full breakfast
P.O. Drawer E	8 rooms, 1 private bath
Fredericksburg, Texas 78624	Children allowed
(512) 997-4916	No pets
Monty & Maria McDonald	Restricted smoking
$95.00	

1883 restored guesthouse on 40 acres in the heart of Texas Hill Country. Furnished with beautiful antiques and collectibles with a Fredericksburg pioneer flair and all the comforts of modern life. Porch with inviting view. Near historic sites, shopping & restaurants.

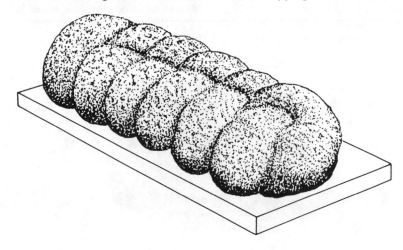

GRANDMA KOST'S GREAT OATMEAL COOKIES

3/4 cup butter
1/2 cup peanut butter
1 cup sugar
1 cup brown sugar
2 eggs
1/4 cup milk
1 teaspoon vanilla
2 cups sifted flour

1 teaspoon baking soda
1 teaspoon salt
1 teaspoon ground cinnamon
1 1/2 cups quick-cooking oats
1 cup raisins

Cream together butter, peanut butter and sugars until smooth and creamy. Add eggs, milk and vanilla, blend well. Sift together flour, baking soda, salt and cinnamon. Stir into creamed mixture. Blend in oats and raisins. Drop by teaspoonfuls onto greased baking sheets. Bake in 350° oven for 15 minutes or until done. Makes 36 - 3" cookies.

Submitted by:

Walden Acres B&B
2965 - 340 Trail
Adel, Iowa 50003
(515) 987-1338
Phyllis & Dale Briley
$55.00 to $60.00

Full breakfast
2 rooms
Children allowed
Pets allowed, with restrictions
Restricted smoking

English style brick home with handsome walnut woodwork, built in 1940 by Cleveland Indians' pitcher, Bob Feller. On 40 acres of beautiful woods with a lake. Convenient location, 15 minutes west of Des Moines. Near I-35 and I-80. Open all year.

HAM ROLLS

1 lb. tub of margarine
2 - 3 teaspoons poppy seed
1 - 2 teaspoons dijon mustard
2 teaspoons Worcestershire sauce

2 teaspoons dehydrated onion
20 Pepperidge Farm party rolls (1 pack)
Sliced Swiss cheese
Sliced Virginia baked ham

Mix margarine with poppy seed, mustard, Worcestershire sauce and onion for spread. It should be made at least the night before serving. Spread will last several days. Take rolls and slice in half. Spread butter mixture on both sides of rolls. Put one slice each of ham and cheese on rolls. Fold rolls back over and keep in pan. Wrap pan in foil and bake at 300° for 30 minutes. Serve warm. Makes 5 servings.

Submitted by:

Applewood Colonial B&B
605 Richmond Rd.
Williamsburg, VA 23185
(800) 899-2753
Fred Strout
$65.00 to $100.00

Continental plus breakfast
4 rooms, 4 private baths
Children allowed
No pets
No smoking
Mastercard & Visa

Flemish-bond brick home built during the restoration of colonial Williamsburg. Parlor is decorated in a colonial style, featuring dentil crown molding. Crystal chandelier above dining room table. Suite has private entrance, fireplace and queen canopy bed.

KEVIN'S BREAKFAST PIE

10 eggs
3/4 cup milk
1/2 teaspoon nutmeg
1/2 teaspoon allspice
1 1/2 teaspoons cream
  of tartar

2 apples, peeled, cored
  and sliced
8 oz. Cheddar cheese,
  shredded
1/2 tablespoon
  cinnamon

Preheat oven to 350°. Blend eggs, milk, nutmeg, allspice, and cream of tartar in blender for one minute. Place sliced apples and shredded cheese in lightly greased fluted flan pan. Pour egg mixture over apples and cheese. Bake 30 - 40 minutes. Makes 8 - 10 servings.

Submitted by:

The Irish Rose B&B
102 South St.
Auburn, N.Y. 13021
(315) 255-0196
Patricia & Kevin Fitzpatrick
$55.00 to $95.00

Full breakfast
5 rooms, 3 private baths
Children allowed
No pets
Restricted smoking
Mastercard, Visa & Discover

Queen Anne Victorian mansion, circa 1872, on Historic Register, with magnificent cherry wood throughout. Irish hospitality & Victorian elegance. Walking distance to museums, shops, historic sites. Large gardens, 20' x 40' inground swimming pool. 5 beautifully decorated rooms, wicker, swings, and decks.

KOLACKY (SLOVAK NUT ROLLS)

First dough:
1 lb. flour
1 teaspoon salt
2 tablespoons sugar
4 egg yolks, unbeaten
2 - 6 oz. cakes yeast, dissolved in 1 cup lukewarm milk or 1 1/2 tablespoons dry yeast

Second dough:
1 lb. flour
1 lb. unsalted butter

Nut filling:
1 1/2 lbs. walnuts (ground)
8 egg whites
2 cups sugar
2 teaspoons vanilla

Beaten egg yolks

Mix all ingredients for first dough to a smooth dough. Then work butter into flour for second dough, and mix well. Combine both doughs and mix well. Let rise 2 hours in covered bowl. Punch down, cover, and let rise again for 2 hours. Punch dough. Roll out on powdered sugared board about 1/4" thick. Mix nut filling ingredients well. For 2 large rolls: Divide dough into 2 parts, roll to rectangular shape & fill with nut filling. Start rolling on short side, press ends so filling stays inside. Place on ungreased cookie sheet, brush with beaten egg yolks. Bake at 350° for 30 minutes. Can also be made into individual rolls. Rolls can be frozen. Makes 120 nut rolls or 40 slices of large nut roll, cut 3/4" thick.

Submitted by:

Leduc's Bed & Breakfast
41 Arrow Drive
Sedona, Arizona 86336
(602) 282-6241
Klaus & Renate Leduck
$60.00 to $80.00

Full breakfast
3 rooms, 3 private baths
Children, over 14
No pets
Restricted smoking

Relax with us in peace and quiet. Our guest rooms are individually decorated. Honeymoon Suite has king size bed with fireplace and jacuzzi tub. Located 2 miles from uptown Sedona. Common room for guest use has view to the Red Rocks.

MAPLE PECAN SCONES

3 cups all-purpose flour
1 cup chopped pecans
1 1/2 tablespoons
  baking powder
3/4 teaspoon salt

3/4 cup grade AA
  unsalted butter
2/3 cup 100% pure Door
  County maple syrup
1/3 cup milk

Combine dry ingredients. Cut in butter with pastry blender. Combine maple syrup and milk; whisk together. Slowly pour liquid into dry ingredients while mixing until combined. Dough should be firm. Roll out about 1" thick. Cut scones with 3" round biscuit cutter. Brush tops with additional maple syrup. Bake on greased and floured cookie sheet for 15 - 20 minutes at 350°. Makes 12 - 18 scones. Yum!

Submitted by:

Inn at Cedar Crossing
336 Louisiana Street
Sturgeon Bay, Wis. 54235
(414) 743-4200
Terry Wulf
$65.00 to $109.00

Continental plus breakfast
9 rooms, 9 private baths
Children, over 5
No pets
Restricted smoking
Mastercard, Visa, Discover

1885 brick vernacular inn in downtown Historic District. Lovingly restored in 1986, with elegant antique-filled guest rooms, double whirlpool tubs, & inviting fireplaces. 95-seat Victorian dining rooms feature fireplaces and "homemade exquisite" cuisine 3 meals a day.

MARY ELLEN'S BREAKFAST COOKIES

2/3 cup sugar
2/3 cup butter
1 egg
1 teaspoon vanilla
   extract
3/4 cup flour
1/2 teaspoon baking
   soda

1/2 teaspoon salt
1 1/4 cups uncooked
   oatmeal
1 cup Cheddar cheese,
   grated
1/2 cup wheat germ
6 slices bacon, fried
   crisply & crumbled

Preheat oven to 350°. In large bowl beat sugar, butter, egg and vanilla. Beat in flour, baking soda, and salt. Stir in oatmeal, cheese, wheat germ and bacon. Drop cookies by tablespoonsful onto greased cookie sheet. Bake for 12 - 14 minutes. Makes 30 cookies.

Submitted by:

Maricopa Manor
15 W. Pasadena Ave.
Phoenix, Arizona 85013
(602) 274-6302
Mary Ellen Kelley

Continental plus breakfast
5 rooms, 5 private baths
Children allowed
No pets
Restricted smoking
Mastercard & Visa

Become a privileged guest, among good friends, in the sumptuous atmosphere of a fine residence. Enjoy all the comforts of home while being catered to with the most attentive service. Fulfill your personal and professional needs in a "home away from home".

NINA'S FRUIT TORTE

1 cup butter
2 cups sugar
4 eggs, beaten
2 cups flour
1/2 teaspoon salt
2 teaspoons baking
  powder

3 or more cups sugared
  blueberries
2 tablespoons lemon
  juice
2 teaspoons flour
4 tablespoons sugar
Cinnamon to taste

Cream together butter and sugar. Add and mix in eggs. Set aside. Mix flour, salt, and baking powder, add to butter. Mix well. Grease 12" springform pan and press dough into it. Cover with blueberries that have been rolled in sugar. Sprinkle with lemon juice, flour, sugar and cinnamon. Bake at 350° for 1 hour and 15 minutes, or until firm. Makes 6 to 8 servings.

Submitted by:

Nauset House Inn
Box 774, 143 Beach Road
East Orleans, Mass. 02643
(508) 255-2195
Diane & Al Johnson
Cindy & John Vessella
$55.00 to $95.00

Full or continental breakfast
14 rooms, 8 private baths
Children, over 12
No pets
Restricted smoking
Mastercard & Visa

A cozy, family-run inn set on over 2 acres of gardens and orchards. Large conservatory with plants & wicker furniture. Large living room & brick-floored breakfast room, with fireplaces. Antiques, art objects, flowers & friendly atmosphere abound. 1/2 mile from Nation Sea Shore beach, 15 miles of ocean and dunes.

NORWEGIAN FRUIT PIZZA

3/4 cup butter
1/2 cup powdered sugar
1 1/2 cups flour
8 oz. softened cream
  cheese
1/2 cup sugar
1/2 teaspoon vanilla
1 canned fruit (your
  choice)

2 fresh fruits, sliced
  (your choice)
Glaze:
1 cup fruit juice
2 tablespoons
  cornstarch
1 tablespoon lemon
  juice
1/2 cup sugar

Mix first three ingredients until crumblike. Do not melt butter. Pat into pizza pan and bake at 350° for about 13 minutes until golden brown. Do not overbake. Mix cream cheese, sugar and vanilla. Spread over cooled crust. Place canned and fresh fruit on top. (Peaches, bananas, kiwi, strawberries or blueberries). Mix glaze ingredients together in pan. Cook over medium heat until clear and thick, stirring constantly. Cool. Spread on top of pizza after slicing. Serves 12.

Submitted by:

The Albert Stevens Inn
127 Myrtle Avenue
Cape May, New Jersey 08204
(609) 884-4717
Curt & Diane Rangen
$65.00 to $135.00

Full breakfast
8 rooms, 8 private baths
Children, over 10
No pets
Restricted smoking
Mastercard, Visa, Am Ex, Disc.

A homey, country inn filled with Victorian treasures, warmth, and heavenly scents from the kitchen. Our guests are nurtured, loved and treasured from the time they enter, until we say goodbye!

THE
Albert
STEVENS
INN

OLD SECRET FAMILY RECIPE FOR APPLE STRUEDEL

2 cups Bisquick
2/3 cup milk
4 oz. cream cheese
1/2 cup powdered sugar
1 teaspoon cinnamon
1 fresh apple, sliced

Icing:
1/2 cup powdered sugar
2 teaspoons milk
1/4 teaspoon vanilla
1 1/2 teaspoons butter, melted

Preheat oven to 350°. Mix biscuit mix and milk. Form dough, roll with rolling pin to rectangle 9" x 14". Fill with mixture of cream cheese, powdered sugar, cinnamon and sliced apple. Roll up into 14" long pastry, bake for 25 minutes. Mix icing ingredients. Dribble icing over struedel and serve hot. Makes 4 servings.

Submitted by:

Falling Pines Inn
300 West French Place
San Antonio, Texas 78212
(800) 880-4580
Grace & Bob Daubert
$67.00 to $97.00

Full breakfast
4 rooms, 5 private baths
Children, over 10
No pets
No smoking
Mastercard & Visa

3 story mansion, 9,000 sq. ft., circa 1911, on 1 acre park-like setting, in Monte Vista Historic District. Designer decorated, magnificent limestone arch, veranda, wood floors, oriental rugs, 2 fireplaces, tiled solarium. Near downtown, riverwalk, convenient to all attractions.

ORANGE BISCUITS

6 cups flour
2 teaspoons baking
powder
1 1/2 teaspoons salt
1 1/2 teaspoons cream
of tartar

1 cup sugar
Grated zest of 1 orange
1 1/2 cups Butter-Flavor
Crisco
1 1/2 cups buttermilk

Mix all dry ingredients together. Add Crisco and buttermilk. Mix until soft dough is formed. Knead on floured board until fully combined. Roll out to 1" thickness, cut with biscuit cutters. Bake on greased cookie sheet at 350° for 20 minutes until golden and bottoms are browned. Makes 24 biscuits.

Submitted by:

Gatehouse Inn
225 Central Ave.
Pacific Grove, Calif. 93950
(408) 649-8436
(800) 753-1881
Doug & Kristi Aslin
$95.00 to $170.00

Full breakfast
8 rooms, 8 private baths
Children, over 12
No pets
Restricted smoking
Mastercard, Visa, Am Ex

Historic seaside Victorian home, circa 1884, with distinctive rooms, stunning views, fireplaces, patios, delicious breakfasts, afternoon refreshments. Walk to the ocean, Cannery Row, Monterey Bay Aquarium, shops & restaurants. 10 minutes from Carmel, Pebble Beach & world-renowned golf courses.

PEACH & RASPBERRY BREAKFAST PIE

Pie crust:
1 1/4 cups all-purpose
flour
1/4 teaspoon salt
6 tablespoons butter or
margarine
3 - 4 tablespoons cold
water

Topping:
3/4 cup all-purpose flour
1/2 cup sugar

Filling:
1 cup Corn Flakes
4 large peaches,
chopped into 1" pieces
1 cup raspberries
1/3 cup sugar
1 teaspoon cinnamon
1/8 teaspoon almond
extract

7 tablespoons chilled
butter

Pie crust: Mix flour and salt with fork. Cut in butter, using a pastry blender or two knives, until the mixture resembles coarse bread crumbs. Add cold water, stirring gently with fork until mixture resembles a rough mass. Roll out on floured board. Makes 1 - 9" crust. Place dough in a greased and floured pie dish. Sprinkle Corn Flakes evenly over pie shell. Mix sugar, cinnamon and almond extract together. Toss peaches and raspberries in sugar mixture until coated. Spread peach mixture over Corn Flakes. Topping: Put flour, sugar and butter into a bowl. Using a pastry blender or two knives, work the butter into the flour until the mixture resembles irregular bread crumbs. Sprinkle the crumbs evenly over fruit mixture. Bake the pie for 10 minutes at 450°, then reduce heat to 350° and continue baking for 35 minutes. Makes 8 servings.

Submitted by:

Preston House B&B
106 Faithway Street
Santa Fe, New Mexico 87501
(505) 982-3465
Signe Bergman
$48.00 to $128.00

Continental plus breakfast
15 rooms, 13 private baths
Children, over 12
Pets allowed
No smoking
Mastercard, Visa, Am Ex

Stay in the historic main house with antiques, Edwardian fireplaces, and stained glass windows; or in the adobe addition with a traditional Southwestern interior. Breakfast includes homebaked breads, bread pudding, coffee cake and fresh fruits. Afternoon tea and dessert.

PEACH & RICE CUSTARD LOAF

1 can sliced peaches, drained	1 cup sifted dry bread crumbs
3/4 cup sugar	4 tablespoons butter or margarine
4 tablespoons flour	
1/4 teaspoon salt (opt.)	4 tablespoons brown sugar
1 1/2 cups milk (divided)	
2 egg yolks	1 egg
1 teaspoon almond extract	1 cup peach juice
2 cups cooked rice	3/4 teaspoon almond extract

Drain peaches, set aside. Combine sugar, flour & salt. Add 1/2 cup milk & egg yolks. Beat well. Add remaining 1 cup milk. Microwave until thick, stirring occasionally. Add extract and fold in rice. Cover bottom of buttered loaf pan with half of bread crumbs. Pour in 1/3 of rice custard, then cover with half of peaches. Repeat layer of custard, remaining peaches and remaining custard. Sprinkle with remaining bread crumbs. Bake in 350° oven about 40 minutes. Let cool 10 - 15 minutes before unmolding. Slice & serve with Peach Sauce: Cream butter & brown sugar. Add egg and beat well. Add peach juice and microwave until slightly thickened. Add flavoring. Makes 8 servings.

Submitted by:

Ironhedge Inn B&B
305 Oregon Ave.
Dundee, Illinois 60118
(708) 426-7777
Sarah & Frank Hejhal
$49.00 to $179.00

Continental plus breakfast
7 rooms, 3 private baths
Children, over 12
No pets
Restricted smoking
Mastercard, Visa, Am Ex, Disc.

Magnificent romantic 28 room mansion on Historic Register, near Fox River & miles of scenic trails. 1/2 hour to airport or Loop. European ambience, floral Tiffany-style windows. Oversize double whirlpools. Luxurious suites, verandahs, library, and gazebo. Perfect for weddings, receptions, corporate seminars and retreats. Formal breakfast.

PEACH COBBLER

2 cups sliced fresh
  peaches
3 tablespoons lemon
  juice
1 cup brown sugar
1 teaspoon cinnamon
3/4 cup flour

1/2 cup sugar
2 teaspoons baking
  powder
1/4 teaspoon salt
3/4 cup milk
1/3 cup butter

Place peaches in bottom of buttered 9" x 13" dish. Sprinkle with lemon juice. Mix all dry ingredients together with milk and pour on top. Melt butter and pour over top of batter. Bake at 350° for 45 minutes - 1 hour. Serves 10.

Submitted by:

Reedley Country Inn B&B
43137 Road 52
Reedley, California 93654
(209) 638-2585
George & Linda Penner
$55.00 to $77.00

Full breakfast
4 rooms, 4 private baths
Children, over 9
No pets
No smoking
Mastercard & Visa

A pink cottage surrounded by 3,500 roses! Each room has either a jacuzzi tub or shower, and patio. Set on a 20 acre farm property growing plums. We're on the "Blossom Trail" (late Feb. - early March) close to King's River rafting and tubing.

PEACH CUSTARD

1 1/2 cups flour	1/2 cup sugar
1/2 teaspoon salt	1/2 teaspoon cinnamon
1/2 cup soft butter	1/2 cup reserved peach
1 lb. 14 oz. can sliced	syrup
peaches, drained	1 egg, slightly beaten
(reserve syrup)	1 cup evaporated milk

Mix flour, salt and butter with pastry blender until coarse. Press into greased 8" square baking pan. Drain peaches well, save 1/2 cup syrup. Arrange peaches in 3 rows over crust. Sprinkle sugar and cinnamon over peach slices. Bake at 375° for 20 minutes. Blend reserved peach syrup, egg, and evaporated milk well. Pour over peach slices. Continue baking approximately 30 minutes or until custard is set. Cool slightly before cutting. Delicious breakfast dessert. Makes 9 servings.

Submitted by:

Benner House
645 Main Street
Historic Weston, Missouri
  64098
(816) 386-2616 (eve.)
Ken & Karen West
$58.00 to $65.00

Full breakfast
4 rooms
Children, over 12
No pets
Restricted smoking

Graciously restored 1890's Victorian home. Relax on wraparound front porch, be serenaded in our sitting room by a Regina music box, and return to yesteryear in our parlor filled with antique toys and dolls. Rest well in comfortable Victorian bedrooms, awaken to delightful aroma of breakfast awaiting you.

PECAN CINNAMON QUICK ROLLS

Dough:
1 1/2 quarts flour
2 1/2 tablespoons
  baking powder
1/2 tablespoon salt
Filling:
1/2 cup (scant) melted
  butter
1 cup brown sugar
Topping: (goes in
  bottom of pan)
1 1/2 cups brown sugar
1 cup corn syrup

3/4 cup sugar
1 cup butter
1 cup shortening
3 eggs
1 cup milk

1 tablespoon cinnamon
2 cups chopped pecans

1 1/2 cups chopped
  pecans
1/2 cup (scant) butter

Blend flour, baking powder, salt, sugar, butter, shortening, eggs and milk. Cover and chill 1 hour. Mix melted butter, brown sugar, cinnamon and pecans together for filling. Roll dough out 1/4" thick and spread cream mixture over it. Roll like a jelly roll and cut. In bottom of baking pan put topping ingredients and cook 3 minutes. Place rolls in pan, bake at 350° for 35 minutes. Turn out of pan while hot. Makes 35 rolls.

Submitted by:

Red Hill Inn
RFD 1, Box 99M
Centre Harbor, NH 03226
(603) 279-7001
Rick Miller & Don Leavitt
$65.00 to $125.00

Full breakfast
21 rooms, 21 private baths
Children allowed
No pets
Smoking allowed
Mastercard, Visa, Am Ex

Country inn on 60 acres overlooking lake and mountains. Fireplaces in rooms, and in country gourmet restaurant. Cross-country ski trails. Small lounge open year-round.

PHEASANT HILL BUBBLE BREAD

4 pkgs. refrigerator biscuits	1/2 cup brown sugar
Melted butter for dipping	1/4 teaspoon nutmeg
3 oz. pkg. instant butterscotch pudding	1 teaspoon cinnamon
	1/2 cup chopped pecans

Cut each biscuit into fourths. Dip in melted butter. After dipping the cut biscuits in butter, arrange a layer in bundt pan. Blend remaining ingredients in small bowl and sprinkle a portion over each layer as you add remaining biscuit pieces to the pan. Bake at 350° for 30 - 35 minutes. Turn out on large plate to cool. Makes 10 - 12 servings.

Submitted by:

Pheasant Hill Farm
HCR 68, Box 12
Bartley, Nebraska 69020
(308) 692-3278
Dona Nelms
$40.00 to $55.00

Full breakfast
5 rooms, 2 private baths
Children allowed
Pets allowed
Restricted smoking

We offer a rural setting on a working farm. Hunting is allowed in season. Area lakes offer recreational opportunities. Golf, restaurants, etc. are a 20 minute drive away.

PUFFED SLICED APPLE DISH

1 stick butter (1/2 cup)	3 tablespoons sugar
5 - 6 large apples, peeled, cored & sliced	1 teaspoon vanilla
6 large eggs, beaten	1 teaspoon cinnamon
1 1/2 cups milk	1/4 teaspoon nutmeg
1 cup flour	Brown sugar to taste

Melt butter in 9" x 13" Pyrex baking dish in 350° oven for 10 minutes. Add apples and return to oven for 10 minutes. Combine eggs and milk, beat well. Add flour, sugar, and seasonings. Pour batter over apples and sprinkle with brown sugar. Continue baking for 30 minutes. Bake until brown & puffed. Serve immediately. Serves 8.

Submitted by:

Victoria-on-Main B&B
622 W. Main St.
Whitewater, Wisconsin 53190
(414) 473-8400
Nancy Wendt
$48.00 to $75.00

Full breakfast
3 rooms, 1 private bath
No children
No pets
No smoking
Mastercard & Visa

Stately 1895 Victorian on National Historical Register, adjacent to UW-Whitewater campus. Guest rooms all feature lace curtains, Laura Ashley wallpapers, fine cotton linens, down comforters & antiques. Near Whitewater Lake & Kettle Moraine State Forest with year-round activities.

QUICK GRAHAM BISCUITS

2 cups Bisquick
4 tablespoons whole
   wheat flour
1 teaspoon baking
   powder

2 tablespoons vegetable
   oil
1/2 cup milk (more if
   needed)
Melted butter for tops

Combine dry ingredients, cut in oil. Starting with 1/2 cup milk, add until dough is moist. Knead as little as possible. Roll out to 3/8" thickness, and cut with regular biscuit cutter. Bake in 450° oven about 5 - 10 minutes until slightly brown. Brush with melted butter. Serve with your favorite jams or jellies. Enjoy! Makes 8 - 10 biscuits.

Submitted by:

The Culpepper House B&B
P.O. Box 462
Senoia, Georgia 30276
(404) 599-8182
Mary A. Brown
$50.00 to $60.00

Full breakfast
3 rooms, 1 private bath
Children, over 10
No pets
Restricted smoking

Browse in the surrounding antique and craft shops, try out tea rooms, look at old houses, visit some of the nearby Georgia State Parks and Gardens, or just enjoy the more leisurely pace of a small friendly town with a flavor of yesteryear.

RASPBERRY CREAM CHEESE TART

2 1/2 cups flour
3/4 cup sugar
3/4 cup butter, unsalted
1/2 teaspoon baking
powder
1/2 teaspoon baking
soda
1/4 teaspoon salt
3/4 cup sour cream

2 eggs (divided)
1 teaspoon almond
extract
8 oz. cream cheese,
softened
1/4 cup sugar
1/2 cup raspberry
preserves
1/2 cup sliced almonds

Preheat oven to 350°. Grease and flour 10" springform pan. In large bowl, combine flour and 3/4 cup sugar. With pastry blender, cut in butter thoroughly. Reserve 1 cup crumb mixture. To remainder add baking powder, baking soda, salt, sour cream, 1 egg and almond extract. Blend well. Spread batter over bottom and up 2" on sides of pan. In small bowl combine cream cheese, 1/4 cup sugar and 1 egg. Blend well. Pour over batter in pan. Carefully spread preserves over filling. Combine reserved crumbs and almonds. Sprinkle over top. Bake 45 - 55 minutes. Cool 15 minutes and remove sides of pan. Refrigerate and serve cold. Makes 16 servings.

Submitted by:

Bedford Inn
805 Stockton Avenue
Cape May, New Jersey 08204
(609) 884-4158
Alan & Cindy Schmucker
$80.00 to $140.00

Full breakfast
11 rooms, 11 private baths
Children, over 7
No pets
Restricted smoking
Mastercard & Visa

Restored 1881 seaside B&B, offering "honeymoon" suites and rooms, all with air-conditioning and authentic Victorian antiques. 1/2 block to beach, on-site parking, close to historic shopping district. Afternoon tea.

RHUBARB COBBLER

7 cups cut-up rhubarb	2 teaspoons baking
1 1/2 cups sugar	powder
6 tablespoons butter	2 cups sugar
1 cup milk	2 tablespoons
2 cups flour	cornstarch
1/2 teaspoon salt	1 cup boiling water

Spread rhubarb in bottom of 9" x 13" pan. Mix sugar, butter, milk, flour, salt and baking powder and spread over rhubarb. Sprinkle sugar and cornstarch on top. Over this pour boiling water. Bake at 350° for 1 hour.

Submitted by:

LaCorsette Maison Inn
629 First Ave. East
Newton, Iowa 50208
(515) 792-6833
Kay Owen
$55.00 to $125.00

Full breakfast
5 rooms, 5 private baths
Children allowed
Pets allowed (Advance notice)
No smoking
Mastercard, Visa, Am Ex

Contemporary comforts blend with turn-of-the-century cham in Mission-style "le mansion" on National Historic Register. Arts & crafts interior with dining room furniture designed by Limbert. Charming French bedchambers & beckoning hearths rekindle those romantic embers. On I-80, 40 minutes from Des Moines.

SALLY LUNN

1/2 cup butter	2 cups flour
2/3 cup sugar	2 teaspoons baking
2 eggs, beaten (room	powder
temperature)	1/2 cup milk

Cream butter and sugar. Add eggs. Combine dry ingredients, add to batter alternately with milk. Bake in 8" x 8" buttered pan, at 375° for 30 minutes. Note: Sally Lunn's bake shop is a museum (with tea shop) in Bath, England. We are located in Bath County, Virginia.

Submitted by:

Anderson Cottage B&B
Box 176
Warm Springs, VA 24484
(703) 839-2975
Jean Randolph Bruns
$55.00 to $110.00

Full breakfast
5 rooms, 4 private baths
Children allowed
Prefer no pets
Restricted smoking

Quiet mountain valley setting near Warm Springs Pools, the Homestead Hotel, hiking trails, and lake swimming. Rambling 18th/early 19th century home with spacious suites and rooms. Brick kitchen is independent 2-bedroom housekeeping unit.

SANDY'S ENGLISH SCONES

4 cups flour
3 tablespoons baking
powder
1 teaspoon salt
1 teaspoon cream of
tartar
3 tablespoons sugar

1 cup butter or
margarine
1 cup currants (or firm
fresh strawberries or
raisins or pecans)
1 1/3 cups milk
Egg wash

Mix first 6 ingredients well in food processor. Put in large bowl and mix in currants. Add milk and mix very gently. On floured board knead 10 - 15 times. Roll to 1 1/4". Cut with 3" cutter. Brush with egg wash. Bake on ungreased cookie sheet in preheated 425° oven 12 minutes. Makes 15 scones. Or divide dough in half and put into 2 ungreased 9" cake pans, and cut each into 8 wedges. Serve warm with butter and your very best homemade jam.

Origin: First prize, New York State Fair, 1984. Many guests say they return year after year just for these wonderful scones.

Submitted by:

The Red House Country Inn
Finger Lakes National Forest
4586 Picnic Area Road
Burdett, New York 14818
(607) 546-8566
Sandy Schmanke &
 Joan Martin
$60.00 to $85.00

Full breakfast
5 rooms, 4 full baths (shared)
Children, over 12
No pets
Restricted smoking
Mastercard, Visa, Am Ex
 Discover

1844 inn in the Finger Lakes National Forest, containing 28 miles of hiking & cross-country ski trails. Beautifully appointed rooms, public room & verandah, acres of lawns and gardens, and an inground pool.

SCALLOPED PINEAPPLE

20 oz. can crushed
   pineapple, undrained
1/3 cup sugar
2 well-beaten eggs

2 tablespoons flour
3/4 stick margarine,
   melted
Bread crumbs for top

Grease 1 1/2 - 2 qt. casserole dish. Mix pineapple, sugar, eggs, and flour. Pour into casserole dish. Drizzle with melted butter. Sprinkle with crumbs. Bake at 350° for 40 - 45 minutes. Serves 6 - 8.

Submitted by:

The Bells
Strawberry Hill St.
Bethlehem, N.H. 03574
(603) 869-2647
Louise Sims
$65.00 to $90.00

Full breakfast
4 rooms, 4 private baths
Children, over 12
No pets
Restricted smoking
Mastercard, Visa, Am Ex

Dramatic Victorian pagoda high in White Mtns. Colorful gardens, stone walls, veranda & gracious interior set the stage for romance. In charming village on Rte. 302 between Mt. Washington and Franconia Notch State Park. Hiking, antiquing, golf, and all attractions close by.

SCOTTISH OATMEAL SCONES

6 oz. plain flour
(1 1/2 cups)
2 oz. medium oatmeal
(1/3 cup)
1/4 teaspoon salt
1 level teaspoon
bicarbonate of soda

2 level teaspoons cream
of tartar
2 oz. margarine (1/4 cup)
About 1/4 pint milk
(2/3 cup)

Mix all dry ingredients together. Add margarine cut into small pieces. Rub into flour, stir in sufficient milk to make a soft but not sticky dough. Knead lightly until smooth. Roll out and cut using 2 1/2" fluted cutter or shape into 8" circle and cut into eight wedges. Bake on lightly greased cookie sheet at 425° for about 10 minutes. Serve with butter and strawberry jam. Makes 7 - 8.

Origin: A Scottish recipe hundreds of years old.

Submitted by:

Brae Loch Inn
5 Albany Street (U.S. Rte. 20)
Cazenovia, New York 13035
(315) 655-3431
James Grey Barr
$75.00 to $125.00

Continental plus breakfast
15 rooms, 12 private baths
Children allowed
No pets
Smoking allowed
Mastercard, Visa, Am Ex

Family-owned and operated since 1946. Originally built in 1805, as close to a Scottish inn as you will find this far west of Edinburgh. Victorian antiques, mellow tartan plaids, original stained glass, all delight the eye and relax the mind. Near shopping, golf and beach.

SIX SISTERS WHOLE WHEAT BISCUITS

2 cups all-purpose flour	3/4 teaspoon cream of
1 cup whole wheat flour	tartar
4 1/2 teaspoons baking	3/4 cup butter or
powder	margarine
2 tablespoons sugar	1 egg, beaten
1/2 teaspoon salt	1 cup milk

Combine flours, baking powder, sugar, salt, and cream of tartar in bowl. Cut in butter until mixture resembles coarse cornmeal. Add egg and milk, stirring quickly and briefly. Knead lightly on floured board. Roll or pat gently to 1" thickness. Cut into 1" - 2" biscuits. Place on greased cookie sheet. Bake at 450° for 12 - 15 minutes. Makes 20 biscuits. (Can add a cup of peeled, diced apples to mix.)

Submitted by:

Six Sisters B&B	Full breakfast
149 Union Avenue	4 rooms, 4 private baths
Saratoga Springs, N.Y. 12866	Children, over 10
(518) 583-1173	No pets
Stephen Ramirez &	No smoking
Kate Benton	Mastercard, Visa, Am Ex
$65.00 to $105.00 (reg. rates)	Mineral bath & massage pkgs.

Beautifully appointed 1880 Victorian recommended by Gourmet. Luxurious, immaculate suites with king beds, a/c and ceiling fans. Antiques, Orientals, hardwoods & Italian marble. Near racetracks, Skidmore College, City Center, SPAC, downtown and restaurants.

SKILLET-SIZZLED BUTTERMILK CORNBREAD

1 cup stone ground yellow cornmeal
1 cup unbleached white flour
1/4 teaspoon salt
1/4 teaspoon baking soda
1 tablespoon baking powder

1 egg
2 tablespoons - 1/4 cup sugar
1/4 cup corn or peanut oil
1 1/4 cups cultured buttermilk
2 - 4 tablespoons butter for skillet

Preheat oven to 375°. Combine cornmeal, flour, salt, baking soda and baking powder. Set aside. Combine egg, sugar, oil, and buttermilk. Set aside. Heat 8" iron skillet with butter in it, over medium heat. Quickly combine wet and dry ingredients, stirring just enough to moisten, and scrape into hot buttery skillet. Bake 20 - 25 minutes until crusty & golden brown. Cut into 8 wedges, like a cake.

Submitted by:

Dairy Hollow House
515 Spring Street
Eureka Springs, Arkansas
 72632
(800) 562-8650
Ned Shank,
C. Dragonwagon
$115.00 to $145.00

Full breakfast
6 rooms, 6 private baths
Children allowed, but advance
 notice is preferred
No pets
Restricted smoking
Mastercard, Visa, Am Ex,
 Discover, Diner's

Woodburning fireplaces in every room, wonderful breakfast delivered daily, right to your door, in a split-oak basket. Called by Gourmet Magazine, "an inn with the finest restaurant in the region. . . all details carefully wrought." Rooms are flower-filled; our cuisine a celebration!

SOUR CREAM CINNAMON TWIST

1 cup sour cream
3 tablespoons sugar
1/8 teaspoon soda
1 teaspoon salt
1 cake compressed
 yeast (1 oz.)
1 large egg
Frosting:
1 cup powdered sugar
1 - 2 tablespoons milk
 or cream

2 tablespoons soft
 shortening
3 cups sifted all-
 purpose flour
2 tablespoons soft
 butter
1/3 cup brown sugar
1 teaspoon cinnamon

1/2 teaspoon vanilla
 or other flavoring

Heat sour cream in large saucepan until lukewarm. Remove from heat and stir in sugar, soda and salt. When cool, crumble yeast into mixture. Stir until dissolved. Add egg, shortening and flour. Mix well (use hands if necessary). Turn dough onto floured surface and knead until smooth. Then roll into an oblong 24" x 6" piece. Spread with 2 tablespoons soft butter. Sprinkle half of dough with a mixture of 1/3 cup brown sugar and 1 teaspoon cinnamon. Fold other half over, cut into 20 strips. Hold both ends of strip and twist (in opposite directions). Place on greased baking sheet. Cover, let rise until light, about 1 hour. Bake at 360° 12 - 15 minutes. Mix frosting ingredients, and frost twists while warm. Serve warm with butter. Makes 20 twists.

Submitted by:

Bed & Breakfast at The Pines
327 Ardussi Street
Frankenmuth, Mich. 48734
(517) 652-9019
Richard & Donna Hodge
$30.00 (sgl.) to $40.00 (dbl.)
Children - $1.00/year of age

Continental plus breakfast
2 rooms, shared baths
No smoking

Traditional ranch-style home in MI's "Little Bavaria." Walking distance to main tourist areas and famous restaurants. Heirloom quilts, ceiling fans, antique accents. Sit-down breakfast: fresh fruits & homemade breads. Recipes shared. "Come as a stranger; leave as a friend."

SWEET POTATO CRISP

8 oz. cream cheese	2/3 cup chopped
40 oz. can cut sweet	cranberries
potatoes, drained	1/2 cup flour
3/4 cup packed brown	1/2 cup raw oatmeal
sugar (divided)	1/3 cup margarine
1/4 teaspoon cinnamon	1/4 cup chopped
1 cup chopped apples	pecans

Preheat oven to 350°. Beat cream cheese, sweet potatoes, 1/4 cup brown sugar and cinnamon in bowl with mixer until well blended. Spoon into 1 1/2 quart casserole or 10" x 6" baking dish. Top with apples and cranberries. Stir together flour, oats, and 1/2 cup sugar in bowl. Cut in margarine and pecans. Sprinkle over fruit. Bake 35 - 40 minutes. Serves 8.

Submitted by:

Whistling Swan Inn	Full breakfast
P.O. Box 791 - 110 Main St.	10 rooms, 10 private baths
Stanhope, N.J. 07874	Children, over 12
(201) 347-6369	No pets
Joe Mulay & Paula Williams	No smoking
$65.00 to $95.00	Mastercard, Visa, Am Ex, Disc.

This house, circa 1900, in the northwestern Skylands portion of N.J., just off I-80 at Route 206, is 45 miles west of N.Y. City; near antiquing, wineries, historic Chester, Waterloo Village, International Trade Center, lakes, Delaware Water Gap, winter activities and restaurants.

FRENCH TOAST, PANCAKES & WAFFLES

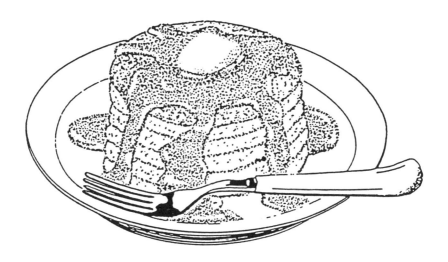

ALLEN VILLA CRISPY FRENCH TOAST

2 cups flour
1 egg
1 tablespoon vanilla

Enough water to make
of dipping consistency
Cinnamon bread

Mix all ingredients for batter. Dip cinnamon bread in batter and fry in Wesson vegetable oil until golden brown. Can be topped with fresh fruit, strawberries, jam, or syrup.

Submitted by:

Allen Villa Bed & Breakfast
434 South Market St.
Troy, Ohio 45373
(513) 335-1181
Robert & June Smith
$45.00 to $65.00

Full breakfast
4 rooms, 4 private baths
Children, over 12
No pets
Restricted smoking
Mastercard, Visa, Am Ex

The Villa is 56' x 42', 3 stories high, with 14 rooms, all finished in the most workmanlike manner with the use of white and black walnut. In 1985, Bob & June Smith purchased the Villa and have since been restoring it to its original condition. Decorated with Victorian furniture.

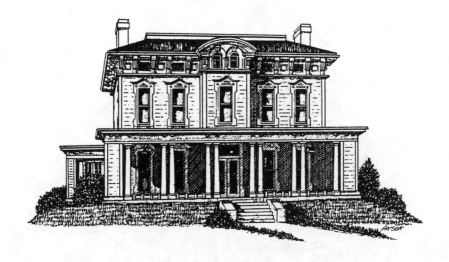

ALMOND FRENCH TOAST

1 loaf Challah bread, unsliced	2 teaspoons brown sugar
6 eggs	1 teaspoon almond extract
1 cup half & half	Toasted slivered almonds for garnish
1/2 teaspoon nutmeg	

Slice Challah bread to desired thickness. Beat eggs well in large bowl, add half & half, nutmeg, sugar, and extract, and beat very well. Heat skillet. Add small amount of oleo or butter. Dip bread slices in batter, grill in skillet until both sides are nicely browned. Serve on plate, garnish with slivered almonds. Serve with maple syrup. Makes 6 servings.

Submitted by:

Silas Griffith Inn
R.R. #1, Box 66F
Danby, Vermont 05739
(802) 293-5567
Paul & Lois Dansereau
$71.00 to $86.00

Full breakfast
17 rooms, 14 private baths
Children allowed
No pets
Restricted smoking
Mastercard, Visa, Am Ex

Gracious 1891 mansion & carriage house on Historic Register. Unique 8' round cherry wood pocket door, cherry and oak woodwork, stained glass windows, furnished with Victorian antiques. In Green Mtn. National Forest, spectacular views, hiking, biking, skiing nearby.

AMISH PANCAKES

1/2 stick butter	Toppings:
6 eggs	Powdered sugar and
1 cup flour	syrup
1/2 teaspoon salt	Strawberries or any
1 cup milk	fruit

Melt butter in 9" x 13" pan. Mix eggs, flour, salt and milk together well. Pour into pan with melted butter. Bake at 425° for 15 minutes. Top with your choice of toppings. Makes 6 servings.

Submitted by:

Pleasant Grove Farm	Full breakfast
368 Pilottown Road	4 rooms
Peach Bottom, Penn. 17563	Children allowed
(717) 548-3100	No pets
Charles & Labertha Tindall	Restricted smoking
$40.00 to $45.00	

Located in beautiful, historic Lancaster County, this 160 acre dairy farm has been family-run for 110 years, earning it the title of "Century Farm". As a working dairy farm, it lets guests experience daily life in a rural setting. 176 years ago, our home was also a country store and post office. Country breakfast by candlelight.

APPLE PECAN BUTTERMILK PANCAKES

2 cups all-purpose flour
1 teaspoon baking soda
1 teaspoon salt
2 tablespoons sugar
2 eggs, slightly beaten
2 cups buttermilk
2 tablespoons melted
   butter

Pinch of cardamom
1 teaspoon cinnamon
2 Golden Delicious
   apples, peeled and
   sautéed in 1 tables-
   spoon butter
1/2 cup toasted
   pecans

Sift flour, baking soda, salt, and sugar into mixing bowl. Combine egg, buttermilk & melted butter. Add spices. Do not overmix. Add sautéed apples and pecans. Bake on hot, lightly greased griddle. Serve hot with butter and real maple syrup. Makes 6 servings.

Submitted by:

The Sand Castle
829 Stockton Avenue
Cape May, New Jersey 08204
(800) 346-5451
Tracie & Daniel Spinosa
$85.00 to $125.00

Continental plus breakfast
10 rooms, 6 private baths
Children allowed
No pets
Restricted smoking
Mastercard & Visa

Experience the charm and atmosphere of a Victorian town in our gothic cottage, circa 1873. Wraparound verandah invites an ocean view while being enticed with homebaked muffins, breads and cakes. Open year round. Near fine restaurants and recreational facilities.

BAKED FRENCH TOAST OLD PARSONAGE

16 slices Pepperidge Farm cinnamon bread	6 large eggs
1 cup brown sugar	1 1/2 - 2 cups milk
1 stick butter	1 teaspoon vanilla
1/4 cup maple syrup	Sour cream & berries for garnish

Melt butter, brown sugar and maple syrup in the bottom of an 11" x 17" pan. Cook until mixture is well-blended and dissolved, 5 minutes. Put pairs of bread into the mixture. Mix eggs, milk and vanilla and pour over bread. Let sit 45 minutes or overnight in refrigerator. Bake at 350° for 30 minutes. Garnish with sour cream and berries. Makes 8 servings.

Submitted by:

Lake Brook B&B
57 Western Ave.
Kennebunk, Maine 04043
(207) 967-4069
Carolyn McAdams
$70.00 to $85.00 + tax
3rd person, $15.00 extra

Full breakfast
4 rooms, 4 private baths
Children allowed
No pets
Restricted smoking

Relax in comfortable rockers overlooking the beautiful flower gardens or stroll into Dock Square just 1/2 mile away. Awaken to our special blend of coffee to start your day. Beaches are just 1 mile away.

BAKED WHOLE WHEAT FRENCH TOAST ROUNDS

2 whole eggs plus 3 egg whites 1 cup lowfat milk 1 tablespoon maple syrup	Zest of 1 lemon Pinch of nutmeg 6 slices whole wheat bread Assorted toppings

Preheat oven to 425°. Cut 4" circle from each slice of bread with empty coffee can. Generously grease large baking pan. Lay rounds in pan. Combine eggs, milk, maple syrup, lemon zest and nutmeg. Beat with electric mixer until thick and smooth. Pour over bread. Let sit about 15 - 20 minutes, until liquid is absorbed. May be refrigerated or frozen at this point. Bake for 6 minutes on each side, until light and fluffy. Serve immediately, topped with 1 quart strawberries, sliced and mixed with 2 tablespoons maple syrup, 1 pint lowfat plain or maple yogurt, and 1/2 cup chopped pecans. Serves 3 - 6 people.

Submitted by:

Liberty Hill Inn on Cape Cod 77 Main St. (Rt. 6A & Willow) Yarmouth Port, Mass. 02675 (800) 821-3977 Jack & Beth Flanagan $75.00 to $125.00	Full breakfast 5 rooms, 5 private baths Children allowed No pets Restricted smoking Mastercard, Visa, Am Ex

150 year old country inn offers a peaceful and unique experience to the discriminating traveler seeking the finest in service & hospitality. Plush carpets & lofty ceilings invite you to linger awhile. Located on the quiet North side, near beach, whale-watching, crafts, and fishing.

BANANA WHEAT BREAD FRENCH TOAST

1 cup butter (2 sticks)	2 teaspoons baking soda
2 cups sugar	1 teaspoon salt
4 large eggs, beaten	4 mashed bananas
2 teaspoons vanilla	1 cup chopped pecans
1 cup sour cream	
1 1/2 cups all-purpose flour	2 eggs
	1 cup milk
1 1/2 cups whole wheat flour	1 stick margarine for frying

For bread dough: Cream butter and sugar. Add eggs and vanilla. Add sour cream and mix well. Add dry ingredients and mix. Add bananas and pecans. Bake in greased loaf tins at 350° for one hour. When cool, slice and dip in mixture of beaten eggs and milk. Fry in 1 stick margarine, as for French toast. Makes 2 loaves, or 8 servings.

Submitted by:

Barrow House	Continental breakfast
524 Royal Street	Full breakfast, $5.00 extra
P.O. Box 1461	4 rooms, 4 private baths
St. Francisville, Louis. 70775	Children allowed
(504) 635-4791	No pets
Shirley & Lyle Dittloff	Smoking allowed
$75.00 to $95.00	

Wicker rockers on front porch, in quiet neighborhood of antebellum homes. Rolling hills and live oaks. 1860's antiques, private gourmet candlelight dinners. Tour six area plantations and enjoy a cassette walking tour of our historic town prepared for our guests.

Camille Leake Barrow House

BELGIAN WAFFLE HOME MIX

1 pkg. dry yeast
2 cups lukewarm milk
4 eggs
1 teaspoon vanilla
2 1/2 cups sifted flour
1/2 teaspoon salt

1 tablespoon sugar
1/2 cup melted butter
1/2 cup drained
   blueberries (or other
   variety of fruit)

Put yeast in lukewarm milk and dissolve. Add eggs and vanilla. Add flour, salt and sugar. Beat well. Add butter and fruit. Stand in warm place for 45 minutes or store in refrigerator overnight. If refrigerated, bring dough to room temperature before baking. Bake in Belgian waffle iron according to instructions. Makes 8 large waffles.

Submitted by:

Skoglund Farm
Route 1, Box 45
Canova, S.D. 57321
(605) 247-3445
Alden & Delores Skoglund
Adults - $25.00, Teens -
   $20.00, Children - $15.00,
   Age 5 & under, free

Full breakfast
4 rooms, 3 shared baths
Children allowed
Pets allowed
No smoking

Enjoy an overnight on South Dakota prairie. Evening dinner. Local attractions: Corn Palace, Indian dig, Doll Museum at Mitchell, Prairie Village at Madison. Local parks, lakes, hiking, animals, farm activities.

BLACKBERRY BUTTERMILK PANCAKES

2/3 cup white flour
1/3 cup whole wheat
  flour
1 tablespoon sugar
2 teaspoons baking
  powder

1 egg, beaten
2 tablespoons oil
1 cup buttermilk
1 cup blackberries (or 2
  ripe mashed bananas)

Combine dry ingredients, set aside. Combine egg, oil and buttermilk, and add to dry ingredients. Stir lightly. Gently stir in blackberries. Drop by 1/3 cupfuls onto 350° griddle. Cook until slightly browned. Makes 12 - 14 pancakes. These are great served with fresh blackberry syrup!

Submitted by:

The Hidden Inn
249 Caroline Street
Orange, Virginia 22960
(703) 672-3625
Ray & Barbara Lonick
$79.00 to $159.00

Full breakfast
10 rooms, 10 private baths
Children allowed
No pets
No smoking
Mastercard & Visa

1880's inn surrounded by 6 wooded acres. Near historic Monticello, Sky Line Drive, Montpelier, & several Civil War battle sites. Have an intimate weekend in the country or simply a refreshing night's stay. Relaxing atmosphere and true Southern hospitality.

BLUEBERRY WILD RICE PANCAKES

3 cups white flour	5 eggs, separated
1 cup whole wheat flour	2 tablespoons oil
3 tablespoons sugar	1 quart buttermilk
1 teaspoon salt	3/4 cup milk
1 tablespoon baking soda	1 tablespoon vanilla
2 tablespoons baking powder	1 pint blueberries
	3 cups cooked wild rice

In large bowl combine flours, sugar, salt, baking soda, and baking powder. Separate eggs. To egg yolks add oil, buttermilk, milk and vanilla. Mix. Beat egg whites stiff but not dry. Pour egg yolk mixture over flour mixture, stir to combine. Fold in berries and wild rice. Gently fold in egg whites. Add extra milk to reach desired consistency. Cook on hot griddle. Serve with butter and maple syrup. Serves 10.

Submitted by:

The Stone Hearth Inn
on Lake Superior
1118 Highway 61 East
Little Marais, Minnesota 55614
(218) 226-3020
Charlie & Susan Michels
$75.00 to $124.00

Full breakfast
7 rooms, 7 private baths
Children, over 12
No pets
No smoking
Mastercard, Visa, Am Ex

Renovated 1920's homestead & boathouse on the shore of Lake Superior. Enjoy four seasons of activities while being treated to relaxed hospitality in North Shore serenity. Unique regional cuisine is served in lakeside dining room. Elegant antiques, some whirlpool tubs and fireplaces.

BLUE CORNMEAL PANCAKES

12 oz. blue cornmeal	1 tablespoon baking
12 oz. all-purpose flour	powder
2 oz. sugar	4 large eggs
1 teaspoon salt	1 quart buttermilk
1 tablespoon baking	4 oz. unsalted butter,
soda	melted

In bowl mix together blue cornmeal, flour, sugar, salt, baking soda, and baking powder. In another bowl, lightly beat eggs, then add buttermilk and melted butter. Sift dry ingredients into wet, and mix until blended. Ladle onto hot, oiled griddle and cook until bubbles form. Turn and brown the second side. Makes 10 servings.

Submitted by:

Friends Lake Inn	Full breakfast
Friends Lake Road	16 rooms, 16 private baths
Chestertown, N.Y. 12817	Children allowed
(518) 494-4751	No pets
Sharon & Greg Taylor	Restricted smoking
$65.00 to $200.00	Mastercard & Visa

A completely restored country inn overlooking Friends Lake with an award-winning dining room and wine list, outdoor hot tub, cross country skiing and mountain bike rentals.

BLUSHING ROSÉ SUPREME FRENCH TOAST

1 loaf homemade or
store baked raisin
bread
6 eggs
1 1/2 cups milk
1 cup half & half
1 teaspoon vanilla
1/4 teaspoon cinnamon

1/4 teaspoon nutmeg
Cinnamon-sugar mixture
Topping:
1/4 cup butter or
margarine
1/2 cup brown sugar
1/2 cup chopped walnuts
(opt.)

Slice bread and overlap lengthwise in 9" x 13" dish. Mix liquid ingredients, including cinnamon and nutmeg. Pour over bread and sprinkle lightly with a cinnamon-sugar mixture. Cover and refrigerate overnight. In the morning mix together topping ingredients. Spread over bread, or may be left plain. Bake at 350° about 40 minutes. Serve hot with syrup.

Submitted by:

The Blushing Rosé B&B
11 William Street
Hammondsport, N.Y. 14840
(607) 569-3402
Ellen & Bucky Laufersweiler
$65.00 to $75.00

Full breakfast/Continental plus
 "Early Bird" breakfast
4 rooms, 4 private baths
Children, over 12
No pets
Restricted smoking

Decorated in period antiques, with spacious guest rooms, and an ambience of warm, cozy, 19th century America. In Hammondsport, the cradle of aviation, and near many points of interest. Stroll to the edge of Keuka Lake, and delight in soft evening breezes off the lake.

CHERRY OATMEAL PANCAKES

1/2 cup dried cherries	2 cups complete
1/2 cup quick cooking	pancake mix
oatmeal	1 1/2 tablespoons sugar
2 cups water	1/2 - 1 teaspoon mace

Combine dried cherries, oatmeal and water. Let stand 10 minutes. Stir in remaining ingredients until moist. Cook on 375° griddle sprayed with vegetable cooking spray. Cook 1 - 1 1/2 minutes each side or until done. Makes 4 servings.

Submitted by:

Manitou Manor B&B	Full breakfast
P.O. Box 864	4 rooms, 4 private baths
Leland, Michigan 49654	Children, over 12
(616) 2546-7712	No pets
Penny & Walt Mace	No smoking
$85.00 to $90.00	Mastercard & Visa

Early 1900's farmhouse, surrounded by cherry orchards and woods. Renovated throughout, with traditional furnishings. Breakfast items indigenous to Leelanau County. Near Leland's historic Fishtown, Manitou Islands, & Sleeping Bear Dunes National Lakeshore. Golf, cross country skiing, wineries and fine dining.

CHOCOLATE WAFFLES WITH CINNAMON BUTTER

Waffles:
2/3 cup all-purpose flour
1/2 teaspoon baking
  powder
1/4 teaspoon salt
1/3 cup sugar
1 1/2 tablespoons cocoa

2 eggs, separated
1/4 cup commercial
  sour cream
3 tablespoons butter or
  margarine, melted
1/8 teaspoon cream of
  tartar

Cinnamon Butter:
1/2 cup unsalted butter
  or margarine, softened
1 tablespoon honey

1/2 teaspoon ground
  cinnamon

Combine first 5 waffle ingredients, set aside. Combine egg yolks, sour cream, and butter. Add to flour mixture, stirring until blended. Beat egg whites (at room temperature) and cream of tartar until stiff peaks form. Carefully fold whites into batter. Bake in preheated, oiled waffle iron. Beat Cinnamon Butter ingredients together well. Serve with waffles. Makes 6 - 4" waffles and 1/2 cup of butter.

Submitted by:

Country Palmer House
R.R. #3, Box 254
Mt. Carroll, IL 61053
(815) 244-2343
Allan & JoAnn Palmer
$40.00 to $75.00

Full breakfast
4 rooms, 2 private baths
Children allowed
No pets
No smoking
Mastercard & Visa

1911 remodeled farm home - fireplace in family room. Quiet, with beautiful view from top of ridge in northwest Illinois. Furnished with many oak antique pieces. Farm tours available. Hayrides and bonfires can be arranged on premises. Country breakfast.

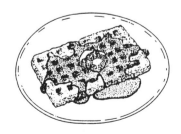

CINNAMON APPLE CREPES

Basic crepe recipe of your choice	6 tablespoons brown sugar
1/4 cup butter	9 apples, peeled & sliced
3/4 cup raisins	12 cooked pork sausage links
1 1/2 teaspoons cinnamon	

Melt butter in large skillet. Add raisins, cinnamon, brown sugar and apple slices. Cook until apples are soft. Add pork sausages. Spread on crepe and roll, tucking sides under. Spoon small amount of apple filling on top. Serve with scrambled eggs. Makes 8 servings.

Submitted by:

Scandia B&B Inn
P.O. Box 166, Hwy. 62 West
Eureka Springs, Ark. 72632
(800) 523-8922
Cynthia Barnes
$65.00 to $99.00

Full breakfast
7 rooms, 7 private baths
Children allowed
No pets
No smoking
Mastercard, Visa, Am Ex, Disc.

Each cottage is a private little dollhouse with private entry. We feature designer linens with Priscilla draperies. Honeymoon suite has private jacuzzi for two, fantasy grapevine and ivy arbor over bed. Large 10-man hot tub outdoors under gazebo.

CORNUCOPIA FRENCH TOAST

4 eggs
1 1/2 cups milk
Dash of salt
1/2 teaspoon almond
  extract
Zest from 1 orange
8 slices thick-cut (1")
  bread
1 tablespoon butter or
  margarine

2 cups sliced peaches
1 banana, sliced
1 teaspoon butter or
  margarine
2 teaspoons fresh
  lemon juice
1 tablespoon brown
  sugar
8 oz. cream cheese,
  softened

Beat eggs, milk, salt, almond extract, and zest until frothy, then refrigerate until later use. Cut a pocket into each bread slice and set aside. Prepare filling: Sauté peaches and banana in butter, lemon juice and brown sugar until carmelized. Combine with cream cheese. Spoon 2 - 3 tablespoons filling into each pocket. Dip bread into egg mixture coating both sides. In melted butter, fry all pieces until golden. Serve with dash of powdered sugar on top and garnish with fresh fruit puree. Makes 8 servings.

Submitted by:

Two Sisters Inn
Ten Otoe Place
Manitou Springs, CO 80829
(719) 685-9684
Wendy Goldstein &
  Sharon Smith
$59.00 to $90.00

Full breakfast
5 rooms, 3 private baths
Children, over 5
No pets
No smoking
Mastercard & Visa

Nestled at base of Pikes Peak, lovingly restored, gracious 1919 rose-colored Victorian bungalow with honeymoon cottage in back garden. Beautiful family collectibles, antiques & fresh flowers fill sunny rooms. Walk to art galleries and mineral springs in Historic District.

CREAM CHEESE FRENCH TOAST WITH FRUIT DRESSING

12 slices raisin bread
4 oz. softened cream
  cheese
Batter:
4 eggs, well-beaten
1/4 teaspoon nutmeg
1 teaspoon vanilla

Dressing:
1 cup whole cooked
  cranberries
1 cup sour cherries
1/3 cup sugar (or to
  taste)
Cornstarch to thicken

Spread 6 slices of bread with a thin layer of cream cheese, top with remaining bread slices and cut each sandwich diagonally. Mix batter ingredients. Dip each sandwich half in batter and fry on very lightly greased griddle (medium high heat) until golden brown on both sides. For dressing: Cook both fruits with the sugar, to near boiling. Add cornstarch to thicken if needed. Serve over the French toast. Makes 6 servings.

Submitted by:

The Loom Room
RD 1, Box 1420
Leesport, PA 19533
(215) 926-3217
Gene & Mary Smith
$45.00 to $50.00

Full breakfast
3 rooms, 1 private baths
Children allowed
No pets
Restricted smoking

A restored 1812 farmhouse with 5 fireplaces and a 1760 log addition where Mary weaves custom clothing. The herb garden, shaded lawn and colonial gazebo create an atmosphere of relaxation. Near tennis, shopping outlets, great antiquing, golf, hiking, fishing and boating.

CURRANT AND CHEESE PANCAKES

1/2 cup flour	1/2 cup cottage cheese
1 tablespoon sugar	2 tablespoons milk
1 teaspoon baking powder	1 tablespoon cooking oil
1/4 teaspoon cinnamon	1 tablespoon vanilla
2 eggs	2 tablespoons currants

Combine flour, sugar, baking powder, and cinnamon. Beat together eggs, cottage cheese, milk, oil and vanilla. Add to dry ingredients, stir until blended but still slightly lumpy. Stir in currants. For each pancake pour one rounded tablespoon batter onto hot, lightly greased griddle. Cook until golden, turning to cook other side when pancakes have a bubbly surface. Serve with butter or margarine and maple syrup. Makes 12 pancakes.

Submitted by:

The Summer House	Full breakfast
158 Main Street	5 rooms, 1 private bath
Sandwich (Cape Cod),	Children, over 6
Massachusetts 02563	No pets
(508) 888-4991	Restricted smoking
David & Kay Merrell	Mastercard, Visa, Am Ex,
$40.00 to $75.00	Discover

Exquisite 1835 Greek Revival B&B featured in Country Living magazine, in the heart of historic village. Antiques, hand-stitched quilts, flowers, large sunny rooms, English-style gardens. Within strolling distance of dining, museums, shops, pond & gristmills and the boardwalk.

DEEP DISH CUSTARD FRENCH TOAST

Butter	3 cups milk
6 slices 1" thick sweet bread (Portuguese, French, Italian or Hawaiian)	2 egg yolks
	1 can evaporated milk
	2 teaspoons vanilla
Cinnamon to taste	Topping:
4 whole eggs	Fruit
3/4 cup sugar or honey	Whipped cream

Lightly grease a 9" x 13" Pyrex dish. Butter both sides of each of six slices of 1" thick sweet bread (Portuguese, preferably). Arrange bread side by side in baking dish, then sprinkle with cinnamon. Mix eggs, sugar or honey, milk, egg yolks, evaporated milk and vanilla with electric mixer until well blended, and pour over bread slices. Bake at 325° approximately 30 - 45 minutes. The French toast is done when knife inserted in egg mixture comes out clean (similar to testing custard). The top should be a golden brown. Top with your favorite fruit, whipped cream or enjoy plain.

Submitted by:

Gloria's Spouting Horn
 Bed & Breakfast Inn
4464 Lawai Road, Koloa
Kauai, Hawaii 96756
(808) 742-6995
Gloria & Bob Merkle
$55.00 to $125.00

Continental breakfast
5 rooms, 5 private baths
Children, over 14
No pets
No smoking
Mastercard & Visa (add $5.00
 a night)

Unique oceanfront B&B featuring restored Hawaiian sugar plantation house nestled between the sea and fields of sugar cane. Relax in a hammock under coconut trees, or whale watch from your bed with the surf 40 feet away from your deck!

DUTCH BABIES/GERMAN PANCAKES

4 eggs	1 teaspoon vanilla
2 cups milk or	extract
half & half	2 teaspoons almond
1/3 cup sugar	extract
1 teaspoon salt	2 cups flour

Beat eggs until fluffy. Add milk/half & half slowly. Do not disturb fluffiness. Add sugar gradually. Add salt, vanilla, almond extract. Mix well. Add 2 cups flour, mixing well. Bake in any type of 12" skillet or baking pan, buttered generously, at 375° for 40 - 45 minutes until puffed and edges are golden brown. Makes 6 - 8 servings.

Submitted by:

Highland Dell Inn	Full breakfast
21050 River Blvd., Box 370	10 rooms, 8 private baths
Monte Rio, California 95462	No children
(800) 767-1759	Pets allowed
Glenn Dixon,	Restricted smoking
Anthony Patchett	Mastercard, Visa, Am Ex,
$65.00 to $255.00	Discover

Landmark beckons to the appreciative traveler through rich stained glass windows, gigantic lobby fireplace, heirloom antiques and a unique collection of historic local photos. On the Russian River, well-known for its recreational activities. Fresh air, and large pool area.

HIGHLAND DELL INN
Bed and Breakfast on the Russian River

FRENCH TOASTED ENGLISH MUFFINS

3 eggs	1/2 teaspoon vanilla
1 cup milk	4 English muffins,
2 tablespoons sugar	split
1/4 teaspoon salt	1 tablespoon butter

Beat first five ingredients until smooth. Soak muffins in mixture until saturated. Heat butter until melted. Brown on each side. Serve with butter and maple syrup. Serves 4.

Submitted by:

Tulip Tree Inn	Full breakfast
Chittenden Dam Road	8 rooms, 8 private baths
Chittenden, Vermont 05737	No children
(802) 483-6213	No pets
Rosemary & Ed McDowell	Restricted smoking
$72.00 to $105.00	Mastercard & Visa

This is the way you have always pictured a country inn. Warm and charming guest rooms, many with their own jacuzzi. Secluded in the Green Mountain National Forest, we offer a bit of backwoods luxury. Fine candlelight dining.

FRUITED GRANOLA PANCAKES

Pancake batter of your choice
Fresh fruit to taste (Blueberries, cranberries, sliced apples, etc.)
4 cups slightly crushed assorted dried cereals
1/2 cup coconut, grated
1/2 cup chopped nut meats
2 tablespoons wheat germ
1/4 cup raisins

Mix cereals, coconut, nuts, wheat germ and raisins for granola topping. Prepare pancake batter of your choice. Fold in fresh fruit to taste. Drop batter onto hot Pam-sprayed grill and immediately top batter with granola mix. Turn and brown. Serve hot with maple syrup or your favorite fruit sauce: rhubarb, apple, blueberry, etc. Leftovers are delicious toasted!

Submitted by:

Island Watch B&B
Freeman Ridge Road
P.O. Box 1359
Southwest Harbor, ME 04679
(207) 244-7229
Maxine Clark (Heidi - standard poodle)
$65.00

Full breakfast
6 rooms, 6 private baths
Children, over 10
No pets
No smoking

Island Watch B&B overlooks the great harbors of Mt. Desert Island and the mountains of Acadia National Park. Spacious rooms, hearty breakfasts, smoke-free, and affordable. Light keeper's daughter.

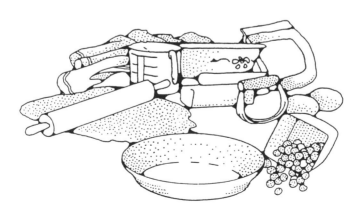

GERMAN FRENCH TOAST (WITH SAUSAGE)

2 cups milk	2 tart apples, peeled,
3 eggs, separated	cored & sliced
1 tablespoon lemon rind	1 tablespoon lemon juice
1 tablespoon sugar	Water
(opt.)	2 - 3 links smoked, sliced
6 - 8 thick slices	bratwurst
day-old French bread	1/4 onion, sliced
1 cup bread crumbs	Cinnamon-sugar mixture

Combine milk, egg yolks, lemon rind and sugar, if desired. Soak bread in this until saturated, then dip in egg whites, then in bread crumbs and place bread on greased cookie sheet. Place in preheated oven for 15 minutes at 425°, turn bread and bake an additional 10 - 12 minutes. Meanwhile, place apple slices and lemon juice in saucepan with water to cover, and bring to boil; then remove from heat. Also lightly sauté sliced bratwurst and onions until lightly browned. Place 2 slices of toast on each plate, sprinkle with cinnamon-sugar, cover with apples and serve with bratwurst. Makes 3 - 4 servings.

Origin: Recipe from my grandmother who came from Alsace-Lorraine. She called it Arme Ritter, meaning "Poor Knights".

Submitted by:

Strawberry Creek Inn
P.O. Box 1818
Idyllwild, California 92349
(714) 659-3202
Diana Dugan & Jim Goff
$80.00 to $125.00

Full breakfast
10 rooms, 10 private baths
Children allowed
No pets
No smoking
Mastercard & Visa

Large cedar shingle mountain home, elevation 5,500', nestled amid the pine and cedar trees of the San Jacinto Mountains of southern California. Country antiques, hand-crafted decorations, queen-size beds, fireplaces, and a glassed-in dining porch.

GINGERBREAD PANCAKES

3 cups unbleached flour	1/3 cup molasses
2 tablespoons baking powder	2 1/4 cups milk
1 teaspoon baking soda	3 eggs, lightly beaten
1 teaspoon cinnamon	6 tablespooons melted butter
1 teaspoon ginger	

Blend flour, baking powder, soda and spices. Combine molasses, milk and egg. Stir in melted butter. Combine mixtures until well-moistened. Cook pancakes on hot griddle. Makes 8 pancakes.

Submitted by:

The Raspberry Patch B&B   Full breakfast
606 Randolph Road   4 rooms, 4 private baths
Stowe, Vermont 05672   Children allowed
(802) 253-4145 or   Pets allowed
(800) 624-0639   No smoking
Linda Jones   Mastercard & Visa
$65.00

Homey comfort, peace and quiet; cozy rooms with antiques & down comforters. A Vermont breakfast is served by the fire in winter, overlooking beautiful Mt. Mansfield. Only 5 minutes from fine restaurants, shops, and activities. Multi-day packages are available. Air-conditioned in summer.

GRANDMA'S WAFFLES

2 cups all-purpose flour	5 tablespoons melted
3 tablespoons sugar	butter
1 teaspoon salt	2 eggs
4 teaspoons baking	1 1/2 cups milk
powder	

Combine all dry ingredients. Beat eggs in blender until frothy and add milk to eggs. Gradually add to dry items and mix. Add melted butter. Heat waffle iron sprayed with Pam. Use 1 ladleful of batter per iron. Bake and enjoy!

Submitted by:

Swatara Creek Inn
Box 692, RD 2
Annville, Pennsylvania 17003
(717) 865-3259
Dick & Jeannette Hess
$50.00 to $70.00 per couple

Full breakfast
10 rooms, 10 private baths
Well-behaved children allowed
No pets
Restricted smoking
Mastercard, Visa, Am Ex, Disc.

Victorian mansion, circa 1860, on 4 acres in the country. Near Hershey, Lancaster (Amish), Reading (outlet shops), and Gettysburg. Canopy beds, large dining room (table seats 20), sitting room and gift shop. Near good restaurant.

GREEN CHILI PANCAKES

1 1/2 cups whole wheat flour
1/2 cup white flour
2 1/2 teaspoons baking powder
1/4 teaspoon salt
2 cups milk
2 eggs
1/3 cup vegetable oil
1/2 cup chopped green chilies
1/2 cup whole kernel corn

Mix dry ingredients together. In separate bowl, mix milk, eggs, and oil. Add dry ingredients. Stir just until mixed. Add chilies and corn. May add more corn if desired. Pour large mixing spoon of batter onto griddle and cook until lightly brown, then turn. Serve with sour cream, jalapeno jelly, or syrup. Makes 18 - 20 pancakes.

Submitted by:

Mildred & Don Cheek's
  Stewart House
P.O. Box 2326
Taos, New Mexico 87571
(505) 776-2913
Mildred & Don Cheek
$75.00 to $120.00

Full breakfast
4 rooms, 4 private baths
Children, over 12
No pets
No smoking
Mastercard & Visa

Built about 20 years ago, its owners in the art business, house is an extraordinary mixture of styles & textures, combining architectural elements from Spanish to Scandinavian, Moorish to Mayan. Inn is filled with art, antiques & handcrafted furniture. Mtn. views, outdoor hot tub, quiet country setting.

LEMON PANCAKES

1 1/4 cups flour
1 tablespoon sugar
1 tablespoon grated
  lemon rind
1 1/2 teaspoons baking
  powder
1/2 teaspoon baking
  soda
1/4 teaspoon salt

1 cup milk
1 egg, beaten
2 tablespoons lemon
  juice
1 1/2 tablespoons butter
  or margarine, melted

Additional butter for
frying

Combine dry ingredients in large mixing bowl. Add milk, egg, lemon juice and melted butter. Stir until flour mixture is moistened through. Do not overmix. Melt 1/2 tablespoon butter on a griddle or in a large skillet and spread around until surface is coated. Pour 1/4 cup of batter for each pancake onto hot griddle. Cook over medium heat, turning when pancakes are bubbly on top and edges are browned, about 2 minutes. Cook other side until done. Makes 12 pancakes.

Submitted by:

Fifth Street Mansion
213 South Fifth Street
Hannibal, Missouri 63401
(314) 221-0445
Mike & Donalene Andreotti
$65.00 to $90.00

Full breakfast
7 rooms, 7 private baths
Children allowed
No pets
Restricted smoking
Mastercard, Visa, Am Ex, Disc.

1858 Italianate mansion offers a happy blend of history & hospitality. Mark Twain visited old school chums here. Gleaming brass, original chandeliers, stained & leaded glass, antique lace & sparkling linens take you back to elegance. Tiffany window dominates front staircase. Walk to Mark Twain Historic District, shops, restaurants, and the river.

"LIGHT AS A CLOUD" PANCAKES

2 eggs, separated
1 1/2 cups buttermilk
1/2 cup sour cream
1/4 cup melted butter

1 cup flour
3/4 teaspoon baking soda
1/2 teaspoon salt

Beat egg whites until stiff. Mix egg yolks, buttermilk and sour cream to blend well. Add melted butter, flour, soda and salt, and blend. Fold in stiffly beaten egg whites. Fry pancakes in moderately hot oil. Especially good served with strawberry or blueberry sauce and whipped cream! Makes 4 servings.

Submitted by:

Cragwood Inn B&B
303 N. Second
Decatur, Indiana 46733
(219) 728-2000
Nancy & George Craig
$50.00 to $60.00

Full breakfast weekends,
Continental plus weekdays
4 rooms, 3 private baths
Children, over 10
No pets
Restricted smoking
Mastercard & Visa

Queen Anne house with magnificent woodwork and beveled leaded glass. Innovative weekends include Victorian crafts, fine needlework seminars, mystery parties, chocolate lovers' weekend, and herbal crafting.

MACADAMIA FRENCH TOAST

4 eggs, beaten
2/3 cup orange
  juice
1/3 cup milk
1/4 cup sugar
1/2 teaspoon vanilla
Strawberry Syrup:
2 - 10 oz. pkgs. frozen,
  sliced strawberries,
  thawed

1/4 teaspoon nutmeg
8 - 1/2" slices Italian or
  French bread
1/3 cup butter, melted
1/2 cup finely chopped
  macadamia nuts

4 teaspoons cornstarch
2 teaspoons lemon
  juice

Combine eggs, juice, milk, sugar, vanilla and nutmeg in medium bowl. Mix well. Arrange bread slices in 9" x 13" baking dish. Pour egg mixture over bread. Cover and refrigerate. Pour butter evenly in jelly roll pan. Arrange bread slices in single layer in pan. Sprinkle with nuts. Bake at 400° about 25 minutes. Serve with strawberry syrup: Drain strawberries, reserving liquid. In medium saucepan, combine 2 tablespoons strawberry liquid and cornstarch. Stir until smooth. Add remaining liquid, berries & lemon juice. Bring to a boil, stirring constantly; will be slightly thickened & translucent. Makes 3 cups.

Submitted by:

Victoriana 1898
622 Washington Street
Traverse City, Mich. 49684
(616) 929-1009
Flo & Bob Schermerhorn
$55.00 to $70.00

Full breakfast
3 rooms, 3 private baths
Children, over 12
No pets
No smoking
Mastercard & Visa

Touch a bit of history and feel a welcoming warmth long-remembered at this Victorian treasure with tiled fireplaces, bubble glass windows, fretwork & oak staircase. Gazebo & carriage house add to the beauty. Quiet, Historic District location near West Grand Traverse Bay.

MARY'S MOUNTAIN OATMEAL PANCAKES

2 cups rolled oats
2 cups milk
2 eggs, slightly beaten
1/4 cup butter, melted & cooled
1/2 cup raisins or currants
1/2 cup flour

2 tablespoons sugar
1 teaspoon baking powder
1 teaspoon baking soda
1 teaspoon ground cinnamon
1/2 teaspoon nutmeg

Mix oats and milk in bowl overnight. Just before cooking, add eggs, butter and raisins until blended. In another bowl mix together flour, sugar, baking powder, soda, cinnamon and nutmeg and add to oat mixture. Mix together. Preheat griddle and grease lightly. Batter will be thick, but add a little more milk if it seems too thick. Pour 1/4 cup batter for each pancake. Cook accordingly. Serve with butter, syrup or jam. Makes about 10 pancakes.

Submitted by:

Butterfield Bed & Breakfast
P.O. Box 1115
Julian, California 92036
(619) 765-2179
Ray & Mary Trimmins
$70.00 to $109.00

Full breakfast
5 rooms, 5 private baths
2 rooms with fireplaces
No children
No pets
Restricted smoking

Quaint inn in Historic District, with country gourmet breakfast served in the Victorian Gazebo. Romantic dinners often served in the Christmas Cottage after a horse drawn carriage ride. Game room for ping pong or pool, and afternoon refreshments. Biking & hiking at their best. Our specialty is intimate weddings with complete catering.

OVERNIGHT ORANGE FRENCH TOAST

3 eggs
1/4 cup milk
1/4 cup frozen orange
   juice concentrate
1 teaspoon baking
   powder
6 slices French bread,
   cut on diagonal to 3/4"
4 tablespoons butter

Orange Syrup:
1 cup granulated sugar
1/2 cup honey or light
   Karo syrup
1/4 cup water
1/4 cup frozen orange
   juice concentrate
2 tablespoons butter
Dash of salt

The night before: Beat first four ingredients together in a bowl. Dip bread slices in this mixture and place in a pan. Cover with waxed paper and refrigerate. Note: This recipe freezes well. Next day melt butter on hot griddle and fry the toast. Do not rush it with a too hot griddle, as it must fry slowly. For syrup: Put first four ingredients in heavy saucepan and boil for two minutes. Add butter and salt. Keeps well for several weeks in refrigerator. Warm before serving. To serve: Place two or more pieces of fried toast on serving plate, with cooked sausage or bacon. Garnish with all or a combination of the following: a dollop of sour cream, a sprinkle of nuts, a twisted orange slice, or a dusting of powdered sugar.

Submitted by:

The Tar Heel Inn
205 Church Street, Box 176
Oriental, N.C. 28571
(919) 249-1078
Dave & Patti Nelson
$55.00 to $75.00

Full breakfast
8 rooms, 8 private baths
Children allowed
No pets
No smoking
Mastercard & Visa

Built in 1899, restored as an English style country inn, with heavy beams, comfortable gathering rooms, country fabrics and wallpaper. Poster, cannonball and pencil post beds & antiques. 2 patios, lawns, lawn games, bicycles, and breakfast "from scratch" each morning.

PEACH POPOVER PANCAKES

1 large can sliced
   peaches, heated,
   thickened with
   cornstarch
Cinnamon to taste
Dash of nutmeg
1 tablespoon vegetable
   oil

4 large eggs
2/3 cup all-purpose flour
2/3 cup milk
1 1/2 tablespoons cold
   butter or margarine, cut
   in small pieces
1 cup sour cream
1/4 cup brown sugar

Heat peaches, thicken with cornstarch to taste. Add cinnamon and nutmeg. Cool to lukewarm. Heat oven to 450°. Pour oil into 9" metal pie pan. Heat in oven 5 minutes. Meanwhile, put eggs, flour, milk and butter into blender or processor and process until well-blended. Scrape down sides and process 30 seconds more. Pour batter into hot pan, bake 20 minutes without opening oven door, until pancake has puffed up high around edges. Reduce temperature to 350° and bake 20 minutes longer until sides are crisp. Can transfer pancake to large platter for serving. Top pancake with warm peach topping. Mix sour cream and brown sugar together. Drizzle sour cream mixture over peaches. Can double peaches if desired for more guests. Serves 4 - 6.

Submitted by:

Canyon Lake Bed & Breakfast
2928 Falls Drive
Rapid City, S. D. 57702
(605) 348-9702
Sandra Shillingstad
$25.00 to $50.00

Full breakfast
3 rooms, 2 private baths
Children, over 10
No pets
No smoking

Located in a residential area in the heart of the Black Hills, 22 miles from Mt. Rushmore. Short walk to Meadowbrook Golf Course, Canyon Lake, and Rapid Creek, with paddleboats and fishing. The Badlands, Custer State Park or Wall Drug, all within a 50 mile radius.

PEACHES 'N CREAM FRENCH TOAST

1 large loaf French bread	1/2 teaspoon vanilla
6 eggs	16 oz. can sliced
1 cup cream (half & half)	peaches in light syrup
1/2 teaspoon nutmeg	
1/2 teaspoon cinnamon	Powdered sugar

Slice French bread into 12 - 1" slices (diagonally looks nicest). Arrange in large baking dish or on cookie sheet with sides. Mix eggs, cream, nutmeg, cinnamon & vanilla, half of a can of peach slices cut into small chunks, and half of the can's syrup. Pour mixture over bread, soaking each piece (top and bottom). Arrange more peach pieces decoratively on top of each piece of toast. Cover pan with plastic wrap and refrigerate overnight. Take out half an hour before serving. Fry on heated griddle. Sprinkle with powdered sugar to serve. Serve with syrup or Peach Butter: 1/4 cup Country Morning butter and 1/4 cup peach preserves. Great with sausage or ham. Makes 6 servings.

Submitted by:

Grand Victorian B&B
402 N. Bridge St.
Bellaire, Michigan 49615
(616) 533-6111
Jill Watson
$55.00 to $85.00

Full breakfast
4 rooms, 4 private baths
No pets
No smoking

Grand 1895 Victorian mansion with period antiques. On National Register, with etched glass windows, birds'-eye maple woodwork, handpainted ceiling decor and original lighting fixtures. Downtown Bellaire, minutes to championship golf courses and the Midwest's finest skiing (Boyne, Shanty/Schuss).

PUMPKIN WHOLE WHEAT PANCAKES

1 cup whole wheat flour
1 cup white flour
1/2 teaspoon salt
2 tablespoons baking
  powder
1 teaspoon cinnamon
1/2 teaspoon nutmeg

1/4 teaspoon ginger
2 tablespoons brown
  sugar
2 eggs
1/2 cup canned pumpkin
2 cups milk
1/4 cup oil

In large bowl, combine dry ingredients. In small bowl, slightly beat eggs, and add remaining liquid ingredients. Make a well in dry mixture, pour liquid mixture in well and stir gently. Let mixture stand 5 minutes. Ladle on hot griddle. Note: May need a bit more milk as batter thickens as it sets. Serves 8.

Submitted by:

A Country Place B&B
Rt. 5, Box 43, North Shore Dr.
South Haven, Mich. 49090
(616) 637-5523
Art & Lee Niffenegger
$65.00 to $85.00 (double)

Full breakfast
5 rooms, 5 private baths
Children, over 7
No pets
No smoking
Mastercard, Visa, Am Ex

Traditional B&B, furnished with American and English antiques, reminiscent of those found in English countryside. 1860's Greek Revival on 6 acres of woodland, has Lake Michigan beach access 1/2 block away. Near Kal-Haven Trail State Park, open all seasons. Breakfast on deck or by fireside.

RAISED ORANGE WAFFLES

1/2 cup water	2 cups flour
1 pkg. yeast	2 eggs
2 cups lukewarm milk	1/8 teaspoon baking
1/2 cup salad oil	soda
1 teaspoon salt	Grated rind of 1 large
1 teaspoon sugar	orange

Night before: Dissolve yeast in water in large ceramic or glass bowl. Add milk, oil, salt, sugar, and flour. Mix, cover, let stand at room temperature overnight. In the morning add eggs, soda, and orange rind. Bake in Belgian waffle iron until crisp. Serve with assorted syrup, honey, fruit, and yogurt. Serves 2 - 3 hearty appetites.

Submitted by:

Deer Run Ranch B&B	Full breakfast
5440 Eastlake,	2 rooms, 2 private baths
Washoe Valley	Children, old enough to sleep
Carson City, Nevada 89704	in separate room alone
(702) 882-3643	No pets
David & Muffy Vhay	No smoking
$75.00 to $85.00	Mastercard & Visa

Western ambience in unique passive solar ranch home on working alfalfa ranch, with pond, pool, and spectacular view of Sierra Nevada Mountains. Convenient to Reno, Tahoe, Virginia City, & Carson City. The owners' woodshop, pottery studio, etc. also on the premises.

RICOTTA CHEESE & APPLE PANCAKES

3 cups ricotta cheese	6 tablespoons chopped
3 cups grated Granny	nuts
Smith apples	1 1/2 teaspoons
2 1/2 cups flour	cinnamon
4 - 6 tablespoons sugar	1 teaspoon nutmeg
3 teaspoons lemon	1 teaspoon vanilla
juice	12 eggs, separated

Mix all ingredients but egg whites. Beat egg whites until stiff. Fold into batter. Sauté in butter on both sides until golden. Serve with warm maple syrup, applesauce, or sautéed apple slices. Makes 36 pancakes.

Submitted by:

Whispers Bed & Breakfast	Full breakfast
409 William St.	6 rooms
Key West, Florida 33040	No children
(305) 294-5969	No pets
Les & Marilyn Tipton	Restricted smoking
$69.00 to $120.00	Mastercard & Visa

Guests enjoy beautiful, comfortable, & romantic antique-filled rooms. Famous breakfast creations served in our gardens each morning. Located in the heart of Old Town, walking distance to all sights.

SAUSAGE AND CHEESE-STUFFED FRENCH TOAST

8 oz. brown & serve sausage patties	4 eggs
1/4 lb. sliced Muenster cheese	1 cup milk
	1 tablespoon sugar
8 Italian bread slices, 1 1/2" thick	1 tablespoon maple syrup
	Oil for frying

Cook sausages, drain. Cut a pocket in each bread slice. Slice almost all the way through. Place sausage and cheese in pockets, cutting to fit. Press together. Beat remaining ingredients. Place stuffed bread in 9" x 13" pan. Pour liquid over bread. Turn until liquid is absorbed. Add about 1 tablespoon oil to electric frying pan (300°). Add bread and cook about 10 minutes until golden brown on both sides. Serve at once with maple syrup and fruit. Makes 8 servings.

Submitted by:

El Presidio B&B Inn
297 N. Main Avenue
Tucson, Arizona 85701
(602) 623-6151
Patti Toci
$85.00 to $105.00

Full breakfast
4 rooms, 4 private baths
Children, over 12
No pets
No smoking

Luxury in award-winning historic Victorian adobe mansion. Romantic, lush garden courtyards filled with Old World ambience, fountains & cobblestones surround richly appointed guesthouses & suites. Walk to the best restaurants, museums and shopping. Mobil 3-star rated.

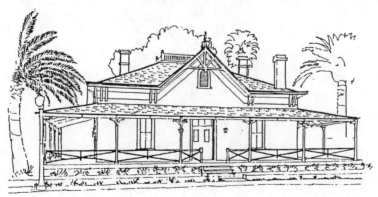

SCARLETT'S BUTTERMILK FRENCH TOAST

14 thick pieces white bread or sliced French bread
8 eggs
1 1/4 cups buttermilk
1 1/4 teaspoons vanilla
Dash of salt, if desired
Cinnamon & powdered sugar to taste
Strawberries for garnish

Beat eggs, buttermilk, and vanilla with a fork in a mixing bowl. Add salt if desired. Grease hot griddle or frying pan with butter. Dip pieces of bread in mixture and place on griddle. Spoon more mixture on top of bread and sprinkle cinnamon on each piece. Fry over medium high heat until brown on the bottom and turn over to brown the other side. Place immediately on plates or platter and sprinkle generously with powdered sugar. Garnish with strawberries. Makes 5 - 6 servings.

Submitted by:

Scarlett's Country Inn
3918 Silverado Trail
Calistoga, California 94515
(707) 942-6669
Scarlett Dwyer
$95.00 to $150.00

Continental plus breakfast
3 rooms, 3 private baths
Children allowed
No pets
Restricted smoking

Secluded 1890 farmhouse set on green lawns, with tall pines overlooking the vineyards. Breakfast in room or by woodland swimming pool. Near spas and wineries. Queen-sized beds, private entrances, a/c, afternoon refreshments, 3 suites, 1 with fireplace.

SEMO CRUNCH WAFFLES WITH APPLE CIDER SYRUP

Waffles:
2 cups baking mix
1/4 cup melted butter

1/4 cup oil
1 egg
1 1/2 cups club soda

Syrup:
2 tablespoons baking mix
2/3 cup sugar
1 tablespoon cinnamon

2 cups apple cider
2 tablespoons lemon juice
2 tablespoons butter

Mix all waffle ingredients together in medium bowl.   Pour onto greased hot waffle iron.   Makes 3 large waffles or 5 small round waffles. For syrup: Mix dry ingredients in saucepan. Add cider and lemon juice. Bring to a boil over medium heat, stirring often. Remove from heat. Add butter and stir until melted.   Serve over waffles. Syrup refrigerates for 3 weeks. Makes 2 1/2 cups syrup.

Submitted by:

Trisha's Bed & Breakfast
203 Bellevue
Jackson, Missouri 63755
(314) 243-7427
Trisha & Gus Wischmann
$65.00 to $75.00

Full breakfast
4 rooms, 3 private baths
Children, over 5
No pets
Restricted smoking
Mastercard & Visa

Located 10 minutes from I-55 and Cape Girandeau, this 1905 Victorian home features 3-course homecooked gourmet breakfast. Handpicked fresh fruits are a speciality. Vintage clothing is on display in bedrooms.   Three blocks from historic steam train, historic tour home, and 20 other county attractions.

SMITH HOUSE FAMOUS FRENCH TOAST

2 eggs	1 tablespoon sugar
3/4 cup milk	1/2 teaspoon salt
1/3 teaspoon orange peel, grated	Softened cream cheese
	Wheat French bread
1 teaspoon orange extract	Fruit toppings of choice
	Powdered sugar

In shallow bowl, combine first six ingredients and beat well. Slice bread 1 1/2" thick and make another cut halfway through the slice. Spread softened cream cheese in between. Heat oil on griddle until hot. Dip bread slices into egg mixture, turning to coat both sides. Place on hot griddle and cook until golden. Serve with powdered sugar and assorted fruit toppings. Makes 6 - 8 servings.

Submitted by:

Smith House Bed & Breakfast	Full breakfast
49 Salmon River Road	5 rooms, 1 private bath
Shoup, Idaho 83469	Children allowed
(208) 394-2121	Pets allowed
Aubrey & Marsha Smith	Restricted smoking
$35.00 to $54.00 For reservations: 1 (800) 238-5915	Mastercard, Visa, Discover

If you really want to get away from it all - including electricity - this is the place! Located in the Salmon National Forest, it provides down home hospitality in a split-level log home and adjacent Guest House. Hiking trails, hot springs, historic gold mine, plus river activities galore.

SOUR CREAM DELIGHTS

4 jumbo or 6 small eggs
(1 1/8 cups)
1/2 teaspoon salt
1/4 cup flour

1/2 teaspoon baking
soda
2 cups sour cream
3 tablespoons sugar

Mix eggs thoroughly, then add all the other ingredients, and beat mixture. This can be done in a blender or food processor. Cook on lightly greased griddle or nonstick pan. They should be made in 1/8 cup portions ("silver dollar" size) and served hot. These pancakes have a custard-like texture and taste. We never have any leftovers when they are served. Makes 18 - 24 small pancakes.

Submitted by:

The Josiah Bellows House
North Main St.
Walpole, N.H. 03608
(603) 756-4250
Lois Ford & Lou Ciercielli
$60.00 to $70.00

Full breakfast
4 rooms, 2 private baths
No children
No pets
No smoking
Mastercard & Visa

1813 Federal home, with 10' ceilings and large windows for the period. Beautifully restored, with eclectic, but elegant decor, combining Colonial and Victorian motifs with Oriental carpets and reproduction brass chandeliers. Homemade breads and muffins.

SOURDOUGH PANCAKES

Cool water in which po-
tatoes have been
boiled. Add flour until
starter batter reaches
desired thickness.
Keep at room tempera-
ture until working;
then refrigerate.

1 cup sourdough starter
1 cup flour
1 cup milk
1/2 teaspoon salt
1/2 teaspoon baking
soda
1 tablespoon cooking oil
1 tablespoon sugar

Remove starter from refrigerator the night before. Mix all ingredients for pancakes. Cook pancakes. Add water and flour to starter to replace that which was used. Important: Use clean utensils when working with mix. For best results, allow batter to work for an hour before cooking. Makes 6 - 7 pancakes.

Submitted by:

Bessemer Bend B&B
5120 Alcova, Rt., Box 40
Casper, Wyoming 82604
(307) 265-6819
Opal McInroy
$30.00 to $50.00

Full breakfast
3 rooms
Children allowed
No pets
Restricted smoking

On the Goose Egg Ranch, 1/2 mile from the site of an Oregon Trail crossing, the Red Butte Pony Express Station, & the first white man's cabin in Wyoming. Scenic area on North Platte River, with deer, bald eagles, pelicans, ducks and geese. Near Casper, a city of 50,000.

SPICED PANCAKES

1 1/4 cups flour	1/4 teaspoon salt
1/8 cup sugar	1 egg
1 teaspoon baking powder	1 1/4 cups buttermilk
1/2 teaspoon baking soda	2 tablespoons oil
1/2 teaspoon cinnamon	Toppings:
1/4 teaspoon nutmeg	Whipped butter
	Warm maple syrup
	Sliced bananas (opt.)

Sift together dry ingredients in large mixing bowl. In separate bowl, mix egg, buttermilk and oil. Make a well in dry ingredients and add liquid, stir until blended. Spoon 1/4 cup batter onto hot griddle or skillet for each pancake, turning once when edges become dry. Serve with sliced bananas if desired, whipped butter and warm maple syrup. Especially good on cold northern New England mornings. Makes 8 - 10 pancakes.

Origin: Concocted in our kitchen one very cold night!

Submitted by:

Sunny Side Inn
Seavey Street
North Conway, N.H. 03860
(603) 356-6239
Chris & Marylee Uggerholt
$45.00 to $70.00

Full breakfast
10 rooms, 3 private baths
Children allowed
No pets
Restricted smoking
Mastercard & Visa

An 1850's restored farmhouse with views of the White Mtns. from flower-trimmed porches in summer. Relax by fireplace or wood stove in winter, minutes from restaurants & outlet shopping. Hiking, rock climbing, swimming, fishing, golf, and skiing at four nearby ski areas.

SWEDISH PANCAKES FROM GRANDMOTHER

3 eggs, beaten
1/2 cup flour
1 1/2 cups 2% milk

2 tablespoons melted
  butter
1/4 teaspoon salt
2 teaspoons sugar

Blend ingredients together in blender, batter will be thin. Must be cooked in an indented cast iron pan available at special kitchen stores. Pan must be very hot, so that a drop of water will sizzle. Serve with powdered sugar and lingonberries. Makes approximately 3 dozen pancakes.

Submitted by:

The Wayside Inn
4344 Columbia Rd.
Ellicott City, Maryland 21042
(410) 461-4636
Margo & John Osantowski
$70.00 to $90.00 plus 5%
  Maryland sales tax

Continental plus breakfast
4 rooms, 2 private baths
Children, over 12
No pets
No smoking
Mastercard, Visa, Am Ex

An historic stone farmhouse on 2 acres with a pond. Two Bicentennial white oaks on the property. 2 rooms have fireplaces, and 2 rooms are suites with sitting rooms.

THE COLBY HILL ALL-PURPOSE FUNCAKES

5 cups all-purpose flour	Reserved fruits for
1/3 cup granulated	garnish
sugar	Powdered sugar
1 teaspoon salt	
1/4 cup baking powder	Topping Variations:
1/2 cup cooking oil	Apple cinnamon
4 eggs	Blueberry
4 cups milk	Raspberry

Mix dry ingredients. Make well in center of bowl, add oil, eggs, and milk and mix well. Great as is, or vary by the cook's whim! Apple cinnamon: Add 2 cups coarsely sliced unpeeled apples, 2 tablespoons cinnamon, 1/2 teaspoon nutmeg, 2 teaspoons vanilla and a dash of almond extract to basic mix. Add more granulated sugar if desired. Blueberry: Add generous amount of fresh or defrosted frozen blueberries just before you turn the pancakes on the grill. Raspberry: Add 2 cups fresh berries or 1 pkg. defrosted frozen raspberries (with liquid), and 1 teaspoon almond extract to batter before cooking. Garnish all fruit pancakes with a dusting of powdered sugar and a few reserved fruits. Makes 8 servings.

Submitted by:

Colby Hill Inn
The Oaks
Henniker, New Hamp. 03242
(603) 428-3281
Ellie & John Day
$85.00 to $140.00

Full breakfast
16 rooms, 16 private baths
Children, over 6
No pets
Restricted smoking
Mastercard, Visa, Am Ex, Disc.

Rambling 1790 farmhouse on five acres in an historic college town. 17 miles west of Concord in south central New Hampshire.

THE TASTIEST-HEALTHIEST WAFFLE IN THE WORLD

1/2 cup whole wheat pancake mix
1/2 cup oat bran
1 1/2 teaspoons "Egg Replacer" (available at health food stores)

1/2 - 2/3 cup pecan pieces
1 cup apple juice
Optional:
Garnish with fresh berries in season

Mix ingredients together. Spray waffle iron lightly with Pam. For a tastier, crispier waffle, allow it to cook for 30 seconds longer than suggested time of waffle iron manufacturer. Top sparingly with maple syrup. Contains no cholesterol, no fat, no animal products. High in fiber, complex carbohydrates, protein and vitamins. The oat bran helps to reduce cholesterol. Yield: 2 waffles.

Origin: Developed by Dr. & Mrs. Mel Rosenthal, our owners.

Submitted by:

Jefferson House
  Bed & Breakfast
5 The Strand
New Castle, Delaware 19720
(302) 323-0999 / Cellar
  Gourmet Restaurant or
(302) 322-8944
Chris Beckstein (Manager)
$49.00 to $85.00

Full breakfast
4 rooms, 4 private baths
Children allowed
No pets
Smoking allowed
Mastercard & Visa

200 year old river front hotel-residence in Historic District, near museums, antique markets, craft fairs and outlet shopping. Outdoor jacuzzi.

CASSEROLES, STRATAS, QUICHES, FRITTATAS & OMELETS

ADMIRAL'S BREAKFAST PIE

1/2 cup butter or
  margarine, melted
1 1/2 cups milk
1/4 teaspoon salt
1/8 teaspoon pepper
1 teaspoon dried chives
  (2 teaspoons fresh)

1/4 teaspoon paprika
1/2 cup biscuit mix
1/2 - 3/4 cup chopped,
  cooked smoked sausage
1 cup Swiss cheese,
  grated
3 eggs, beaten

Mix first 7 ingredients in blender for 1 - 2 minutes. Pour into greased 10" glass pie plate. Sprinkle batter with sausage. Push down into batter. Follow with grated cheese. Pour beaten eggs over all. Bake 30 - 40 minutes at 375°. Cool somewhat before cutting and serving. Plan on serving seconds! Makes 4 - 6 servings.

Submitted by:

Admiral Peary House
9 Elm Street
Fryeburg, Maine 04037
(207) 935-3365
Nancy & Ed Greenberg
$89.00 to $98.00

Full breakfast
4 rooms, 4 private baths
Children, over 12
No pets
No smoking
Mastercard & Visa

Charming historic home & former residence of Arctic explorer, Robert E. Peary. Clay tennis court, outdoor spa, bicycles, billiard table, fireplace, spacious grounds & perennial gardens. Walk to village, fine restaurants. Near White Mtns., hiking, canoeing, skiing, theater, outlet shopping & golf.

ARTICHOKE OMELET

6 eggs	Prepared mild salsa
Salt & pepper to taste	Grated Monterey Jack
6 cooked or canned	cheese, to taste
artichoke hearts	

Beat eggs with salt and pepper to taste. Divide into 2 omelet skillets and cook until just set. Top with cut-up artichokes heated in salsa. Save some of the salsa for topping. Sprinkle with cheese. Fold omelet over. Cook for one more minute in microwave. Top with warmed salsa. Makes 2 servings.

Submitted by:

Lodge at Manuel Mill
P.O. Box 998
Arnold, California 95223
(209) 795-2622
Jerry & Pat King
$85.00 to $105.00

Full breakfast
5 rooms, 5 private baths
No children
No pets
Restricted smoking

Unique Sierra B&B resort nestled in Stanislaus National Forest, overlooking historic millpond. Hiking, swimming, fishing, mountain biking, & boating all featured in our serene and romantic hideaway. Open year-round.

AUNT GAY'S CHIPPED BEEF BRUNCH

16 eggs
1 cup evaporated
  milk
3/4 cup butter (divided)
1/2 cup flour
2 teaspoons pepper

1 quart milk
8 oz. can mushrooms
6 slices bacon, cooked
  & crumbled
1/2 lb. chipped beef,
  rinsed

Beat eggs and evaporated milk. Melt 1/4 cup butter in skillet and scramble egg mixture until soft and wet. Set aside. Melt 1/2 cup butter, stir in flour and pepper. Add milk slowly to make a white sauce. Stir in mushrooms, bacon, and chipped beef, and heat. Grease a 9" x 13" x 2" pan. Layer sauce, eggs, sauce, eggs, sauce. Cover with foil. Bake at 275° for about 1 1/2 hours. Makes 8 - 12 servings.

Submitted by:

The Inn at Mitchell House
Box 329, RD 2
Chestertown, Maryland 21620
(410) 778-6500
Jim & Tracy Stone
$75.00 to $95.00

Full breakfast
6 rooms, 5 private baths
Children allowed
No pets
Smoking allowed
Mastercard & Visa

Nestled on ten rolling, wooded acres, this 18th century manor home greets you with warmth and a touch of tranquility. Awake to birdsong or migrating geese. See deer, fox or an eagle at sunset. A mere 1/2 mile from the Chesapeake Bay. A true nature lover's paradise.

BREAKFAST DISH

5 slices white bread	2 cups milk
1 lb. mild sausage, browned & drained	1/2 teaspoon dill
	1 teaspoon dry mustard
6 eggs	2 tablespoons chopped chives
1 cup shredded Cheddar cheese	

Cut bread into small cubes, and line baking pan with bread. Fry sausage and drain. Spread meat over bread. Combine eggs, cheese, milk, dill, mustard, and chives. Pour over bread and meat. Refrigerate overnight. Bake in a greased 9" x 13" pan at 350° for half an hour. Makes 6 - 8 servings.

Submitted by:

Herr Farmhouse Inn
2256 Huber Drive
Manheim, Penn. 17545
(717) 653-9852
Barry Herr
$70.00 to $95.00

Continental plus breakfast
4 rooms, 2 private baths
Children, over 12
No pets
Restricted smoking
Mastercard & Visa

Fully restored 1750 stone plantation home on 11.5 scenic acres. All original trim, doors, cabinets, and flooring. Take a step into yesteryear amidst Early American antiques and reproductions. Breakfast served in country kitchen with large walk-in fireplace. Antiques, quilts, and other attractions within 10 minutes of inn.

BREAKFAST POTATO CASSEROLE

2 tablespoons chopped onion
2 tablespoons diced red, green & yellow peppers
4 tablespoons margarine
1 cup cooked diced ham, or cooked sausage, or cooked bacon

8 eggs
1 cup milk
1 teaspoon dry mustard
4 medium potatoes (baked or boiled)
1 cup grated Cheddar cheese

Sauté onions and peppers in margarine, and place in lightly greased glass baking dish. Add cooked meat. Beat eggs, milk, and dry mustard. Pour egg mixture over meat. Slice cooked potatoes and layer on top of egg mixture. Bake at 375° for 25 - 30 minutes (until egg mixture is set). Turn off oven. Sprinkle grated cheese over casserole. Leave in oven until cheese is melted. Remove from oven and cut into 6 - 8 pieces.

Submitted by:

Magnolia Inn Bed & Breakfast
601 East Main - Highway 9
Dillon, South Carolina 29536
(803) 774-0679
Jim & Pam Lannoo
$40.00 to $50.00

Full breakfast
4 rooms, 3 private baths
Children allowed
No pets
No smoking
Mastercard & Visa

Southern hospitality and decor grace this century-old Southern Colonial home. Library and Victorian parlor are available for TV and relaxing. 4 guest rooms: Azalea - Southern Rice bed with canopy; Camellia - white iron bed; Dogwood - oak Victorian mansion bed; Wisteria - Victorian roll-top bed. All rooms have decorative fireplaces.

COUNTRY GRITS CASSEROLE

4 cups water
1 cup old-fashioned
  grits (uncooked)
3 slices chopped bacon
2 eggs, slightly beaten
1 cup chopped
  pineapple chunks

1/2 teaspoon coarse
  ground black pepper
2 cups (8 oz.) shredded
  sharp Cheddar cheese
1/4 teaspoon garlic salt
3 tablespoons whole milk
1 teaspoon table salt

Boil water and stir in grits. Add bacon. Cover and simmer 10 minutes, stirring occasionally. Stir a spoonful of hot grits mixture into eggs and then add eggs to grits, stirring constantly. Remove grits from heat and stir in chopped pineapple, pepper, cheese, garlic salt, milk and table salt. Pour mixture in a lightly greased 2-quart casserole. Bake at 350° for 40 - 45 minutes to a light brown. Makes 6 servings.

Submitted by:

Woodruff Bed & Breakfast
223 Ponce De Leon Ave.
Atlanta, Georgia 30308
(404) 875-9449
1-800-473-9449
Joan & Douglas Jones
$54.00 to $79.00

Full breakfast
12 rooms, 9 private baths
Children allowed
Restricted smoking
Mastercard, Visa, Am Ex,
  Discover

Southern hospitality and charm await you in historic, beautifully restored B&B inn. Located in midtown Atlanta, convenient to everything. Lots of antiques. Near Atlanta entertainment traditions: the Fox Theatre, Carter Presidential Library, and the High Museum.

DICED POTATO SOUFFLÉ

2 tablespoons parsley	1/2 lb. Colby or Velveeta
2 tablespoons onion	cheese, diced
1 lb. potatoes (sliced	1/4 cup butter, melted
and cooked)	1/4 cup flour
8 hard-boiled eggs,	1 teaspoon salt
diced	1 1/2 cups sour cream

Mix parsley, onion, potatoes, eggs, and cheese together. In separate bowl mix melted butter, flour, salt and sour cream. Then mix all ingredients together. Bake at 375° for 45 minutes. Makes 10 servings.

Submitted by:

Patchwork Quilt Country Inn   Full breakfast
11748 County Road 2   9 rooms, 6 private baths
Middlebury, Indiana 46540   Children, over 5
(219) 825-2417   No pets
Maxine Zook   No smoking
$50.95 to $95.00   Mastercard & Visa

Our inn is located in the country where one can relax, away from the hustle and bustle of everyday life. In the evening deer often graze in the fields. We also offer Amish Backroads Tour, country dining, and a gift shop.

DIXIELAND SAUSAGE-RICE CASSEROLE

1/2 - 1 lb. bulk sausage
1 cup onion, chopped
1 cup celery, chopped
1/2 cup green pepper,
  chopped
1/8 teaspoon pepper
  (or use hot sausage)
1/2 teaspoon garlic
  powder

1/4 teaspoon salt
1 cup rice, uncooked
  (white or converted)
1 can cream of
  mushroom soup
1 can cream of
  chicken soup
1 soup can water

Crumble up sausage and brown in big frying pan. Drain. Add remainder of ingredients. Mix together and bake, tightly covered in 9" x 13" x 2" Pyrex baking dish at 350° for 1 1/2 hours. If convenient, after about 45 minutes cooking time, stir mixture. After allotted cooking time you may need to add some additional water to the casserole if rice has become too dry. Just gradually pour in warm water and stir to moisten. Serves 6.

Submitted by:

Sims-Mitchell House B&B
242 Whittle St., P.O. Box 429
Chatham, Virginia 24531
(804) 432-0595
1-800-967-2867 (reserv.)
Henry & Patricia Mitchell
$45.00 to $70.00

Full breakfast
2 suites, 2 private baths
Children allowed
No pets
No smoking
Mastercard & Visa

Historic 1870 home with family atmosphere, in charming Victorian town. Main house's raised English basement is spacious guest suite with 2 bedrooms, sitting room & private entrance. Adjacent cottage suite has 2 bedrooms, sitting room & kitchen. Hostess is nationally-known cookbook writer; host, a planetarium specialist; both natives.

DUNBAR HOUSE SMOKED SALMON PIE

1 - 9" unbaked wheat
pie shell
1 cup broccoli spears,
blanched & drained
8 oz. flaked, smoked
salmon
1/3 cup celery, finely
minced
1/3 cup sliced scallions

1 cup grated Swiss
cheese
2 hard-cooked eggs,
diced
1 cup mayonnaise
1/2 teaspoon dillweed,
chopped
Salt & pepper,
to taste

Preheat oven to 375°. With fork, prick small holes in pie shell. Place broccoli spears in bottom of shell. In bowl, fold together flaked salmon, celery, scallions, Swiss cheese, eggs, mayonnaise and dill. Adjust seasonings if needed. Spoon mixture over broccoli. Bake for 30 minutes. Serve warm or chilled, cut into wedges. Serves 8.

Submitted by:

Dunbar House, 1880
271 Jones St., P.O. Box 1375
Murphys, California 95247
(209) 728-2897
Barbara & Bob Costa
$105.00 to $145.00

Full breakfast
4 rooms, 4 private baths
Children, over 10
No pets
Restricted smoking
Mastercard & Visa

Stay where history has a home, in the heart of California's Gold Rush Country. Comfortably decorated, TV's, VCR's and refrigerators. Complimentary bottle of local wine and appetizer buffet upon arrival. Breakfast in dining room by the fire, or in the century old gardens.

EGG & BACON CASSEROLE (OEUF ENTRALLES)

9 hard boiled eggs, sliced
1/2 lb. drained, crisp bacon, crumbled into bite-size pieces
1/2 lb. grated sharp Cheddar cheese
2 cups white sauce recipe of your choice
Buttered bread crumbs

In 9" x 9" x 2 1/2" casserole, start with layers of sliced eggs. Sprinkle crumbled bacon over eggs. Add cheese to 2 cups of your favorite white sauce recipe. Spread cheese sauce over casserole to cover. Sprinkle with buttered bread crumbs. Bake at 350° for 20 - 30 minutes. Makes 4 servings.

Submitted by:

Valley Forge Mountain B&B
P.O. Box 562
Valley Forge, Penn. 19481
(215) 783-7838
1-800-344-0123
FAX 215-783-7783
Carolyn Williams
$40.00 to $65.00

Guests' choice of full, continental plus, or continental breakfast
2 rooms, 1 private bath
Children allowed
Some pets allowed
Restricted smoking
Mastercard, Visa, Am Ex, Diners Club

French Colonial adjacent to Valley Forge Park. TV, phone, a/c, computer/printer for business. Minutes from shopping, antiquing, restaurants, theatre, cross-country skiing, horseback riding, golf. Featured in Philadelphia Magazine. Call/write for free brochure.

EGGS À LA WEDGEWOOD

16 eggs
1 teaspoon nutmeg
Salt & pepper to taste
1 teaspoon fresh parsley
1/2 - 3/4 cup sour cream
1/4 cup finely chopped
   green onions

1/2 - 1 cup crisply fried
   bacon
8 - 12 fresh mushrooms,
   sliced
2 cups grated Cheddar
   cheese

Night before: Beat eggs and nutmeg well. Scramble in skillet. Add salt, pepper, and parsley. Place cooked eggs in greased baking or quiche dish as first layer. Now layer sour cream, green onions, bacon, mushrooms, and cheese. Refrigerate overnight. Next morning: Bake at 300° for 20 - 30 minutes until warm through, and cheese is melted. Serves 8. May be adapted to serve any number. Use 2 eggs per person and layer other ingredients generously.

Submitted by:

The Wedgewood Inn
11941 Narcissus Road
Jackson, California 95642
(209) 296-4300
For reservations, call:
1-800-WEDGEWD
Vic & Jeannine Beltz
$85.00 to $130.00

Full breakfast
6 rooms, 6 private baths
Children, over 12
No pets
Restricted smoking
Mastercard, Visa

Elegant 1987 Victorian replica with wraparound porch and swing, nestled on wooded acreage. Lavishly furnished with antiques and family heirlooms. Some balconies & wood burning stoves. Terraced gardens, spectacular gazebo, walking paths, hammocks, croquet, sparkling fountains. Afternoon refreshments. Romantic getaway! Mobil Travel Guide *** Rating.

EGG STRATA

9 slices French bread
(crusts removed)
Butter for bread
6 - 9 eggs
3 cups milk
1/2 teaspoon salt
Dash of dry mustard

Dash of Worcestershire
sauce
Seasoning salt/grated
onion to taste (opt.)
Assorted toppings
1/2 lb. grated Cheddar
cheese

Butter and cube bread. Beat eggs, milk, and seasonings. Butter 9" x 13" baking dish. Put layer of cubed bread in bottom. Pour egg mixture over bread. Layer minced ham, green pepper, chicken, bacon (cooked & crumbled), drained mushrooms or sautéed fresh mushrooms, etc. over cubed bread. Cover with grated cheese. Cover and refrigerate overnight. Bake covered for 45 minutes - 1 hour (or until done) at 325° - 350°, depending on oven. Serves 8.

Submitted by:

Vichy Springs Resort & Inn
2605 Vichy Springs Rd.
Ukiah, California 95482
(707) 462-9515
Gilbert & Marjorie Ashoff
$80.00 to $150.00

Continental plus breakfast
14 rooms, 14 private baths
Children allowed
No pets
Restricted smoking
Mastercard, Visa, Am Ex, Disc.

Our facilities consist of warm, naturally carbonated and naturally 90° mineral baths, 104° hot pool, and Olympic-size swimming pool. Also available by appointment are Swedish massage and facials. Located on 700 acres ideal for hiking, with beautiful waterfall.

FANTASTIC SPINACH DELIGHT

1 1/2 cups biscuit
mix
2 eggs
1/2 cup milk
15 oz. can spinach
1 pint small curd
cottage cheese

1 1/2 cups Cheddar
cheese, shredded
1/2 cup grated
Parmesan cheese
2 teaspoons garlic
granules
4 large eggs

Mix first 3 ingredients in bowl and spread in greased 9" x 13" pan. Let stand. In same bowl put drained spinach, cut into small pieces. Add cottage cheese, Cheddar and Parmesan cheeses, and garlic. Mix in eggs, and spread over first mixture covering it all. Smooth out, and refrigerate all night. Next morning bake at 350° for half an hour, until set. Let stand 5 minutes until firm and cut into 12 servings. Can sprinkle top with cheese. Freezes well before baking or after.

Submitted by:

Columbia River Inn B&B
1681 Franklin Avenue
Astoria, Oregon 97103
(503) 325-5044 or
(800) 847-2475
Karen N. Nelson
$65.00 to $80.00 plus 7% tax

Full breakfast
5 rooms, 5 private baths
Children allowed
No pets
No smoking
Mastercard & Visa

Gracious Victorian home with elegant furnishings, and a feeling of historic elegance which surrounds you as you enter. Enjoy browsing through "Krafty's Korner", a unique gift shop with creations made by your hostess. Double living room & large dining room with fireplace.

FORBESTOWN INN VEGETABLE OMELET

1 tablespoon margarine
1 cup total of desired
 vegetables: Bell pep-
 pers, mushrooms, to-
 matoes, green onion,
 broccoli, cauliflower
2 tablespoons
 margarine

1/2 teaspoon Italian
 seasoning
Salt & pepper to taste
3 eggs
2 tablespoons cream
 cheese, softened
1/4 cup grated Cheddar
 cheese

Heat skillet with 1 tablespoon margarine and bring to a "bubble heat". Add vegetables and stir-fry until tender. Remove from heat. Heat skillet with 2 tablespoons margarine and bring to "bubble heat" again. Mix seasonings, eggs and cream cheese together and pour into skillet. Let this cook for one minute, then lift sides of egg mixture to let liquid egg run under the edges all around skillet. Add vegetable mixture on one side of omelet and spread evenly. Add cheese to top when mixture has finished cooking. Flip over the other half of omelet to make a half moon shape. Serve and enjoy.

Submitted by:

Forbestown Inn
825 North Forbes St.
Lakeport, California 95453
(707) 263-7858
Jack & Nancy Dunne
$85.00 to $105.00

Full breakfast
4 rooms, 1 private bath
Children, over 12
No pets
Restricted smoking
Mastercard, Visa, Am Ex

Step back in time to the days of clawfoot tubs, iron beds, and hearty country breakfasts. Our history dates back to the Civil War. This charming Victorian home features oak antiques & fabrics by Bill Blass & Laura Ashley. Pool & spa, only 1 block from lake and main street.

FRITTATA HACIENDA

6 slices bacon, diced
1/4 cup butter
10 eggs
17 oz. can cream style
corn
3/4 lb. sharp Cheddar
cheese, grated
4 oz. can diced green
chilies

1 tablespoon Worcester-
shire sauce
1/2 teaspoon
pepper
1/4 teaspoon garlic
powder, or to taste
1/4 cup chopped
pimiento (opt.)

Cook bacon until crisp, set aside, but do not drain. Melt butter in 9" x 13" baking dish. Beat eggs in large mixing bowl. Add bacon with about half of drippings, and stir until blended. Add rest of ingredients, again stirring until blended. Pour into baking dish. Bake at 325° for 35 - 40 minutes, or until top is golden. Serve with salsa and sour cream for garnish. Serves 6 - 8.

Submitted by:

Calistoga Wayside Inn
1523 Foothill Boulevard
Calistoga, California 94515
(707) 942-0645 or
(800) 845-3632
Deborah & Leonard Flaherty
$100.00 to $135.00

Full breakfast
3 rooms, 3 private baths
Children allowed
No pets
Restricted smoking
Mastercard, Visa, Am Ex

Warm and inviting, situated in a park-like setting under stately shade trees. King & queen beds, hot tub and lovely patio; curl up by the fireplace. Savor a country breakfast, and afternoon refreshments. Close to wineries, restaurants and spas.

GRITS CASSEROLE

4 cups water
1 teaspoon salt
1 cup quick-cooking grits
4 eggs, lightly beaten
1 lb. pork sausage,
   browned & drained

1 1/2 cups shredded
   sharp Cheddar cheese,
   divided
1/2 cup milk
1/4 cup butter,
   softened

In saucepan, bring water and salt to a boil. Slowly stir in grits. Reduce heat and cook 4 - 5 minutes, stirring occasionally. Remove grits from heat and add a small amount of hot grits to the eggs. Return to saucepan. Stir in browned and drained sausage, 1 cup cheese, milk and butter. Stir until the butter melts. Pour into greased 9" x 13" pan. Sprinkle with remaining cheese. Bake at 350° for 50 minutes or until the top begins to brown. (Leftover portions are even tasty served cold.) Makes 10 - 12 servings.

Submitted by:

Dicus House Bed & Breakfast
609 E. Broadway St.
Streator, IL 61634
(815) 672-6700
Felicia & Art Bucholtz
$45.00 to $55.00

Full breakfast
4 rooms, 3 private baths
Children, over 10
No pets
No smoking
Mastercard & Visa

Situated near 3 state parks, this historic 1890 home welcomes you to a bygone era. 6 marble fireplaces, carved walnut woodwork, and original brick walks, all in a park-like setting. Buffet breakfast in formal dining room. Lunch & dinner by advance request. Evening snacks.

HAM & BROCCOLI BREAKFAST PUFF

8 slices white bread, trimmed & cubed
1 1/2 cups shredded Monterey Jack cheese
10 oz. pkg. frozen chopped broccoli, thawed
1 cup cooked ham, chopped
2 tablespoons minced onion
8 eggs
1 1/2 cups milk
1 tablespoon dry mustard
1/2 teaspoon salt
1/4 teaspoon white pepper

Alternate layers of bread cubes, cheese, broccoli, ham and onion in buttered 2 quart casserole dish. Beat remaining ingredients together and pour over layers. Cover and refrigerate overnight. Uncover and bake for 50 - 60 minutes at 350° until puffed and golden brown. Makes 8 servings.

Submitted by:

Swift Street Inn B&B
1204 Swift St.
Perry, Georgia 31069
(912) 987-3428
Wayne & Jane Coward
$55.00 to $75.00

Full breakfast (gourmet)
4 rooms, 4 private baths
Children, over 12
Pets allowed, outside kennels
No smoking
Mastercard, Visa, Am Ex, Disc.

Antebellum, coastal plantation style home offers deluxe service and accommodations, with each guest room filled with antiques. Step back to a time of Southern charm, romance & luxury of 135 years ago. We take pride in making your stay restful, peaceful and memorable!

HAM AND POTATO BREAKFAST CASSEROLE

1/2 lb. diced ham
1/4 lb. mozzarella cheese, shredded
1/4 lb. Cheddar cheese, shredded
8 eggs
3 tablespoons chicken flavor granules or 1 tablespoon bouillon powder
1 teaspoon Tabasco
1 tablespoon mixed herb seasoning
1 tablespoon finely minced onion
1 teaspoon prepared mustard
4 cups milk or half & half
16 - 20 oz. bag frozen hash brown potatoes
1/4 cup melted butter

Night before: Mix ham and cheeses together and refrigerate. Beat eggs and flavorings, then add milk or half and half. Refrigerate overnight separately from ham. In the morning: Spray or grease baking dishes (2 - 1 1/2 quarts or a 3 quart flat casserole). Place frozen potatoes in dish and drizzle with melted butter. Bake at 400° for 20 minutes. Scatter ham and cheeses over potatoes, pour eggs over this. Reduce heat to 325° and bake for 20 - 30 minutes, or just until eggs have set. Remove from oven, and cover lightly with aluminum foil for 10 minutes. This will improve flavor and texture. Cut into squares. Serves 18 to 20.

Submitted by:

Mason House at Bentonsport
Route #2, Box 237
Keosauqua, Iowa 52565
(319) 592-3133
Sheral & Bill McDermet
$49.00 to $74.00

Full breakfast
9 rooms, 5 private baths
Children allowed
No pets
No smoking
MasterCard & Visa

Charming 1846 steamboat river inn, with a tradition of quality hosting continuing into the 1990's. In National Historic District, near antique shops, state park and state forest, canoeing and cross-country skiing. Blacksmith, potter, sculptor, and artists in the village.

ITALIAN CHEESE PIE

2 - 9" pie crusts
4 eggs (divided)
1 cup cubed cooked ham
1 cup ricotta cheese
1 cup shredded
mozzarella cheese
1 cup cubed Swiss
cheese

5 tablespoons grated
Parmesan cheese
(divided)
1 tablespoon chopped
fresh parsley
1/4 teaspoon
oregano
1 egg

Preheat oven to 375°. Prepare pie crusts for 9" pan. Mix all ingredients, except 1 egg and 1 tablespoon Parmesan, together, blend well. Spoon mixture into pie crust. Top with second crust. Brush top with remaining beaten egg, sprinkle with remaining Parmesan cheese. Cut slits into top of crust. Bake 50 minutes or until golden brown. Makes 6 - 8 servings.

Submitted by:

Frederick House
18 East Frederick Street
Staunton, VA 24401
(800) 334-5575 or
Joe & Evy Harman
$45.00 to $95.00

Full breakfast
14 rooms, 14 private baths
Children allowed
No pets
No smoking
Mastercard, Visa, Am Ex,
Discover

A small hotel across from Mary Baldwin College, in Staunton, the oldest city in the Shenandoah Valley. Together with us on Frederick Street are Chumley's Tearoom, the Town Center Athletic Club, and McCormick's Restaurant. Breakfast is served at Chumley's, lunch and dinner at McCormick's. Swim in the Town Center.

216

LINDA'S 'MOM'S' STRATA

1 loaf sourdough
French bread,
cubed
1 1/2 lbs. Cheddar
cheese, grated
4 green onions, diced
9 eggs
3 teaspoons brown
sugar (divided)
1/2 teaspoon paprika
(divided)

1 1/2 teaspoons salt
(divided)
1 1/2 teaspoons garlic
salt (divided)
2 teaspoons cayenne
pepper (divided)
1/2 teaspoon Worcester-
shire sauce (divided)
1 1/2 teaspoons dry
mustard (divided)
2 3/4 cups milk (divided)

Spray 9" x 12" pan with Pam. Layer half of French bread, half of cheese, and half of green onions. Mix eggs, 1 1/2 tsps. brown sugar, 1/4 tsp. paprika, 3/4 tsp. salt, 3/4 tsp. garlic salt, 1 tsp. cayenne, 1/4 tsp. Worcestershire, 3/4 tsp. mustard, and 1 1/2 cups milk. Pour over bread layers. Repeat layers. Mix 1 1/2 tsps. brown sugar, 1/4 tsp. paprika, 3/4 tsp. salt, 3/4 tsp. garlic salt, 1 tsp. cayenne, 1/4 tsp. Worcestershire, and 3/4 tsp. mustard with 1 1/4 cups milk, and pour over layers. Bake 1 1/2 hours at 325°. Makes 10 - 12 servings.

Submitted by:

The Zaballa House
324 Main St.
Half Moon Bay, Calif. 94019
(415) 726-9123
Linda Malone, Sharon Tedrow
$65.00 - $150.00

Full breakfast
9 rooms, 9 private baths
Children allowed
Pets allowed
No smoking
Mastercard, Visa, Am Ex, Disc.

Our house, circa 1859, is the oldest standing building in Half Moon Bay. Set in a garden-like setting in the heart of downtown. Our Room #6 is reported to have a ghost in residence - $10.00 off to those who see it!

LINDA'S SOUTHERN APPLE & SAUSAGE QUICHE

1 1/2 cups sausage, ground
1/2 cup minced onion (or 2 - 3 green onions could be added for color)
1 tablespoon thyme
Salt & pepper to taste

1 1/2 cups Swiss cheese grated
1/2 cup Cheddar cheese grated
1 1/2 cups Granny Smith apples, chopped
1 1/2 cups half & half
3 eggs

Cook sausage, onion, and thyme. Add salt and pepper. Layer cheeses, then sausage mixture, and finally apples. Mix half & half and eggs. Pour this custard mixture over layers. Bake at 350° for 30 - 40 minutes. Serves 5 - 6.

Submitted by:

Storybook Inn
P.O. Box 362
28717 Highway 18
Skyforest, California 92385
(714) 336-1483
Kathleen & John Wooley
$105.00 to $200.00

Full breakfast
10 rooms, 10 private baths
Children allowed, over 12 preferred
No pets
No smoking
Mastercard, Visa & Discover

Great escape to elegant mountain inn by Lake Arrowhead. Luxurious living room and den with wood-burning fireplaces and spectacular view. Morning paper, hot tub, fresh flowers. AAA 3-Diamond rating.

LITTLE RIVER INN QUICHE LORRAINE

9" pie shell, baked
4 slices onion, sautéed
  (1 small)
4 slices cooked bacon,
  crumbled
4 slices ham, cubed

1 cup grated Cheddar
  cheese
4 eggs
1 cup whipping cream
1/4 teaspoon dry
  mustard

Bake pie shell at 425° for 10 minutes. Put onion, bacon, ham and cheese in pie shell. Beat eggs, cream and dry mustard. Pour over other ingredients. Bake at 350° until custard is set and top is nice golden brown, about 45 minutes. Cut into wedges. Serves 4 - 6.

Submitted by:

Little River Inn
Route 130
Pemaquid, Maine 04558
(207) 677-2845
Kristina de Khan
$50.00 to $70.00

Full breakfast
6 rooms, 1 private bath
Children allowed
No pets
Smoking allowed
Mastercard & Visa

An 1840's Cape farmhouse located on the coast in one of Maine's most historic and scenic areas. Select a traditional room or a rustic gallery room. Minutes from the lighthouse, beach, archeological digs, New Harbor, galleries and shops.

OVEN BAKED OMELET

6 eggs
1/2 cup low-fat cottage
  cheese
1/2 cup sour cream
1/2 cup mild salsa

1 cup shredded
  Monterey Jack cheese
1 cup shredded Cheddar
  cheese

Mix the first 3 ingredients with a whip. Spray 9" pie pan with no-stick cooking spray. Spread salsa in pan and add cheese. Pour egg mixture over cheese. Bake at 350° for 45 minutes. Serves 5 - 6.

Submitted by:

Gate House Inn
1330 Jackson Gate Road
Jackson, California 95642
(209) 223-3500
Stan & Bev Smith
$75.00 to $105.00

Full breakfast
5 rooms, 5 private baths
Children, over 12
No pets
Restricted smoking
Mastercard, Visa & Discover

Charming turn-of-the-century Victorian offering five elegant guest rooms, (4 in main house, 1 private cottage) all with queen beds. Breakfast served in formal dining room. Swimming pool in summer. A quiet country setting. 3-star Mobil rating.

PACIFIC NORTHWEST BREAKFAST CASSEROLE

12 - 14 slices white sandwich bread	8 eggs (or 2 cartons Egg Beaters)
1/2 lb. sharp cheese, grated (can use low fat)	2 cups milk (can use non-dairy milk)
1 lb. hot bulk pork sausage, crumbled, fried & drained	1/2 teaspoon salt
	1 teaspoon dry mustard
	Dash of pepper

Grease 9" x 13" baking dish. Line bottom with about half of bread slices, cutting some of them into pieces. Sprinkle cheese on top, then sausage. Mix remaining ingredients together. Pour about half over top of casserole. Arrange remaining bread slices over top, cutting to fit. Pour remainder of egg mixture over all the bread slices. Cover with plastic wrap; refrigerate overnight. Bake at 350° for 30 - 35 minutes. Slice, garnish with parsley & serve. Makes 8 - 10 servings.

Submitted by:

Hill Top Bed & Breakfast	Continental plus breakfast
5832 Church Road	3 rooms, 2 private baths
Ferndale, Washington 98248	Children allowed
(206) 384-3619	No pets
Paul & Doris Matz	Restricted smoking
$44.00 to $54.00	Mastercard & Visa

We overlook Mt. Baker & Cascade Mtn. Range, are near state & local parks. Large, comfortable rooms with beautiful quilts made by your hostess. Fireside Room has kitchenette, cable T.V., & player piano. Cascade Room has kingsize bed, sitting area and 1/2 bath. Queen Room is reserved for longer stays with private bath across hall.

POTATO CASSEROLE

2 cans cream of chicken
 soup
2 small onions, diced
1/2 stick margarine

2 lb. bag frozen French
 fries, chopped
Salt & pepper to taste

In large bowl, mix together undiluted cream of chicken soup, diced onion, and margarine. Then add chopped French fries, salt, and pepper. Place mixture in greased 9" x 13" x 2" casserole dish. Bake in preheated 350° oven for 30 minutes. Makes 8 servings.

Submitted by:

River Forest Manor
600 East Main St.
Belhaven, N.C. 27810
(919) 943-2151 or
(800) 346-2151
Melba Smith, Axson Smith, Jr.
$45.00 to $75.00

Continental plus breakfast
9 rooms, 9 private baths
Children allowed
No pets
Smoking allowed
Mastercard, Visa, Am Ex

Enjoy Victorian splendor surrounded by modern facilities. Built in 1899 and converted to a restaurant/country inn and marina in 1947. Featuring the world famous smorgasbord served nightly 6:00 P.M. to 8:30 P.M.

POTATO-CHEESE CASSEROLE

1 pkg. instant mashed
  potatoes (for 8)
1/2 cup sour cream
4 slices bacon, cooked
  crisply and crumbled
  (save grease)

3/4 cup grated Swiss
  cheese
3/4 cup grated Monterey
  Jack cheese
1 cup chopped green
  onions (including tops)

Follow directions on box for making mashed potatoes. Spread in baking pan that has been liberally greased with bacon grease. (The bacon fat gives the casserole an excellent flavor.) Spread sour cream over top of potatoes, sprinkle with bacon pieces, grated cheese and chopped onion. Bake at 385° for 15 minutes, until it is nicely browned. Makes 8 servings. Rather than double this recipe, it is better to make 2 separate casseroles of it. It's delicious!

Submitted by:

Sutter Creek Inn
75 Main Street, Box 385
Sutter Creek, Calif. 95685
(209) 267-5606
Jane Way
$45.00 to $97.00

Full breakfast
19 rooms, 19 private baths
Children, over 10
No pets
Restricted smoking

Large living room, huge library and game tables, a/c, electric blankets, and hammocks under the trees. There are 10 fireplaces and 4 rooms with swinging beds, (very romantic) which can be stabilized. Huge lawns surround the inn. A hot breakfast is included.

POTATO DELIGHT

8 cups cooked diced potatoes
6 slices diced bacon, uncooked
1 large onion, diced

1/4 lb. Velveeta cheese
1/4 cup chopped green olives
1 cup mayonnaise

Mix all ingredients and chill overnight. Bake in ungreased 9" x 13" casserole at 350° for 1 hour. Serves 10.

Submitted by:

The Chicago Street Inn
219 Chicago Street
Brooklyn, Michigan 49230
(517) 592-3888
Karen & Bill Kerr
$55.00 to $65.00

Full breakfast
4 rooms, 4 private baths
Children, over 13
No pets
Restricted smoking
Mastercard & Visa

Return to yesteryear. 1880's Victorian decorated with family and area antiques, located in the Irish Hills area. Close to antiquing, shopping, hiking, biking, county and state parks, swimming and golfing.

REDNECK SOUFFLÉ

2 lbs. frozen, Southern
style hash browns
1/4 cup dried or 1/2 cup
fresh minced onion
Granulated or fresh
garlic, to taste
Lawry's® Pinch of Herbs
& Mixed Peppers,
to taste

Cayenne pepper (opt.)
1/2 lb. cooked, ground,
lean country ham (or
crumbled cooked bacon
or corned beef) *
9 eggs, beaten
1/4 lb. crumbled
Cheddar cheese
Sesame seeds to taste

Lightly oil a 12" skillet, then add potatoes and onion. Season liberally with Herbs and Peppers, garlic, and a dash of cayenne if desired. Fry over medium heat until potatoes begin to brown. Add meat and/or mushrooms & continue to cook, turning frequently. When potatoes are done, add eggs, lower heat. Quickly, mix thoroughly, pat into a firm cake shape away from sides of pan & cover. When eggs brown on bottom, flip, or turn into another 12" pan. Sprinkle Cheddar cheese over the "done" side, then sesame seeds. Cover until eggs are cooked through, then pie-slice into 8 pieces. Note: Proportion into a 10" pan for 6 slices, an 8" - 9" pan for 4 slices, or a 7" pan for 2 slices. *Mushrooms may be substituted for or added to the meat.

Submitted by:

The Osceola Mill Country Inn
Steele's Tavern, VA 24476
(703) 377-MILL (6455)

Full breakfast
11 rooms, 11 private baths &
Honeymoon Cottage with bath
Children allowed
Pets considered
No smoking

A warm, friendly & unpretentious alternative to both hotels or motels and other inns. Charming accommodations, two parlors, music room, game room and dining room. Pool, porches and babbling brook for relaxation. Biking, hiking, antiquing, exploring, golf, & fishing nearby.

SALMON QUICHE

Pie crust:
1 1/3 cups flour
1/3 cup milk

3 tablespoons vege-
table oil
1/2 teaspoon salt

Filling:
1 1/2 cups baked
salmon, flaked
4 green onions,
chopped

8 eggs
4 cups whipping cream
1/2 teaspoon sugar
1/4 teaspoon cayenne

For pie crust: Measure flour into medium bowl. Blend together milk and vegetable oil, and add to flour, just until combined. Lightly flour pastry cloth, and roll out to fit 9" pie crust. (Makes 2 crusts) Filling: Divide salmon and onions evenly between the two crusts. Beat eggs well, add whipping cream, sugar and cayenne. Heat oven to 425°. Pour half of egg mixture on salmon and onions in each pie plate. Bake 15 minutes. Reduce oven temperature to 300° and bake about 45 minutes. Let stand 10 minutes before cutting. (Egg mixture can be made the night before.) Serves 12. A favorite with our guests!

Submitted by:

Alaska's 7 Gables B&B
P.O. Box 80488
Fairbanks, Alaska 99708
(907) 479-0751
Paul & Leicha Welton
$45.00 to $105.00

Full breakfast
12 rooms, 5 private baths
Children allowed
No pets
Restricted smoking
Mastercard, Visa, Am Ex, Disc.

Fraternity house, walking distance to UAF, yet close to river & airport. 10,000 sq. ft. Tudor home has floral solarium, antique stained glass decorated foyer with indoor waterfall, cathedral ceilings, and rooms with dormers. Cable TV, phones, laundry, jacuzzi, bikes and canoes.

SAUSAGE QUICHE

1 lb. pork sausage	1 1/2 cups light cream
1 onion, minced	1/2 teaspoon salt
1/2 lb. Swiss cheese, grated	1/4 teaspoon freshly ground pepper
1 tablespoon flour	1/4 teaspoon nutmeg
1 unbaked 10" pie shell	2 tablespoons chopped parsley
4 eggs, lightly beaten	1/2 teaspoon sage

Preheat oven to 375°. Cook sausage and onion in skillet until brown and crisp, and drain. Toss grated cheese with flour. Scatter sausage meat over bottom of pie shell. Arrange cheese over meat. Place remaining ingredients in blender; cover and blend on low until mixed. Pour over meat and cheese. Bake 45 minutes or until knife inserted into center comes out clean. Makes 8 servings.

Submitted by:

Chester House
43 Chester Street
Front Royal, Virginia 22630
(703) 635-3937 or
(800) 621-0441
Bill & Ann Wilson
$55.00 to $150.00

Continental plus breakfast
7 rooms, 3 private baths
Children, over 12
No pets
Restricted smoking
Mastercard, Visa, Am Ex

Georgian mansion with extensive formal gardens in Historic District. Quiet, relaxed atmosphere in elegant surroundings, an "oasis" in the heart of town. Walk to antique & gift shops & historic attractions. Short drive to Skyline Drive/Caverns, Shenandoah River, golf, tennis, hiking, skiing and restaurants.

SPINACH FRITTATA

3 medium potatoes	1/2 cup shredded
6 large eggs	Cheddar or Monterey
1 1/2 cups cream	Jack cheese
1 pkg. frozen chopped	4 oz. cream cheese
spinach	Garnishes: Sour cream
1/4 teaspoon white	& dill, tomato wedges,
pepper	black olives

Preheat oven to 375°. Cut potatoes into chunks (we leave them unpeeled), steam, and arrange in bottom of a 9" buttered Pyrex pie pan. Whisk eggs and cream, blend in spinach, white pepper, and cheese. Pour over potatoes. Dot mixture with small chunks of cream cheese. Bake 30 - 40 minutes until firm and a knife comes out clean. Cut into wedges, garnish with sour cream mixed with dill, tomato wedges and black olives. This is also good served at room temperature. Makes 6 - 8 servings.

Submitted by:

DeHaven Valley Farm Country	Full breakfast
Inn & Restaurant	4-course dinners
39247 North Highway One	9 rooms, 7 private baths
Westport, California 95488	Children allowed
(707) 961-1660	No pets
Jim & Kathleen Tobin	Restricted smoking (outside)
$85.00 to $125.00	Mastercard, Visa, Am Ex

115 year old Victorian farmhouse on 20 acres of pastures, meadows and woods, across the street from the Pacific Ocean. Guests enjoy horses, donkeys, llamas, goats, sheep, and 10 cats. Hiking, tidepooling, hot tubbing & "just kickin' back" are popular activities.

VEGETABLE QUICHE

9" pie shell	2 tablespoons onion
2 eggs	1/2 cup green
1/2 cup mayonnaise	pepper
1 tablespoon flour	1/2 cup tomatoes
1 cup whole milk	2 tablespoons parsley
1/2 teaspoon salt	1/2 cup grated Swiss
1/4 teaspoon mustard	cheese

Beat 2 eggs. Add mayonnaise, flour, milk, salt & mustard, and beat.
Dice onion, green pepper, tomatoes, and parsley. Sprinkle grated
cheese and all vegetables into pie shell. Pour egg mixture over all.
Bake at 375° for 40 minutes or until set. Cool 5 minutes and serve.
Note: May use other fresh vegetables if desired.

Submitted by:

The 1661 Inn & Guest House
Spring Street
Block Island, R.I. 02807
(401) 466-2421
Joan & Justin Abrams/
Rita & Steve Draper
$70.00 to $300.00

Open May 1 to November 1
Full breakfast
19 rooms
No pets
Smoking allowed
Mastercard, Visa, Am Ex

Charming inn and guest house overlooking the Atlantic Ocean. Most
rooms with ocean view decks, some with jacuzzis. Buffet breakfast
and wine & nibble hour included. Petting Zoo with llamas, Sicilian
donkeys, black swans, emus, Pygmy goats, and Indian runner ducks.

YANKEE SPOILER CASSEROLE

1 lb. hot sausage
1 3/4 cups milk
1 stick butter or
margarine
1 cup cooked grits
4 eggs, beaten

1 box Jiffy Corn Muffin
mix
Salt & pepper to taste
2 cups shredded
Cheddar cheese

Brown sausage and drain on paper towels. Place on bottom of 9" x 13" baking pan. Heat milk and butter together, add cooked grits, eggs, and corn muffin mix. Salt and pepper to taste. Pour over sausage. Top with cheese. Bake at 325° for 45 minutes. Makes 8 - 10 servings.

Submitted by:

The Inn on Providence
6700 Providence Road
Charlotte, N.C. 28226
(704) 366-6700
Dan & Darlene McNeill
$59.00 to $79.00

Full breakfast
5 rooms, 3 private baths
Children, over 12
No pets
Restricted smoking
Mastercard & Visa

A 3-story brick Colonial nestled on 2 acres amidst gardens and an outdoor swimming pool. Early American antiques, quilts and family heirlooms. Special egg dishes, apple pannekoeken, home-made breads and muffins for breakfast; served on our verandah, weather permitting.

ZUCCHINI AND CRAB FRITTA

1 tablespoon oil	7 eggs
1 tablespoon butter	1/2 cup milk
1/4 yellow onion, chopped	Salt, pepper & nutmeg to taste
1/2 red bell pepper, chopped	1 1/2 cups Swiss cheese, shredded
1 zucchini, sliced	Paprika
1/2 cup crab, chopped	Parsley

Sauté onion and bell pepper in oil and butter until soft. Add zucchini and crab, sauté 2 minutes longer. In bowl, beat eggs, add milk, and mix together. Season with salt, pepper, and a dash of nutmeg. Add cheese. Generously grease one large quiche pan. Pour vegetable mixture in pan and then egg mixture. Sprinkle with paprika and parsley. Bake at 350° for 35 minutes. Serves 8.

Submitted by:

Eagle River Inn	Full breakfast
P.O. Box 100	12 rooms, 12 private baths
Minturn, Colorado 81645	Children, over 12
(303) 827-5761	No pets
Jane Leavitt	No smoking
$89.00 to $170.00	Mastercard, Visa, Am Ex

Guests are welcomed with down comforters, fresh flowers, and views of the river or mountains, colorful tiles, thick towels and fine toiletries. Southwestern decor, hot tub to enjoy secluded backyard. Walk to colorful restaurants. Near summer and winter sports and attractions.

ZUCCHINI AND HAM FRITTATA

3 tablespoons margarine	1/2 cup cream
1 small onion, chopped (1/4 cup)	1 1/4 teaspoons salt
	1/8 teaspoon pepper
2 small zucchini, sliced (2 cups)	1 cup diced cooked ham
1/2 teaspoon Italian seasoning	1/2 cup Parmesan cheese
10 eggs	1 large tomato, sliced

Melt margarine in 10" round ovenproof casserole. Add onion, zucchini, and Italian seasoning. Sauté over high heat, stirring often until zucchini is lightly browned. Beat eggs, cream, salt and pepper in medium bowl. Pour into casserole with zucchini. Mix well. Add ham. Top with Parmesan cheese and sliced tomatoes. Bake in 350° oven for 25 minutes. Cut into wedges to serve.

Submitted by:

Goose Chase	Full breakfast
200 Blueberry Rd.	5 rooms, 3 private baths
Gardners, Penn. 17324	Children, over 12
(Gettysburg)	No pets
(717) 528-8877	No smoking
Marsha Lucidi	Mastercard & Visa
$69.00 to $89.00	

Lovingly restored, circa 1759 home, on 25 acres. Colonial hospitality with the emphasis on gourmet breakfasts, which use our homegrown blueberries. Breathtaking views, swimming pool, woodland trails. 15 minutes from Battlefield. Skiing, antiquing, golf nearby.

EGG, MEAT
&
CHEESE DISHES

AMBER CRAB SOUFFLÉ

12 eggs
1/2 cup 2% milk
1/2 teaspoon white
  pepper
1/2 teaspoon dillweed

1 cup imitation crab, cut
  into identifiable pieces
6 oz. cream cheese,
  cut into small cubes
Paprika to taste

Spray 6 - 8 ramekins with Pam. Beat eggs, milk, pepper and dillweed. Stir in crab and cream cheese cubes. Pour mixture into individual ramekins, place on cookie sheet, cover with plastic wrap, and refrigerate overnight or up to 24 hours. In morning, uncover, sprinkle with paprika and bake at 350° for 40 - 45 minutes. Makes 6 - 8 servings.

Submitted by:

Garden Street Inn
1212 Garden St.
San Luis Obispo, Calif. 93401
(805) 545-9802
Dan & Kathy Smith
Rooms: $90.00 to $120.00
Suites: $140.00 to $160.00

Full breakfast
9 rooms, 4 suites, 13 private
  baths
Children, over 16
No pets
Restricted smoking
Mastercard, Visa, Am Ex

1887 Italianate/Queen Anne Victorian in the heart of a quaint downtown, featuring spacious decks and a classic restoration. Each room has unique decor: Victorian wallcoverings, custom-designed bedding and antiques. Many rooms with fireplaces and jacuzzis.

APPLE-SAUSAGE BREAKFAST RING

2 lbs. Bob Evans herb/
    sage roll sausage
2 eggs, slightly beaten
1/2 cup cream or milk
1 cup unpeeled apple,
    finely chopped

1 1/2 cups Italian or herb
    flavored bread crumbs
    or stuffing mix,
    finely ground
1/4 - 1/2 cup onion,
    finely minced

Combine all ingredients and mix thoroughly. Press lightly into greased (Pam is great) 6 - 8 cup ring mold. Bake at 350° for 1 hour on aluminum cookie sheet to catch the drippings. Cool and invert. You can make this the day before. Slice into wedges and fry until heated and brown. Makes 18 - 20 average slices, according to how thickly it's sliced. Great served cold for sandwiches!

Submitted by:

The Old Appleford Inn
218 Carlisle Street
Gettysburg, Penn. 17325
(717) 337-1711
Frank & Maribeth Skradski
$83.00 to $123.00

Full breakfast (gourmet)
12 rooms, 12 private baths
Children, over 14
No pets
No smoking
Mastercard, Visa, Am Ex, Disc.

Welcome to Gettysburg's first B&B, in the Historic Pathway, 1867 Italianate Victorian mansion features fine 20th century hospitality. Tour the battlefield in summer . . . enjoy brilliant autumn foliage, and relax with a quiet, romantic Victorian holiday!

AUSSIE BACON & EGG ROLLS

10 round crisp bread
   rolls
10 spinach leaves,
   chopped
1 oz. butter
2 medium onions,
   chopped

10 strips of bacon,
   chopped
3 tablespoons barbecue
   sauce
10 eggs
1 cup grated Cheddar
   cheese

Cut slice from top of bread rolls and set aside. Scoop out inside of bread rolls leaving a thin shell. Drop spinach into pan of boiling water and boil one minute, drain. Sauté spinach in hot butter for one minute, drain. Divide spinach among bread rolls. Sauté onions and bacon in pan until tender, stir in barbecue sauce, spoon over spinach. Break an egg into each bread roll, top with cheese, and replace the roll tops. Wrap rolls in foil, place on tray, and bake in oven at 350° for 15 minutes. Remove from oven, let stand 5 minutes before removing foil.

A favorite with dairy farmers in Australia. Richard & his brother looked forward to their grandmother baking this treat, after milking the cows.

Submitted by:

The Walkabout Inn
P.O. Box 294, 837 Village Rd.
Lampeter, Penn. 17537
(717) 464-0707
Richard & Margaret Mason
$69.00 to $99.00

Full breakfast
5 rooms, 5 private baths
Children allowed
No pets
Restricted smoking
Mastercard, Visa, Am Ex

Australian host has created an authentic British style B&B in the heart of the Amish countryside. English gardens, fountains, balconies, fireplaces and antique furnishings. Recipient of international acclaim for its famous recipes at the Royal Easter Show in Australia.

BAKED EGGS FOR TWO

4 ham patties, partially cooked	3/4 cup toasted croutons
4 large eggs	1 cup shredded Cheddar cheese (or your choice)

Preheat oven to 350°. Grease 2 - 10 oz. ramekins. Place 2 ham patties in each dish. Place 1 egg on top of each patty. Place croutons around eggs. Sprinkle top with cheese. Place both ramekins on baking sheet. Bake for 18 minutes. Serve with pride!

Submitted by:

Log Home Bed & Breakfast
R.R. #2, Box 93 H
Millville, Pennsylvania 17846
(717) 458-4681
(717) 458-6654
Wes & Bette Swanson

Full breakfast
3 rooms, 1 private half bath
  and 1 full shared bath
No pets
Restricted smoking

Located in a peaceful country setting with a spectacular view of neighboring mountains and villages. A covered porch, facing the view, invites one to come and relax. Bedtime snacks. Near state parks, fishing, shopping, golf, universities and an amusement park.

BAKED SPINACH EGG "NESTS"

4 slices Canadian bacon	4 eggs
8 fresh spinach leaves (approximately)	Salt & pepper to taste
4 teaspoons butter	4 teaspoons shredded Cheddar cheese

Brown Canadian bacon on both sides in skillet, then cut into 1/4" strips. Wash, dry, and remove stems from spinach. Stack leaves and roll up tightly, then slice in narrow strips. Put 1 teaspoon butter in each of 4 - 4 oz. baking cups. Add about 1/4 of the spinach, then about 1/4 of the Canadian bacon. Break an egg on top of each nest, then top each egg with 1 teaspoon of shredded Cheddar cheese. Place baking dishes on cookie sheet and bake in preheated 325° oven for approximately 15 - 20 minutes. Serves 4.

Submitted by:

Spring Bayou Inn
32 W. Tarpon Avenue
Tarpon Springs, Florida 34689
(813) 938-9333
Ron & Cher Morrick
$55.00 to $85.00

Continental plus breakfast
5 rooms, 4 private baths
No children
No pets
No smoking

For a taste of old winter resort residences, we are in the center of Historical District, near shops, restaurants, and waterfront park. Charming small Greek village known as sponge capital of the world. Sponge docks are an easy walk from the inn.

BREAKFAST FRITTAS

2 - 10 oz. pkgs. frozen chopped spinach, thawed & squeezed dry	4 tablespoons chopped onion
1 1/2 cups ricotta cheese	1/2 teaspoon oregano
1 cup Parmesan cheese	1/4 teaspoon Sea salt
1 cup chopped mushrooms	1/4 teaspoon freshly ground pepper
	2 eggs, beaten
	Chopped chives

Preheat oven to 375°. Coat individual baking dishes/ramekins with cooking spray. In a bowl combine spinach, ricotta and Parmesan cheeses, mushrooms, onion, oregano, salt and pepper. Beat in the eggs. Divide mixture into ramekins. Bake 20 - 25 minutes or until firm, but not dry (still moist looking). Top with chopped chives. Serve hot. Serves 8.

Submitted by:

North Coast Country Inn
34591 S. Highway #1
Gualala, California 95445
(707) 884-4537
(800) 959-4537
Loren & Nancy Flanagan
$135.00, all rooms

Full breakfast
4 rooms, 4 private baths
Children, over 12
No pets
No smoking
Mastercard, Visa, Am Ex

Rustic redwood buildings on a forested hillside overlooking the Pacific Ocean. Fireplaces, mini-kitchens, decks, authentic antiques. Romantic hot tub under the pines, and hilltop gazebo garden. Near beaches, lighthouse, hiking, golf, tennis, state parks, & restaurants.

BREAKFAST PASTA

1 lb. bacon, chopped
1 medium onion, chopped
1/3 cup flour
Salt & pepper to taste
4 cups milk
2 cups grated Swiss cheese

1/2 cup grated Parmesan cheese
3/4 lb. lasagna noodles, cooked & drained
1 dozen hard cooked eggs, sliced
Fresh chopped parsley

Cook bacon until crisp, and then drain and set aside. Sauté onion in bacon drippings until opaque. Add flour, salt and pepper, and cook until paste forms. Add milk slowly and cook until thickened. Add 1 cup Swiss cheese and Parmesan cheese. Stir until cheese is melted, and set aside. Meanwhile, cook and drain lasagna noodles and slice hard cooked eggs. Grease 9" x 13" baking dish and spoon a thin layer of sauce over bottom. Layer noodles, chopped bacon, sliced eggs, sauce and remaining cup of Swiss cheese until completely used (2 or 3 layers). Sprinkle with fresh chopped parsley and bake at 350° for 30 minutes. Cut into squares. Serves 12 - 16.

Submitted by:

Windward House
24 Jackson Street
Cape May, New Jersey 08204
(609) 884-3368
Sandy & Owen Miller
$80.00 to $135.00

Full breakfast
8 rooms, 8 private baths
Children, over 12
No pets
Restricted smoking
Mastercard & Visa

Edwardian seaside inn, in Historic District, 1/2 block to beach and shopping mall. Spacious guest rooms, queen beds, a/c, amid a trove of high Victorian furnishings & treasures. Spectacular summer porches & wintertime coziness, afternoon refreshments, bicycles. Christmas is our special time.

BREAKFAST PIZZA

1 small onion, finely
  chopped
1/2 cup green pepper,
  chopped
1 tablespoon butter
1/2 lb. bulk pork sausage
1 medium tomato,
  seeded & chopped
2 cups biscuit baking mix

1/2 cup cold water
1 1/2 cups shredded
  Cheddar cheese
1/4 cup half & half
  (or milk)
2 large eggs
2 tablespoons dried
  parsley

Heat oven to 350°. Grease 12" pizza pan. Cook onion and pepper in butter until just tender. Set aside. Cook sausage, breaking it up, drain, and set aside. Mix baking mix and water, forming a soft dough. Pat dough into pan with floured hands, pressing 1/2" up on sides. Spread sausage over dough, then peppers, onions, tomatoes, and cheese. Beat half & half and eggs with whisk until foamy. Pour carefully over cheese. Add parsley over top. Bake uncovered 30 minutes. Serve immediately. Makes 6 - 8 servings.

Submitted by:

The Inn at New Ipswich
Porter Hill Road, P.O. Box 208
New Ipswich, N.H. 03071
(603) 878-3711
Ginny & Steve Bankuti
$45.00 (sgl.) to $60.00 (dbl.)

Full breakfast
6 rooms, 5 private baths
Children, over 8
No pets
No smoking
Mastercard & Visa

Gracious 1790 farmhouse with classic red barn instantly welcomes you. Six fireplaces, wide pine floors, and cozy country furnishings will remind you of Grandma's. To quote guests, "Breakfast alone is worth the visit." Located in unspoiled Monadnock Region where activities abound: skiing, golf, antiques, hiking, concerts and more.

THE INN AT
NEW IPSWICH

BRUNCH ENCHILADES

2 cups ground, fully-cooked ham
1/2 cup sliced green onions
1/2 cup finely chopped green bell pepper
2 1/2 cups shredded Cheddar cheese
8 - 7" flour tortillas

4 eggs, beaten
2 cups light cream or milk
1 tablespoon flour
1/4 teaspoon salt (opt.)
1/4 teaspoon garlic powder
Few drops hot liquid pepper sauce

In bowl, combine ground ham, onion & green pepper. Place 1/3 cup mixture and 3 tablespoons cheese at one end of tortilla. Roll up. Arrange tortillas seam-side down in greased 12" x 7 1/2" x 2" ovenproof casserole. Combine eggs, cream, flour, salt, garlic powder and hot pepper sauce. Pour over tortillas. Cover and refrigerate several hours or overnight. Bake uncovered in 350° oven 45 - 50 minutes or until set. Sprinkle with remaining cheese. Bake 3 minutes more until cheese melts. Let stand 10 minutes. Serve with garnish of avocado slices, fresh salsa and sour cream. Serves 8.

Submitted by:

Blue Spruce Inn
2815 Main Street
Santa Cruz (Soquel), California
  95073-2412
(800) 559-1137
Pat & Tom O'Brien
$80.00 to $125.00

Full breakfast
5 rooms, 5 private baths
Children, over 12
No pets
Restricted smoking
Mastercard, Visa, Am Ex

1873 farmhouse in Soquel Village. Walk to fine dining, antique shops, local wineries. Trellised gardens, quiet decks. Explore Monterey Bay - Redwood Forest, pounding surf, golf, hiking, fishing.

CHEESE 'N EGG CROISSANTS

3 tablespoons butter or margarine
3 tablespoons flour
2 cups milk
8 oz. Cheddar cheese, grated

12 eggs, poached
6 croissants, warmed & halved
12 half slices of avocado
White pepper to taste
Paprika to taste

Melt butter in heavy saucepan. Add flour and blend with a wire whisk stirring constantly (4 - 5 minutes). Stir in milk, whisking until smooth. Add cheese and stir frequently while sauce heats and thickens. Do NOT boil. Poach eggs and warm croissants. Place croissant halves on plate. Add a poached egg to each half and sprinkle with white pepper. Spoon sauce over egg and croissant. Place half a slice of avocado on top of each egg and sprinkle with paprika. Serve with link sausage. Garnish with wedges of fresh melon or grape cluster. Makes 6 servings.

Submitted by:

Colonial Capital
  Bed & Breakfast
501 Richmond Road
Williamsburg, VA 23185-3537
(800) 776-0570
Barbara & Phil Craig
$90.00 to $125.00 (suite)

Full breakfast
5 rooms, 5 private baths
Children, over 6
No pets
Restricted smoking
Mastercard & Visa

Elegantly furnished Colonial Revival, circa 1926, only 3 blocks from historic area. Cozy Canopy Beds, and Breakfast With Class. Classic plantation parlor with woodburning fireplace, afternoon tea and wine. Complimentary bikes, Off-street parking, central a/c, screened porch, patio and deck.

CHEESE PIE

3 cups seasoned croutons	4 large eggs, slightly beaten
2 cups coarsely grated sharp Cheddar cheese	2 1/2 cups milk, half & half, or combination
1 cup cooked ham, cut into 1/4" cubes (opt.)	1 large tomato, cut into wedges

Spray 8" x 8" baking dish with non-stick coating. Combine croutons, cheese, and ham in dish and mix well. In bowl, combine eggs and milk. Pour mixture over croutons and stir to combine. Push tomato wedges down into mixture spacing evenly over dish. Bake uncovered at 350° until puffed and brown and firm in the center, 30 - 45 minutes. Serve hot. Makes 12 servings.

Submitted by:

Glen-Ella Springs
Route 3, Bear Gap Road
Clarkesville, Georgia 30523
(706) 754-7295
Barrie & Bobby Aycock
$75.00 to $135.00

Full/Continental plus breakfast
16 rooms, 16 private baths
Children allowed, some rooms
No pets
Restricted smoking
Mastercard, Visa, Am Ex

1890 inn on National Register combines the past with modern comfort and amenities. Renovated in 1987, pine-paneled guest rooms feature antiques, local reproductions, private entrance/porch, views of 17 acres of meadows, with herb, perennial and vegetable gardens, a 20' x 40' swimming pool and large sun deck.

CHILI CHEESE EGG PUFFS

10 eggs (or equivalent
in EggBeaters)
1 pint lowfat cottage
cheese (small curd)
1 lb. shredded Monterey
Jack cheese
2 - 4.5 oz. cans chopped
mild green chilies

1/2 cup melted butter
or margarine
1/2 cup flour
1 teaspoon baking
powder
1/2 teaspoon salt

Beat eggs in large bowl till light. Add rest of ingredients, blending thoroughly. Pour into 10 - 3 1/2" x 2" deep individual baking dishes or a 9" x 13" pan whch has been buttered or sprayed with Pam. Bake at 350° for 35 - 40 minutes for individual dishes or 1 - 1 1/4 hours for a large pan. Bake until browned and center is firm. Serve with warm mild salsa and cornbread, corn sticks or corn muffins. Makes 10 servings.

Submitted by:

Village Green Inn
40 West Main Street
Falmouth, Mass. 02540
(508) 548-5621
Linda & Don Long
$75.00 to $110.00

Full breakfast
5 rooms, 5 private baths
Children, over 16
No pets
Restricted smoking
Mastercard, Visa, Am Ex

Gracious 1804 Colonial on historic village green, well-groomed lawns and flower gardens. Tastefully decorated in soft colors, antiques and reproductions. Lovely formal parlor with fireplaces and large porches, 19th century charm, warm hospitality and thoughtful amenities. Walk to fine shops, restaurants, beaches, tennis, bike path and ferry.

CHILI SOUFFLÉ

Tortillas
1 1/2 cups cheese,
  grated
5 chilies, peeled
Thin slices of ham, diced

5 eggs
2 cups lowfat milk
1/2 teaspoon salt
Pepper to taste

Spray 5 ramekins with nonstick spray. Layer tortillas, cheese, chilies, ham, then tortillas and cheese. Mix eggs, milk, salt, and pepper, and pour into cups. Bake 30 minutes in 350° oven. Makes 5 servings.

Submitted by:

Cottonwood Inn B&B
123 San Juan Avenue
Alamosa, Colorado 81101
(719) 589-3882
Julie Mordecai &
  George Sellman
$52.00 to $75.00

Full breakfast
6 rooms, 4 private baths
Children allowed
No pets
No smoking
Mastercard & Visa

Lovely, historical turn-of-the century home. Local artwork and antiques, hearty breakfast. Visit Great Sand Dunes, cross-country ski, ride the Cumbres-Toltec Railway, bike, hike, fish, hunt or visit nearby bird sanctuaries.

246

CORNED BEEF HASH WITH EGGS

4 large baked potatoes	1 tablespoon fresh basil
2 tablespoons olive oil	or parsley
1 large onion, chopped	1 can corned beef
1 tablespoon fresh	2 tablespoons butter
rosemary	8 - 12 eggs

Chop baked potatoes and skins. Sauté onion in olive oil until tender, add potatoes and seasonings. Add corned beef, and cook until well warmed through & beginning to get crisp. In another saucepan, melt butter and cook eggs sunny side up. To serve, spoon hash onto each plate, top with one or two fried eggs and garnish. Serves 4 - 6.

Submitted by:

Peppertrees B&B Inn
724 E University
Tucson, Arizona 85719
(602) 622-7167
Marjorie Martin
$65.00 to $130.00

Full breakfast
5 rooms, 1 private bath
Children allowed
No pets
Restricted smoking
Mastercard & Visa

1905 house by the main gates of the University of Arizona. Furnished in period furniture, with lovely courtyard and 2 comfortable guesthouses. Known for great hospitality, homey ambience, wonderful food & interesting guests. Walk to theatres, museums, shops, restaurants & campus.

COUNTRY INN SCRAMBLE

1 sheet puff pastry, frozen or homemade	2 oz. cream cheese
8 large eggs	4 oz. smoked turkey
2 cloves garlic, finely minced	1 tablespoon freshly snipped herbs
Pinch of salt	1 tablespoon butter or oil
Pinch of white pepper	

Prebake puff pastry shells in 350° oven until well browned and dry in the center. They can be cut into any shape desired, we use 5" x 5" squares. Cut lengthwise in half before serving. Scramble the remainder of ingredients in the oil in a nonstick pan. To serve, place eggs on bottom half of shell, and top with top of shell. Garnish with sprigs of fresh herbs and a beautiful flower. Makes 4 servings.

Submitted by:

Wine & Roses Country Inn
2505 W. Turner Rd.
Lodi, California 95242
(209) 334-6988
Kris Cromwell,
Del & Sherri Smith
$69.00 to $125.00

Full breakfast
10 rooms, 10 private baths
Children allowed
No pets
No smoking
Mastercard, Visa, Am Ex

90 year old historical estate on secluded 5 acres of towering trees & old-fashioned flower gardens. Reflecting the past with nostalgia, rooms are filled with handmade comforters, antiques, art, collectibles & fresh flowers. Browse through library, warm by the crackling fire, or stroll through the gardens. Enjoy casually elegant "wine country" dining in our restaurant.

CRAB-FILLED CREPES

Crepes:
4 eggs
4 egg yolks
3/4 cup sifted flour
2 teaspoons sugar
1 quart milk
Clarified butter
Sauce:
White sauce recipe of
   your choice
1/4 cup white Cheddar
   cheese, grated

Filling:
1 1/2 cups crab
1/2 cup minced celery
1/4 cup scallions
2 heaping teaspoons
   horseradish
Sour cream to taste

1/4 cup yellow Cheddar
   cheese, grated
1/2 cup chunk crab
   meat

Crepes: Beat eggs, add to flour and sugar. Add milk. Mix. Pour 2 - 3 ozs. batter into medium hot crepe pan coated with one tablespoon melted clarified butter per pan. Cook until very lightly browned, then flip. When done, cool on waxed paper, using waxed paper to separate crepes. Cool thoroughly or refrigerate before using. Makes 24 crepes. Mix filling ingredients together with enough sour cream to moisten to taste. Fill the crepes with filling, put in a warm oven with a wet towel over the crepes to give a steam effect. Warm for 2 - 3 minutes. To a simple white sauce recipe add cheeses and chunk crab meat. Spoon warm sauce over crepes. Serves 12.

Submitted by:

The Martine Inn
255 Oceanview Boulevard
Pacific Grove, Calif. 93950
(408) 373-3388
Marion & Don Martine
$115.00 to $225.00

Full breakfast
19 rooms, 19 private baths
Children allowed
No pets
Restricted smoking
Mastercard & Visa

Grand old home, established in late 1890's, overlooks magnificent rocky coastline of Monterey Bay. Elegantly furnished with authentic museum quality antiques. Breakfast served on Old Sheffield silver, Victorian china, crystal and lace. Creating a world of ease and grace.

CURRIED EGGS MIMOSA

6 tablespoons butter	3 cups milk
1 tablespoon curry powder	1/2 teaspoon Tabasco sauce
6 tablespoons flour	9 hard-cooked eggs, shelled
1 teaspoon salt	

Melt butter in saucepan. Add curry and cook 3 - 5 minutes. Add flour and salt. Remove from heat and stir in milk. Cook over medium heat, stirring constantly, until smooth and thickened. Stir in Tabasco. Quarter eggs, slip into sauce, and stir very gently. Keep hot in chafing dish. Serve with hot fruit compote. Serves 6.

Submitted by:

The Lyon & The Lambe Inn	Full gourmet breakfast
988 Lawrence St. at Tenth	4 rooms, 4 private baths
Eugene, Oregon 97401	Children, over 12
(503) 683-3160	Well-behaved dogs allowed
Barbara & Henri Brod	Restricted smoking
$55.00 to $83.00	Mastercard & Visa

Lovely, elegant inn, committed to your comfort. Luxuriously appointed tub room with jacuzzi bath, candles, bubbles and music. "Delectables" featured at breakfast each day. Centrally located, close to everything, yet in a quiet neighborhood.

EGG POT PIE

1/2 cup butter
1/2 cup flour
2 cups milk
8 oz. extra sharp
  Cheddar cheese,
  grated
1 cup sour cream
2 pkgs. Herb Ox
  chicken bouillon
1/2 teaspoon thyme
  leaves

1/2 teaspoon salt
3/4 teaspoon freshly
  ground pepper
1/2 lb. cooked smoked
  ham, in 1/2" cubes
18 hard boiled eggs,
  peeled & quartered
Pastry crust to cover
  tops of pies

Slowly melt butter, then add flour. Stir until well-blended. With wire whisk, beat in milk. Cook over low flame until thick. Stir in cheese, sour cream and seasonings. After cheese has melted, add the ham and hard boiled eggs. Stir until the eggs and ham are thoroughly heated. Spoon into individual ramekins. Cover with crust, poke 3 holes in top with a knife. Bake approximately 20 minutes at 450°. Makes 6 individual servings.

Submitted by:

Pig Hill Inn
73 Main Street
Cold Spring, New York 10516
(914) 265-9247
Wendy O'Brien/Joe Heavey
$85.00 to $150.00

Full breakfast
8 rooms, 4 private baths
Children allowed
No pets
No smoking
Mastercard, Visa, Am Ex

1 hour from New York City, and known for our decor, as well as incredible breakfasts, served in your room by the fireplace, in the dining room, or in the wonderful, terraced garden. Styles range from rustic Adirondack, to French Provençal, to country English. All furnishings are for sale.

EGGS BATTENKILL WITH LEMON-CHIVE HOLLANDAISE

Egg dish:
4 English muffins
8 large eggs
1/4 cup heavy cream
Salt & pepper to taste
1 tablespoon olive oil
2 smoked trout fillets
  (boned, skinned &
  chopped)

Hollandaise sauce:
2 egg yolks
Juice of 1 lemon
Pinch of salt
Dash of cayenne pepper
1 tablespoon water
1 tablespoon chopped
  chives
12 oz. clarified butter

Split and toast muffins. Put on plate and hold warm. Whisk eggs, cream, salt and pepper together. Heat olive oil in nonstick pan. Add trout and heat through. Add eggs and lightly scramble. Divide eggs into equal portions on top of muffins. For sauce: Combine first six ingredients in a double boiler. Whisk until yolks are fluffy and ribboning. Whisk in butter in slow steady steam. Hold in a warm but not hot area. Top eggs with Hollandaise sauce and serve. Serves 4.

Submitted by:

Barrows House
Dorset, Vermont 05251
(802) 867-4455
Sally & Tim Brown
$160.00 to $210.00 MAP

Full breakfast
28 rooms, 28 private baths
Children allowed
Pets allowed in 2 cottages
Restricted smoking
Personal checks, Visa,
  Mastercard

Early 19th century inn and eight historic buildings, set on 11 acres. Tennis courts, a heated outdoor swimming pool, bicycles, cross-country ski shop, and a gourmet restaurant are all available on the property.

EGGS BENEDICT CALEDONIA

2 quality split English muffins	4 eggs, poached
Butter or margarine	1 pkg. Hollandaise sauce mix
4 slices Canadian bacon or ham	3 tablespoons lemon juice

Toast or broil muffin halves and spread with butter. Top with slices of Canadian bacon or ham. Warm at 160° in oven. Poach eggs for 3 1/2 minutes in cups sprayed with vegetable oil. With whites set and yolks liquid, place inverted eggs upon muffins. Prepare Hollandaise sauce replacing 3 tablespoons of water with lemon juice. Cover eggs with sauce. Garnish with fresh parsley, kiwi slice, strawberry half, or a favorite garnish of your choice. Makes 2 servings.

Submitted by:

Caledonia Farm
Route 1, Box 2080
Flint Hill, Virginia 22627
(703) 675-3693
Phil Irwin
$80.00 to $140.00-Sat. surch.

Full breakfast-hourly intervals
2 suites/2 rooms
Children, over 12
No pets - kennel nearby
No smoking
Mastercard, Visa & Discover

National Register landmark adjacent Shenandoah National Park. Beautifully restored 1812 stone home and romantic summer kitchen surrounded by pasturelands & accented by 3,300' Blue Ridge Mtns. Working fireplaces, individual heat and a/c, Skyline Drive views, hayrides, porches, bicycles, & lawn games. Evening dining nearby. Washington, VA, 4 miles, & Washington, D.C., 68 miles.

EGGS IN A GARDEN

2 medium onions, or more
1 green pepper
4 whole tomatoes, or large sections
1 handful fresh chives
1 handful parsley
4 garlic cloves, minced, or equivalent

Other vegetables as desired & available, all coarsely chopped
6 eggs
Salt & pepper to taste
Garnish:
Crushed oregano or English thyme
Paprika

In a large (9" - 11") stainless steel covered skillet, add enough coarsely chopped fresh vegetables to make a thick layer on bottom (about 1 1/2"). We use mainly onions, but heavily laced with other vegetables. Tomatoes are arranged to alternate nicely with eggs. Cover skillet, steam vegetables on low heat until juicy and softened. Make indentations for eggs with back of spoon. Break eggs into indentations. Salt & pepper to taste. Sprinkle with garnish choice. Juices will fill in the holes and furnish poaching liquid for each egg. Cook until eggs are done. Serve from skillet at table. Serves 4.

Submitted by:

West Shore Farm B&B
2781 West Shore Drive
Lummi Island, Wash. 98262
(206) 758-2600
Polly & Carl Hanson
$75.00 to $85.00

Full breakfast
2 rooms, 2 private baths
Children allowed
No pets
No smoking
Mastercard & Visa

Visitors will enjoy and remember: our quiet natural beach, 180° view of islands, sunsets, Canadian mountain backdrop for passing boats, eagles, seabirds, seals on offshore rocks, our unique octagonal owner-built home of native woods, healthy meals served family-style.

EGGS PICANTE

4 eggs
1/4 cup yogurt
2 tablespoons salsa
  sauce

1/2 cup grated Cheddar
  and Swiss cheeses,
  mixed

Beat eggs and yogurt. Bake at 350° for 15 minutes or until eggs are set. Spread salsa sauce over eggs, and sprinkle grated cheese over top. Bake until bubbly, about 10 minutes. Serve immediately. Vary the salsa sauce from mild to hot depending on your choice of flavor. Makes 2 servings. This recipe is very easy to double for 4 people.

Submitted by:

Just-N-Trails Bed & Breakfast/
  Farm Vacation
Route #1, Box 274
Sparta, Wisconsin 54656
(608) 269-4522
1-800-488-4521
Donna & Don Justin
$60.00 to $195.00

Full breakfast
8 rooms, 7 private baths
Children allowed
No pets
No smoking
Mastercard & Visa

We specialize in recreation, relaxation and romance. Choice of 4 rooms in 1920 farmhouse, or "The Woodshed," "The Granary," or "Little House on the Prairie,", each with double whirlpool & fireplace. Near Elroy-Sparta Bike Trail, Amish community, & canoeable rivers.

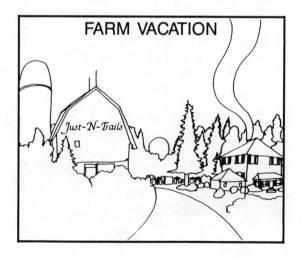

EGGS RANCHO

1 large onion
1 small green pepper
3 tablespoons olive oil
3 tablespoons flour
1 large can tomatoes
1 teaspoon salt

1/2 teaspoon chili powder
1/2 teaspoon oregano
8 eggs
1/2 cup grated Swiss or mozzarella cheese
Several sliced ripe olives

Preheat oven to 350°. Slice onion and green pepper. Cook in oil until tender but not brown. Stir in flour. Add tomatoes, salt, chili powder and oregano. Cook slowly until sauce thickens slightly, about 20 minutes. Pour into shallow baking dish and drop eggs in, one at a time, carefully. Scatter cheese on top, then olives. Bake until firm. Makes 8 servings.

Submitted by:

Heritage House, Inc.
Main & Piedmont Streets
Washington, Virginia 22747
(703) 675-3207
Jean & Frank Scott
$95.00 to $125.00 (suite)

Full breakfast
4 rooms, 4 private baths
No children
No pets
No smoking
Mastercard & Visa

1837 manor house in "Little" Washington, VA, a village surveyed by young George Washington. Used as a Civil War headquarters. Heirloom antiques, international collectibles, gourmet breakfasts and gorgeous Blue Ridge views. Central to fine dining, antiquing, hiking, and nature. Relaxed, comfortable, pretty!

EGGS SUMMIT PLACE

6 strips cooked bacon,
  or 1 cup cooked
  sausage, drained &
  crumbled
4 eggs
1 cup milk

1 heaping tablespoon
  flour
Dash of Worcestershire
  sauce
2 tablespoons grated
  cheese

Preheat oven to 350°. Cook bacon well in frying pan. Drain all but 1 tablespoon of the fat. Mix other ingredients with beater. Spread bacon in bottom of frying pan and pour mixture over it. Bake until brown on top. Serves 4.

Submitted by:

Summit Place B&B
1682 W. Kimmel Rd.
Jackson, Michigan 49201
(517) 787-0468
Douglas & Marlene Laing
$50.00 (sgl.) to $60.00 (dbl.)

Full breakfast
2 rooms, 1 1/2 private baths
Children, over 3
No pets, dog in residence
No smoking
Mastercard & Visa

Enjoy warmth and elegance where the past blends with the present in a beautiful, quiet countryside. Fireplace, formal dining room, deck surrounded by wisteria in summer. Books, music, & piano in living room, or enjoy TV in your room. Near golf, antiques, and attractions.

FANCY EGG SCRAMBLE

6 oz. Canadian bacon, diced	Topping:
1/4 cup green onions, chopped	4 teaspoons butter, melted
3 tablespoons butter	2 1/2 cups bread crumbs
12 eggs, beaten	1/8 teaspoon paprika
1 cup mushrooms, sliced thin	
Cheese sauce:	
2 tablespoons butter	1/8 teaspoon pepper
2 tablespoons flour	2 cups milk
1/2 teaspoon salt	4 oz. American cheese, shredded

Cook bacon and onion in 3 tablespoons butter until tender. Add beaten eggs, and scramble until set, but not dry, set aside. Melt butter. Blend in flour, salt and pepper. Add milk. Stir and cook until bubbly. Stir in American cheese (no sharp cheese). Add cooked eggs and mushrooms to cheese sauce. Pour into 9" x 13" baking dish. Combine topping ingredients. Sprinkle on top. Cover and chill. Bake uncovered at 350° for 30 minutes. Makes 8 - 10 servings.

Submitted by:

Grey Whale Inn	Full breakfast
615 North Main St.	14 rooms, 14 private baths
Fort Bragg, California 95437	Children, over 12
(707) 964-0640 or	No pets
(800) 382-7244	No smoking
John & Colette Bailey	Mastercard, Visa, Discover
$75.00 to $150.00	

Named "one of the 1991 top 50 inns in America" by The Inn Times. Extra comfortable rooms, one with whirlpool, some fireplaces. Ideal for special occasions, couples, business people & groups. 6 blocks from beach, walk to Skunk Train, shops and sights.

FLUTED QUICHE CUPS

Crepes:	**1/2 lb. bulk sausage**
4 eggs	**1/4 cup chopped onions**
1/4 teaspoon salt	**1/2 cup milk**
2 cups flour	**3 eggs**
2 1/4 cups milk	**1/2 cup mayonnaise**
1/4 cup melted	**2 cups shredded**
butter	**Cheddar cheese**

Crepes: Combine all ingredients in blender, blend for 1 minute. Scrape down sides & blend another 15 seconds or until smooth. Refrigerate batter 1 hour or more. Cook crepe until bottom is browned, then carefully turn with spatula. Brown other side for a few seconds. Remove from pan with spatula, stack on plate or tray. Freeze in muffin tins, & store in plastic bags. Yield: 32 - 36. Filling: Brown sausage and onion and drain. Combine remaining ingredients with sausage. Line greased muffin tins with crepes. Fill 3/4 full with sausage mixture and bake at 350° for 15 minutes. Cover loosely with foil and bake additional 15 minutes or until set. Fills 12 - 14 crepes.

Submitted by:

Garth Woodside Mansion
R.R. #1
Hannibal, Missouri 63401
(314) 221-2789
Diane & Irv Feinberg
$58.00 to $90.00

Full breakfast
8 rooms, 8 private baths
Children, over 12
No pets
Restricted smoking
Mastercard & Visa

Chosen "1 of the Midwest's 10 best Country Inns," an historic country estate at its finest! Mansion contains mostly original furnishings. Stroll our 39 acres or fish in our pond. Enjoy pampered elegance and hospitality with afternoon tea, and nightshirts to wear.

"GOOD MORNING" SAUSAGE BALLS

1 lb. good quality sausage	1 egg
2 teaspoons cornstarch	2 teaspoons soy sauce
1 cup fresh bread crumbs	1/2 cup chopped pecans

Mix ingredients together. Roll into small balls. Fry or bake, until done. Serve with warm applesauce.

Submitted by:

Candlelight Cottage B&B
910 Vassar St.
Alma, Michigan 48801
(517) 463-3961
Ron & Yvonne Wolfgang
$45.00 to $55.00

Full breakfast
2 rooms, 2 private baths
Children allowed
No pets
No smoking

Within view of Alma College, a delightful Cape Cod cottage secluded behind a picket fence. Elegant furnishings, beautiful decor, fresh flowers, crisp linens, cleanliness and home baking add to the pleasure and comfort of your holiday homestay. Afternoon tea & evening snacks.

HUEVOS SHENANDOAH

6 oz. chopped chorizo
  sausage, browned &
  drained
1/2 med. red bell pepper
  & 1/2 med. green bell
  pepper, chopped
1/2 medium onion,
  chopped
1 cup frozen Ore Ida
  Potatoes O'Brien,
  cooked per package
  instructions

10 large eggs
1/2 cup milk
2 tablespoons butter
  or margarine
1/2 tablespoon Schilling
  Mexican seasoning *
16 - 7" flour tortillas
  (or 8 - 10" tortillas)
  warmed in aluminum foil
2 cups grated Monterey
  Jack/Cheddar cheese

* Note: May substitute 1/4 teaspoon crushed dried red chilies, 1/4 teaspoon cumin, and 1/2 teaspoon dried oregano for Mexican seasoning. In large frying pan sauté bell peppers and onions in small amount of oil until tender. Remove from heat, stir in cooked sausage and cooked potatoes, transfer to large bowl. In same pan, melt butter. Whip eggs with milk, pour into pan and scramble eggs over medium heat. As eggs begin to congeal, add sausage-vegetable mixture and seasonings. Cook just until medium-set, and remove from heat. Fill centers of tortillas with 1/3 cup egg mixture (1/2 cup if using large tortillas) and roll up. Place seam-down on lightly greased cookie sheet, cover with cheese, and place under broiler until cheese melts. Cut large tortillas in half. Garnish with cilantro leaves, and serve with salsa and sour cream. Serves 8 hungry people!

Submitted by:

Shenandoah Inn
0600 Frying Pan Rd., Box 578
Basalt, Colorado 81621
(303) 927-4991
Bob & Terri Ziets
$60.00 to $75.00

Full breakfast
4 rooms, 2 semi-private baths
Children, over 12
No pets
No smoking
(Rooms higher at Christmas)

Contemporary western B&B, on 2 private riverfront acres on Frying Pan River, a premier gold metal trout stream! 1/2 hour from Aspen & Glenwood Springs, year-round access to the best of the Colorado outdoors. Warm, friendly atmosphere, exceptional cuisine.

JAN'S BAKED POTATOES FOR POACHED EGGS

1 medium potato per serving plus 2 more	Chopped green onion to taste
1 cup grated Monterey Jack cheese, or Havarti (per 10 potatoes)	Salt & pepper to taste
	Half & half to taste
	Assorted toppings

Boil potatoes. When tender, drain, peel, (except red potatoes), and chop or grate into buttered baking dish or individual ramekins. Layer potatoes, green onions, cheese and seasonings. Add half & half, piercing with a fork so liquid will go to the bottom of dish. Not too much - you don't want to see it! Bake casserole 45 minutes at 375°, ramekins 20 minutes. To serve: Casserole - Spoon out a portion, make a hollow with back of spoon and slip in poached eggs. Sprinkle with Parmesan cheese, paprika and parsley. Ramekins: Bake on cookie sheet. Remove ramekins from oven after 20 minutes, make hollows, and break an egg in each. Cover eggs with 1 more tablespoon cream. Sprinkle with paprika and Parmesan cheese. Return to oven 10 minutes or until eggs are set. Great brunch dish!

Submitted by:

Kangaroo House
P.O. Box 334
Eastsound, Wash. 98245
(206) 376-2175
Mike & Jan Russillo
$65.00 to $100.00 plus tax

Full breakfast (3-course)
5 rooms, 2 private baths
Children allowed
No pets
Restricted smoking
Mastercard & Visa

1907 Craftsman-style home on Orcas Island, convenient to shops, restaurants, beaches, & airport. All rooms are bright and airy. Each decorated with blend of period, antique & contemporary furnishings. Sitting room with stone fireplace. Expansive decks, lawns & gardens.

KIRSCHKE HOUSE SPECIAL BREAKFAST

1/4 cup butter	1/4 cup butter
2 medium onions, minced	16 slices bacon, cooked & crumbled
2 large red apples, cored & diced	16 large eggs, beaten
2 tablespoons parsley	Pecans
	Blue cheese

Sauté onions, apples and parsley in 1/4 cup butter. Add cooked, crumbled bacon. Cook eggs in 1/4 cup butter until they begin to set. Add bacon mixture. Scramble to desired consistency. Sprinkle with pecans and blue cheese to taste. Garnish with a slice of apple. Makes 8 servings.

Submitted by:

Kirschke House	Full breakfast
1124 West 3rd St.	4 rooms
Grand Island, Nebraska 68801	Children allowed
(308) 381-6851	No pets
Lois Hank	No smoking
$45.00 to $55.00 (double)	Mastercard, Visa, Am Ex, Disc.

Vine covered 2-story brick has windowed cupola, turret, stained glass windows and open oak staircase. Old World atmosphere: Victorian lace, period furnishings and antiques. Wooden hot tub in lantern-lit brick wash house. Meals served on fine china, with crystal and silver.

MEXICAN BAKED EGGS

Mild salsa or picante
  sauce
8 eggs
Salt & pepper to taste
Shredded mozzarella
  or Monterey Jack
  cheese

Freshly grated Parmesan
  cheese
Dry or fresh cilantro
Toasted English muffins
  or thick slices of
  bakery bread, toasted

Spray 8-cup muffin tin with no stick Mazola oil. Place 3 tablespoons salsa or picante sauce in each muffin cup. Crack an egg in each cup over salsa. Salt and pepper each egg. Sprinkle shredded mozzarella or Monterey Jack cheese over egg. Sprinkle Parmesan on top of shredded cheese. Sprinkle cilantro over Parmesan. Bake in 350° oven for 20 - 25 minutes. Serve on toasted English muffins or on toasted halves of thickly sliced bakery bread. Spoon extra sauce in the muffin cups over eggs before serving. Makes 4 servings.

Submitted by:

Lamb's Mill Inn
RR #1, Box 676
Lamb's Mill Rd.
Naples, Maine 04055
(207) 693-6253
Laurel Tinkham, Sandra Long
$75.00 to $85.00

Full breakfast
6 rooms, 6 private baths
Children, over 12
No pets
No smoking
Mastercard & Visa

Charming country inn in foothills of Maine's western mountain and lake region. Romantic atmosphere on 20 acres of fields and woods. Country breakfast, hot tub. Near lakes, antique shops, skiing, canoeing. Ewe hike, ewe bike, ewe ski, ewe z-z-z-z-z-z-z-z!

MONTEREY JACK/DILL SOUFFLÉ

1 tube of 8 crescent rolls	2/3 cup half & half
Sweet mustard or dijon	2 1/2 cups grated cheese
8 eggs, beaten	Dill to taste

Preheat oven to 350°. Line bottom of 9" x 13" baking pan with unbaked crescent rolls to form a crust. Paint rolls lightly with mustard. Combine eggs, milk and cheese, and spread evenly in pan. Sprinkle with dill. Bake for 45 minutes. Let sit covered 5 - 15 minutes. Cut into squares and serve. Serve with side dish of chutney or with sausage patties and fruit salad.

Submitted by:

Chambered Nautilus B&B Inn	Full breakfast
5005 22nd Avenue N.E.	6 rooms, 4 private baths
Seattle, Washington 98105	Children, over 12
(206) 522-2536	No pets
Bill & Bunny Hagemeyer	No smoking
$72.50 to $95.00 (double)	Mastercard, Visa, Am Ex

Combine the warmth of a country inn with access to city's theaters, restaurants, and shopping. Fine views of Cascade Mtns., the inn perches on a green & peaceful hill in the University district. Large, airy guest rooms furnished in American & English antiques. Fireplaces, piano, well-stocked bookshelves.

OSCAR'S BREAKFAST PINWHEELS

1/4 cup shortening
2 cups unsifted self-
rising flour
1 cup buttermilk

1 1/2 lbs. raw bulk pork
sausage
1/2 - 3/4 teaspoon sage
1/4 - 1/2 teaspoon white
pepper

With pastry blender, cut shortening into flour. Add buttermilk and mix. Knead on lightly floured board for a few seconds. Add additional flour if necessary. Roll dough to 12" x 9" rectangle. Spread with sausage. Roll up in jelly roll style. Cut into 1/2" slices. Place on lightly greased baking sheet. Bake at 425° for 25 minutes or until brown. Makes 8 servings.

Submitted by:

Chateau Du Lac
P.O. Box 1098
911 Hospital Road
Lake Arrowhead, Calif. 92352
(714) 337-6488
FAX # (714) 337-6746
Oscar & Jody Wilson
$95.00 to $250.00

Full breakfast
6 rooms, 4 private baths
Children, over 14
No pets
Restricted smoking
Mastercard, Visa, Am Ex,
Discover

Overlooks Lake Arrowhead. Sparkling sun in the morning, mist and gentle breezes in the afternoon make this a romantic place to be. Wonderful for weddings, showers, parties. We have a great gazebo with a hammock for two. Fabulous views, teddy bears for sale.

PANCETTA-CHEVRE EGG SCRAMBLE

1/4 lb. pancetta, cut into small pieces
3 tablespoons extra virgin olive oil
7 fresh eggs
3 tablespoons heavy cream
Salt & pepper to taste
1 - 2 tablespoons sweet butter
2 oz. Chevre, crumbled
1 teaspoon fresh chives, finely cut
1 teaspoon Italian parsley
1 teaspoon fresh thyme

In sauté pan, cook pancetta with olive oil. Drain off excess fat and oil, and dab pancetta with paper towels to dry. Set aside. In bowl, beat eggs, cream, and salt & pepper until well-blended. Melt butter to coat the cooking surface of a pan, & pour in egg mixture. Cook eggs slowly, stirring gently. Before eggs are set, add Chevre, pancetta, chives, parsley, and thyme, and stir into mixture. Cook eggs to desired doneness, and serve immediately. Serves 2 - 3.

Submitted by:

The Carter House
1033 Third Street
Eureka, California 95501
(707) 445-1390
Mark & Christi Carter
$69.00 to $299.00

Full (4-course) breakfast
7 rooms, 4 private baths
Children, over 10
No pets
No smoking
Mastercard, Visa, Am Ex, Disc.

Elaborate Victorian mansion, in Historical District, built in 1982 from century-old architectural drawings, graciously awaits visitors with hospitality, decor, & cuisine which have won great praise across the nation. California Magazine says, "The best breakfast in California!"

RICHMONT EGGS AND ZUCCHINI

6 zucchini, cut into
  chunks
3 sprigs fresh mint
  leaves

8 eggs
2 tablespoons butter
Salt & pepper to taste

Cut ends off zucchini and peel 3 of them. Cut all 6 into large pieces. Place zucchini and mint in saucepan, cover and cook over medium heat until tender. Drain and press dry with a towel. Place into food processor and purée. In a bowl, beat eggs, then stir in zucchini puree. In large saucepan, melt butter over low heat. Add zucchini-egg mixture and cook, stirring frequently until eggs have the texture of soft scrambled eggs. Season to taste with salt and pepper. Makes 4 servings.

Submitted by:

Richmont Inn
220 Winterberry Lane
Townsend, Tenn. 37882
(615) 448-6751
Susan & Jim Hind
$85.00 to $130.00

Full breakfast (gourmet)
10 rooms, 10 private baths
Children, over 12
No pets
No smoking

Appalachian barn beautifully furnished with 18th century English antiques & French paintings. Breathtaking mtn. views. Graciously appointed rooms with sitting areas, king beds, fireplaces, spa-tubs for two, balconies. 10 minutes to Great Smoky Mtns. National Park. Art/craft shops, Cades Cove, golf nearby.

SALSA EGGS

2 tablespoons water	4 eggs
3 tablespoons picante or salsa sauce	Grated Cheddar cheese to taste

Spray 8" nonstick skillet with pan coating. Place water and picante or salsa sauce in pan over medium heat. Crack eggs into pan, grate Cheddar over eggs, cover, and reduce heat to low. Cook 2 - 4 minutes or until eggs are cooked to desired consistency. Serves 2.

Submitted by:

Creede Hotel & Restaurant
Main Street, Box 284
Creede, CO   81130
(719) 658-2608
Cathy & Rich Ormsby
$49.00 to $59.00

Full breakfast
4 rooms, 4 private baths
Children allowed
No pets
Restricted smoking
Mastercard, Visa, Discover

A community focal point, dating back to the wild silver boom days. We offer four restored guest rooms. The old Hotel dining room is open to the public, and is noted for its delicious food. "Warm hospitality . . . . capturing the lure of the 1890's."

SCOTCH EGGS

1 lb. bulk breakfast
  sausage, hot or mild
1/4 teaspoon basil
1/4 teaspoon cayenne
  pepper
1 tablespoon grated
  onion

6 hard-cooked eggs,
  shelled
2/3 cup all-purpose flour
2 eggs, beaten
1 cup fine saltine
  cracker crumbs
Vegetable oil for frying

Preheat oil in deep fryer to 370°. In medium bowl combine sausage, basil, cayenne and onion, mixing well. Divide into 6 portions; form each into a patty. Place an egg on each and mold sausage mixture around egg, making sure eggs are totally covered. Roll eggs in flour to lightly coat, shake off excess. Dip eggs into beaten egg, then roll in cracker crumbs. Deep fry the eggs in oil for 5 - 6 minutes, or until sausage coating is a deep brown. Serves 6.

Submitted by:

Grant Corner Inn
122 Grant Avenue
Santa Fe, N.M. 87501
(505) 983-6678
Louise Stewart & Pat Walter
$65.00 to $130.00

Full breakfast
13 rooms, 7 private baths
Children, over 6
No pets
No smoking
Mastercard & Visa

A colonial manor home with lush gardens, two blocks from Santa Fe's Historic Plaza. Beautifully appointed guest rooms with antiques and collectibles. Public restaurant serving gourmet breakfast and brunch is open daily.

SPINACH SOUFFLÉ

2 - 10 oz. pkgs. frozen chopped spinach	12 oz. Cheddar cheese, shredded
9 eggs	1/2 cup margarine or butter, melted
1/2 cup flour	
24 oz. cottage cheese	3/4 teaspoon seasoned salt
12 oz. Monterey Jack cheese, shredded	

Thaw and drain spinach. Beat eggs, stir in spinach and remaining ingredients. Pour into greased 9" x 13" pan. Bake at 350° for 1 hour or until top is light brown. Let stand 10 minutes before serving. Can be prepared ahead and frozen. Makes 12 servings.

Submitted by:

The Inn at Palisade
384 Highway 61 East
Silver Bay, Minnesota 55614
(218) 226-3505
Bob & Mary Barnett
$70.00 to $85.00

Full breakfast
5 rooms, 5 private baths
Children, over 10
No pets
No smoking
Mastercard & Visa

Cozy, country style on beautiful Lake Superior, with its magnificent sunrises & wildlife. Quilts, antiques, easy access to beach. Next to Tettegouche State Park. Open June to mid-October.

STUFFED MEXICAN PANCAKE

Chopped tomatoes
Chopped onions
1 tablespoon oil
1/2 lb. sausage, fried &
   drained
4 eggs, beaten

1 tablespoon fresh
   cilantro or parsley
1/2 cup picante
   sauce
Floured tortillas or
   feta bread

Sauté tomatoes and onions in oil. Brown and drain sausage. In separate pan, mix eggs, and scramble. Add tomatoes & onions, and sausage. Add cilantro and picante sauce. Fill warmed floured tortillas or stuff feta bread. Makes 2 - 4 servings.

Submitted by:

Bed & Breakfast - South Reno
136 Andrew Lane
Reno, Nevada 89511
(702) 849-0772
Caroline Walters,
Robert McNeill
$64.00 to $70.00

Full breakfast
3 rooms, 2 private baths
Children, over 10
No pets
Smoking on decks
Am Ex

Ranch style, surrounded by mountains & animals, with early American antiques, beamed ceilings, poster beds. Heated swimming pool, decks everywhere, 1 suite. Queen beds in 3 rooms. Close to Reno - 10 miles to casinos, golf, Virginia City, Lake Tahoe.

SUGAR PLUM BACON

Bacon   **Cinnamon to taste**
Sugar to taste

Let bacon come to room temperature for about an hour. Cut strips in half, roll in sugar and cinnamon mixture. (to taste) Twist the bacon and lay in glass baking dish. Bake for 20 - 23 minutes in oven at 350°. Watch closely as it burns easily. Serve lukewarm.

Submitted by:

The Travelling Companion   Full breakfast
4314 Main   3 rooms
Elk Horn, Iowa 51531   Children allowed
(712) 764-8932   No pets
Duane & Karolyn Ortgies   No smoking
$45.00 to $50.00

Velkommen (Welcome). This charming 1909 home is nestled in a peaceful town in the heart of the largest Danish settlement in the U.S. Comfortable furnishings. The inn's name is from Hans Christian Andersen's fairy tales, with each room named after a different story.

TEX-MEX EGGS

1 can quality canned tamales	Shredded Cheddar cheese
4 large or 6 small eggs, scrambled	Parsley or coriander for garnish
Shredded Monterey Jack cheese	Paprika for garnish

Distribute bite-sized pieces of tamales (remove any surplus fat) in four ramekins. Put in 400° oven for 10 minutes. Scramble eggs softly. Place on top of tamales. Combine the two cheeses. Sprinkle cheese mixture over eggs. Garnish with parsley or coriander, and paprika. Place in oven until cheese melts. Makes 4 servings.

So easy, but a "10" with guests on a snowy morning.

Submitted by:

Eagles Landing B&B
27406 Cedarwood
Lake Arrowhead, California
Mail to: Box 1510,
Blue Jay, California 92317
(714) 336-2642
Dorothy & Jack Stone
$95.00 to $175.00

Full breakfast
4 rooms, 4 private baths
Children, over 14
No pets
No smoking
Mastercard, Visa, Discover

European-style hospitality at its best, by the shores of beautiful Lake Arrowhead in the San Bernadino Mountains. Common room & decks overlook sparkling blue waters. Enjoy boating, fishing & swimming, toasty fires, skiing & skating, in season. Have a mountain adventure!

FRUITS, CEREALS, BEVERAGES & MISCELLANEOUS DISHES

ALMOST-A-MEAL BREAKFAST DRINK

2 - 5 1/4 oz. cans
  pineapple tidbits
2 medium bananas
1/2 cup milk

16 oz. pineapple
  sherbet or lowfat yogurt
2 - 4 tablespoons
  orange juice

In food processor combine all ingredients. Blend until smooth. Makes 4 servings. Recipe may be doubled for more servings.

Submitted by:

Maple Leaf Inn B&B
831 N. Grand
Connersville, Indiana 47331
(317) 825-7099
Gary & Karen Lanning
$45.00 to $55.00

Continental plus breakfast
4 rooms, 4 private baths
Children allowed
No pets
Restricted smoking
Mastercard & Visa

Surrounded by lovely maple trees, this 1860's Victorian home offers warm hospitality. Bedrooms furnished with period furniture and paintings by local artists. Area attractions include state parks, antique shops, IN's largest lake & Whitewater Valley Railroad & Old Metamora.

APPLE FRITTERS

1 beaten egg
1 cup milk
1 cup finely chopped
  apple (unpeeled &
  cored)
1/4 cup sugar
1/4 teaspoon salt
3 tablespoons orange
  juice

1 teaspoon grated
  orange peel
1/2 teaspoon vanilla
2 cups flour
3 teaspoons baking
  powder
Sifted confectioner's
  sugar

Combine first 8 ingredients. Sift flour and baking powder, and add to wet ingredients until flour is moistened. Drop by rounded teaspoons into deep hot fat. Fry until golden. Drain on paper towels. Dust with confectioner's sugar. Makes 3 1/2 dozen fritters.

Submitted by:

The Inn at Manchester
Route 7A
Manchester, Vermont
 05254
(802) 362-1793
Stan & Harriet Rosenberg
$65.00 to $130.00

Full breakfast
20 rooms, 15 private baths
Children, over 8
No pets
Restricted smoking
Mastercard, Visa, Am Ex,
 Discover

Historic country inn, charming rooms & suites, gracious hospitality. Bountiful breakfasts included. Antiques, plus 3 fireplaced lounge areas, cross country & downhill skiing. Secluded pool in meadow with mountain views, marble terrace, great front porch, a/c. Seasonal packages, tennis, shopping, theater.

APPLE SYRUP

3 cups sugar	2 cans water (24 oz.)
9 tablespoons Bisquick	6 tablespoons lemon
3 teaspoons ground	juice
cinnamon	1 stick butter
3 - 12 oz. cans apple	
juice concentrate	

Mix dry ingredients in saucepan. Add liquid and bring to slow boil. Stirring, add butter. Makes 2 quarts of syrup.

Submitted by:

Applebutter Inn   Full breakfast
152 Applewood Lane   11 rooms, 11 private baths
Slippery Rock, Penn. 16057   Children allowed
(412) 794-1844   No pets
Gary & Sandra McKnight   No smoking
$69.00 to $115.00   Mastercard, Visa, Am Ex

Charming, original 1844 farmhouse restored, then added-to, beautifully appointed rooms with antiques & decorator linens. Gourmet breakfast served at adjacent Wolf Creek School Café where food is prepared: quaint atmosphere of a one-room schoolhouse recently restored to its original state.

BAKED ORANGE CUPS

3 large oranges
3 Granny Smith apples
1/2 cup white sugar
6 tablespoons butter

1/2 teaspoon vanilla
extract
1/2 cup finely chopped
pecans

Preheat oven to 325°. Shave a little off top & bottom of each orange, cut into equal halves. Loosen and scoop out orange flesh, without breaking skin. Place cups in 9" x 13" baking pan. Place orange flesh in heavy saucepan. Peel, core & dice apples, add to saucepan with sugar and butter. Cook gently 30 - 40 minutes until thick. Remove from heat and add vanilla. Fill each orange cup with hot mixture and sprinkle with pecans. Pour about 1/2 cup hot water in bottom of pan and bake for 30 minutes. Serve immediately. Makes 6 orange cups.

Submitted by:

The Inn at Union Pier
9708 Berrien - P.O. Box 222
Union Pier, Michigan 49129
(616) 469-4700
Bill & Madeleine Reinke
$95.00 to $140.00

Full breakfast
15 rooms, 15 private baths
Children, over 12
No pets
Smoking allowed
Mastercard, Visa, Discover

Elegantly refurbished inn blending barefoot informality with all the comforts of a country home. Enjoy gardens and courtyard. Lake Michigan beach across the street. Sauna, outdoor hot tub, porches, and Swedish fireplaces. Special midweek packages all year.

BAKED "SNOWBALL" GRANOLA APPLES

1 large Macintosh apple
  for each serving
Granola to taste

Maple syrup to taste
Flavored or plain
  yogurt for topping

Core each apple, fill cavity with granola, a teaspoon at a time. Drizzle maple syrup into cavity. Place in ovenproof dish and add 1" water (you can add 1/2 cup raw oatmeal to this water). Bake at 350° for 35 - 45 minutes. Serve topped with yogurt - they look like snowballs!

Submitted by:

Golden Dreams B&B
6412 Easy Street - Whistler,
  B.C., Canada   VON 1B6
(604) 932-2667
FAX# (604) 932-7055
1-800-668-7055 (reserv.)
Ann & Terry Spence
$55.00 to $85.00

Full breakfast
3 rooms, 2 private baths
Children allowed
No pets
Restricted smoking
Mastercard & Visa

Relax in Victorian, Oriental, or Aztec theme rooms. Enjoy private jacuzzi bath and awake to Ann's nutritious, hearty breakfast including homemade jams. Mountain bike/cross country ski trails at doorstep, TV/VCR in fireplace lounge.

BARK EATER GRANOLA

8 cups old-fashioned oats	3/4 cup cashews
1 1/2 tablespoons cinnamon	3/4 cup almonds
	1/4 cup butter
1 cup coconut	1 cup oil
1/2 cup wheat germ	1/2 cup honey
1/2 cup sunflower seeds	1/4 cup molasses
1/4 cup poppy seeds	1/2 cup brown sugar
1/4 cup sesame seeds	1/2 cup peanut butter
1 teaspoon salt	1 tablespoon vanilla

Combine oats, cinnamon, coconut, wheat germ, sunflower seeds, poppy seeds, sesame seeds, salt, cashews, & almonds in large bowl. Stir. Combine remainder of ingredients in microwaveable bowl. Heat on high for 3 minutes. Stir well. Pour mixture over dry ingredients. Stir until well mixed. Spread granola onto large baking sheet. Bake for 40 - 45 minutes at 375°, stirring every 15 minutes. Let granola cool and add currants or raisins, if desired. Freezes well or keeps up to 1 month in sealed container. Makes approximately 18 cups.

Submitted by:

Bark Eater Inn	Full breakfast
Alstead Hill Road	16 rooms, 6 private baths
Keene, New York 12942	Children allowed
(518) 576-2221	No pets
Joe-Pete Wilson	Restricted smoking
$90.00 to $110.00	Mastercard, Visa, Am Ex

Homey & informal inn nestled in the heart of the Adirondack High Peak Region. Simple but gracious accommodations, memorable dining, & easy access to the great outdoors. In winter, try our cross-country ski center and rental shop. Year-round, enjoy horseback trail rides, from beginner to expert.

BEECHMONT QUARK

2 cups plain yogurt	1 1/2 teaspoons
1/2 cup sour cream	cinnamon
1/4 cup sugar	1/2 teaspoon nutmeg
1 1/2 teaspoons vanilla	

Mix all ingredients together until smooth and well blended. The spices and sugar are approximate measures; taste to decide whether the proportions are correct for you. Serve over granola or fresh fruit.

Submitted by:

Beechmont Inn	Full gourmet breakfast
315 Broadway	7 rooms, 7 private baths
Hanover, Penn. 17331	Children, over 12
(800) 553-7009	No pets
Terry & Monna Hormel	Restricted smoking
$70.00 to $125.00	Mastercard, Visa, Am Ex

Elegant 1834 Federal Period inn, fireplaces, a/c, antiques, afternoon refreshments. Large suite with private whirlpool, canopy bed & working fireplace. Convenient to Gettysburg Battlefield & Lake Marburg. Great antiquing, Farmers' Market, golfing, outlet shopping. Honeymoon/anniversary, weekend pkgs. offered. Picnics available.

BREAKFAST RED POTATOES

4 medium size, new red potatoes, boiled   **2 - 3 tablespoons butter**

Boil new red potatoes until nearly cooked through, but still firm. Cool and slice once lengthwise, & then in 1/4" slices. Brown in butter over medium heat, turning once, about 15 - 20 minutes total. Serves 2.

Submitted by:

Milton Hall B&B Inn
RR #3
Covington, Virginia 24426
(703) 965-0196
John & Vera Eckert
$75.00 to $140.00

Full breakfast
6 rooms, 6 private baths
Children allowed
Pets allowed
Smoking allowed
Mastercard & Visa

English country manor house, circa 1874, with spacious rooms, antiques, period reproductions and unique collectibles, fireplaces, and queen size beds. Hiking, bicycling, fishing, hunting, mineral baths, covered bridges, and the many attractions at The Homestead.

BROILED TOMATOES

5 fresh tomatoes
1/2 cup bread crumbs
1/2 cup grated Parmesan
cheese

2 tablespoons snipped
chives or chopped
onions
1/4 cup minced parsley
1/4 cup melted butter

Peel and slice tomatoes 1/2 inch thick or thicker. Small tomatoes can be cut in half. Place on broiler pan. Mix remaining ingredients and place equal portion on top of each tomato slice. Broil 5 minutes until hot and slightly browned. Serve immediately.

Submitted by:

Halfway House
  Bed & Breakfast
Route #2, Box 80
Oxford, Wisconsin 53952
(608) 586-5489
Dr. & Mrs. J. A. Hines
$28.00 to $42.00

Full breakfast
4 rooms
No children
No pets
No smoking

We were once a stop on the logging road that went north out of Portage in the 1800's. A comfortable, peaceful working farm with Herefords in the pastures; there are wild birds and animals. Your host is a veterinarian, working with all animals, but mostly dairy cattle.

CAROLA'S BAKED BANANAS

1/3 cup melted butter	1 teaspoon cinnamon
1/3 cup brown sugar	6 firm ripe bananas

Preheat oven to 375°. Pour melted butter in shallow baking dish. Put sugar and cinnamon in bowl. Mix together thoroughly. Place bananas in baking dish, turn over to coat with butter, sprinkle with sugar mixture. Bake 10 minutes. Turn bananas over and sprinkle again with sugar mixture. Bake another 10 minutes. Serve on warm dishes. Makes 6 servings.

Submitted by:

Amber Lights Inn B&B	Full/Continental breakfast
Route 3	5 rooms, 1 private bath
W. Thornton, N.H. 03223	Children, over 7
(603) 726-4077	No pets
Carola Warnsman & Paul Sears	No smoking
$45.00 to $75.00	Mastercard, Visa, Discover

1815 Colonial in country setting on 5 lovely acres with brook, between Loon Mtn. & Waterville Valley in White Mtns. Queen beds, handmade quilts, antiques & collectibles. Sumptuous homemade breakfasts. Meticulously clean. Murder mystery weekends available.

CINNAMON-BLUEBERRY JAM

4 pints blueberries,
  washed and sorted
3 cups sugar

2 tablespoons water
4 cinnamon sticks

Place blueberries, sugar, and water in heavy saucepan over low heat. Cook, stirring constantly, until berries begin to release their juice. Add a bit more water if necessary to prevent sticking. Raise the heat slightly and add cinnamon sticks. Boil mixture gently, stirring frequently, until thick and syrupy, approximately 20 minutes. Remove cinnamon sticks. Transfer to sterilized pint jars, seal with lids or melted paraffin. Store in a cool, dark place. Makes 2 pints of jam.

Submitted by:

Interlaken Inn
15 Interlaken Avenue
Lake Placid, New York 12946
(518) 523-3180 or
(800) 428-4369
Roy & Carol Johnson
$100.00 to $160.00 (MAP)

Full breakfast and dinner
12 rooms, 12 private baths,
  1 carriage house
Children, over 5
No pets
Restricted smoking
Mastercard, Visa, Am Ex,
  Encore

Lovely Victorian in the heart of Lake Placid. Individually decorated rooms, three with balconies, some king, queen, and double beds. Gourmet weekend dining in dining room with tin ceiling, walnut paneling, and lots of lace! Family-owned and operated inn - our son a CIA graduate chef, and Carol head the kitchen.

CRANAPPLE FRAPPÉ

2 cups Cranapple juice
2 cups freshly squeezed
  orange juice
1/4 cup whipping cream
1 tablespoon lemon
  juice

2 bananas
3/4 cup crushed ice
3 drops red food
  coloring
Sweeten to taste
Fresh mint for garnish

Combine all ingredients (except fresh mint) in blender container.
Blend on high speed for one minute. Serve in a frosted stem glass
and garnish with mint. Serves 6.

Submitted by:

Maple Leaf Cottage Inn
P.O. Box 156
Historic Elsah, Illinois 62028
(618) 374-1684
Mrs. Patty Taetz
$65.00 Single or Double

Full breakfast
6 rooms, 6 private baths
Children, over 12
No pets
Restricted smoking
Mastercard & Visa

Private grounds cover one village block, surrounded by an English
garden, facing the spectacular limestone bluffs of Elsah. Stenciling &
lace tablecloths add to country elegance. Screened front porch, with
wicker chairs and swing, is a great place to enjoy a peaceful evening.

FRIED GREEN TOMATOES

4 large green tomatoes, sliced thickly	1/2 teaspoon salt
2 large eggs, lightly beaten	1/2 teaspoon pepper
1/2 cup water	1 cup yellow cornmeal
1 1/2 cups all-purpose flour (divided)	1 quart frying oil or shortening

Slice tomatoes into 1/4" thick slices. Mix eggs and water until well-blended, set aside. Combine 1 cup flour, salt & pepper. Coat tomato slices in seasoned flour and then dip into egg wash mixture until thoroughly coated. Mix 1/2 cup flour and cornmeal together. Remove tomatoes from egg wash and coat with cornmeal mix. Place in skillet or frying pan and cook at 350° until golden brown, turning and cooking on each side. Makes 6 servings.

Submitted by:

Richmond Hill Inn   Full breakfast
87 Richmond Hill Dr.   21 rooms, 21 private baths
Asheville, N.C. 28806   Children allowed
(800) 545-9238   No pets
Susan Michel   No smoking
$125.00 to $300.00   Mastercard, Visa, Am Ex

Century old Victorian mansion overlooking Blue Ridge Mtns. and city skyline. On National Register of Historic Places, with rich oak paneling, handcarved fireplaces, & high ceilings. 12 guest rooms in mansion and 9 in Victorian-style cottages, many with fireplaces, canopy & 4-poster beds.

FRUIT SALAD

4 bananas, sliced
21 oz. can cherry pie
   filling

15 1/4 oz. can pineapple
   tidbits, drained

Combine all ingredients. Chill and serve. Makes 10 - 12 servings.

Submitted by:

Laurel Hill Plantation
P.O. Box 190
8913 N. Highway 17
McClellanville, S.C. 29458
(803) 887-3708
Jackie & Lee Morrison
$65.00 to $75.00

Full breakfast
4 rooms, 4 private baths
No children
No pets
Restricted smoking

The original house was destroyed by Hurricane Hugo on September 21, 1989. The reconstruction is nestled beside a picturesque tidal creek. Wraparound porches overlook a sweeping panorama of Cape Romain's salt marshes, islands, waterways, and the Atlantic Ocean.

VIEW FROM THE PORCH

GOLDEN PARSLEY POTATOES

1/2 stick of butter, melted
6 large potatoes, peeled & quartered into 1" chunks

1/3 cup flour
1/3 cup Parmesan cheese
1/3 teaspoon salt
1/8 teaspoon pepper
Parsley to taste

Melt butter in bottom of baking pan. Mix flour, cheese, salt and pepper in a bowl. Pour potatoes into bowl of flour mixture. Cover all sides of potatoes, then cover bottom of buttered pan with potatoes. Do not overlap them. Sprinkle with parsley. Bake at 350° for 1 hour, turning potatoes over after 1/2 hour. Note: You can save flour mixture to use again. Makes 6 - 8 servings.

Submitted by:

Liechty's Homestead Inn
7830 Pine Forest Road
Pensacola, Florida 32526
(904) 944-4816
Neil & Jeanne Liechty
$59.00 to $79.00

Full breakfast
6 rooms, 6 private baths
Children allowed
No pets
No smoking
Mastercard, Visa, Am Ex

Williamsburg atmosphere, with delicious Mennonite-prepared food, now famous in northwest Florida. Outside gazebo-courtyard area is perfect for reading, or quietly catching your breath. Near Pensacola Beach, Historic Downtown, Naval Air Museum & the USS Lexington.

GOVERNOR'S AMBROSIA

1 can chunk pineapple, drained	1/2 cup red seedless grapes, halved
1 can mandarin oranges, drained	1/2 cup flaked coconut
1 can grapefruit sections cut in bite-size pieces, drained	1/3 cup orange juice
	1/4 cup light corn syrup
	Strawberry garnish (opt.)

Combine first 5 ingredients in large bowl. Combine orange juice and corn syrup. Pour over fruit mixture and toss lightly. Chill for several hours before serving. Garnish with strawberries if desired. Serve in chilled stemmed glasses or in fancy individual bowls. Serves 6.

Submitted by:

Governor's Trace B&B
303 Capitol Landing Road
Williamsburg, Virginia 23185
(804) 229-7552
Sue & Dick Lake
$95.00 to $115.00

Continental plus breakfast
2 rooms, 2 private baths
No children
No pets
No smoking
Mastercard & Visa

Rekindle romance in the closest B&B to Colonial Williamsburg. Lovely old Georgian brick lets you step into history just one door away. Candlelit, antique-furnished, spacious rooms offer choice of tall four-poster king size bed with working fireplace, or full Colonial style canopy bed with private screened porch.

HEALTHY GRANOLA MIX

1 stick oleo or butter
1 cup brown sugar or
  honey
2 tablespoons water
4 cups whole rolled oats
  (old-fashioned)

1 cup nut meats (pecans
  or walnuts)
1 cup sunflower seeds
1 cup whole wheat flour
1 teaspoon cinnamon
1 cup raisins (added
  after baking)

Melt oleo in 9" x 13" pan, add sugar and water. Remove from heat and after sugar is dissolved, add the next 5 ingredients. Stir well. Place in oven at 350° and bake for 45 minutes, stirring every 10 minutes. When you remove from the oven, add the raisins and mix in well. Store in dry, cool place. Serves 15 - 30.

Submitted by:

Country Gardens
  Bed & Breakfast
HCR 4   Lakeshore Drive
Branson, Missouri 65616
(417) 334-8564
Bob & Pat Cameron
$70.00 to $95.00

Full breakfast
3 rooms, 3 private baths
Children, over 12
No pets
Restricted smoking
Mastercard, Visa, Discover

Amidst the new country music capital of the world, this Bed & Breakfast offers a quiet park-like setting. A pretty waterfall, colorful gardens and many trees all make it restful. A private spa in one room and the other two share a spa overlooking the lake. Romantic - yes!

HOMEMADE CINNAMON APPLESAUCE

**4 lbs. apples (Red De-
licious are prettiest)
2 cups water**

**2 tablespoons cinnamon
hearts candies**

Wash the apples but do not peel. Core and cut into wedges directly into cooking pan. Add water to make 1" - 2" in the bottom of pan. Cook until apples are soft. Force through a food mill or sieve. Add cinnamon hearts while the apple mixture is still hot. Stir well to color and give a good sweet cinnamon flavor. Makes 1 quart applesauce.

Submitted by:

Lewrene Farm B&B
9738 Downsville Pike
Hagerstown, Maryland 21740
(301) 582-1735
Irene & Lewis Lehman
$50.00 to $75.00

Full breakfast
6 rooms, 3 private baths
Children allowed
No pets
No smoking

Spacious Colonial country farm home near I-70 & I-81. Large living room, fireplace, piano, antique family heirlooms. Bedside snacks, canopy poster bed & other period beds. Home away from home for tourists, business people, families. Peacocks, old-fashioned swing, gazebo. Quilts for sale. Near attractions.

HONEYDEW FRUIT RINGS

1 honeydew melon
2 tablespoons lime
   juice
2 tablespoons
   honey

1 cup red cherries,
   halved & pitted,
   or grapes
2 kiwi fruits, peeled &
   cut into bite-size pieces

Cut honeydew crosswise into 3/4" slices. Remove seeds and rind. Cut a decorative edge on 4 - 5 center rings. Cut remaining melon into bite-size pieces. In medium bowl combine lime juice and honey for dressing, blend well. Add cherries, kiwi pieces and melon pieces to gently coat. Spoon into center of honeydew rings. Garnish with mint sprig. Makes 4 - 5 servings.

Submitted by:

Cantwell House
107 High Street
Odessa, Delaware 19730
(302) 378-4179
Carole F. Coleman
$50.00 to $85.00

Continental breakfast
2 rooms, 2 private baths
Children allowed
No pets
Restricted smoking

Built in the 1840's, the house has been completely refurbished and furnished in country antiques. Featured in Mid-Atlantic Country Magazine in 1992. Third story room affords a view of historical Odessa, showcasing its fine architecture from several periods.

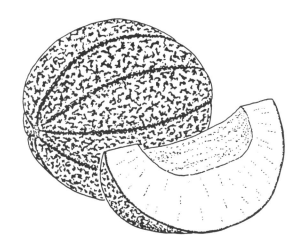

HOPTON'S POTATO PANCAKE

6 medium potatoes	Salt & pepper to taste
1 small onion	Dash of nutmeg
6 eggs	3 tablespoons flour

Grate potatoes and onion. Cook both in hot water for 5 minutes, not boiling them. In bowl, put drained potato and onion. Add 3 eggs, salt, pepper, nutmeg, and flour. Mix well. Cook on hot grill, adding small amount of remaining eggs which have been beaten. Serve with applesauce or sour cream. Makes 8 - 10 servings.

Submitted by:

State House Inn B&B
43 Jewett Street
Providence, R.I. 02908
(401) 785-1235
Monica & Frank Hopton
$79.00 to $99.00

Full breakfast
10 rooms, 10 private baths
Children allowed
No pets
No smoking
Mastercard, Visa, Am Ex

100 year old Colonial Revival in quiet, quaint neighborhood. Newly renovated country B&B with queen or king beds. Some rooms with fireplace, and canopy bed. Cable TV and telephones.

HOT SPICED NECTAR

3 cups apricot nectar
2 cups orange juice
1 cup water
2 teaspoons lemon juice

1/2 cup brown sugar
12" stick cinnamon
1 teaspoon cloves

Combine nectar, orange juice, water, lemon juice and brown sugar. Place in coffeepot. Put spices in coffeepot basket. Run through coffee cycle. This can also be made on top of the stove, but do not boil!

Submitted by:

The Strawberry Inn
17 W. Main St., P.O. Box 237
New Market, Maryland 21774
(301) 865-3318
Jane & Ed Rossig
$75.00 to $95.00 (double)

Full breakfast
5 rooms, 5 private baths
Children, over 10
No pets
Smoking allowed

1837 restored Maryland farmhouse serving guests for the past 20 years. Breakfast served from 7:30 to 10:00 A.M. on grapevine-covered porch or in dining room. Afternoon tea in Victorian gazebo and small conference facilities in restored log building on property.

LEMON FRUIT SOUP

2 large cans fruit
  cocktail, drained
1 pkg. instant lemon
  pudding
1/2 cup sour cream

1/2 cup orange juice
1/4 cup milk
For garnish: Blackber-
  ries, blueberries, or
  raspberries

In a very large bowl combine all ingredients just to mix together. Depending on size of food processor or blender, mix 1/4 - 1/2 of fruit mixture at a time, on process or blend until smooth. If mixture is very, very thick (like paste) when finished blending, just stir in a little more orange juice. Chill mixture in refrigerator for several hours. Serve in soup bowls garnished with berries. Makes 8 - 10 servings.

Submitted by:

Sea Holly Bed & Breakfast Inn
815 Stockton Ave.
Cape May, N.J. 08204
(609) 884-6294
Christy & Chris Igoe
$85.00 to $180.00

Full breakfast
Children, over 16
No pets
Restricted smoking
Mastercard, Visa, Am Ex

We offer Victorian decor, designer sheets, bath sheets (large towels), a/c, beach tags, towels, & bikes. But all of our guests' "thank-you's" say, "What a great breakfast, can we take the cook home?" and "Can we have the chocolate chip cookie recipe?"

LOTTIE'S BEET JELLY

4 cups beet juice	6 cups sugar
1/2 cup lemon juice	1 box Sure Gel

In heavy pan: Mix beet juice with lemon juice, add Sure Gel and mix. Stir while bringing to a boil, then add the sugar. Stir while mixture comes to a rolling boil. Then boil for three minutes. Pour into hot jars. Cover at once. Makes about 4 half-pint jars.

Submitted by:

The Thorpe House
  Country Inn
Clayborne Street
P.O. Box 36
Metamora, Indiana 47030
(317) 647-5425 or 932-2365
Mike & Jean Owens
$60.00 to $100.00

Full breakfast
5+ rooms, 5 private baths
Children allowed
Pets allowed
Smoking allowed
Mastercard, Visa, Discover

1840 Canal town home, where steam engine still brings passenger cars, and gristmill still grinds cornmeal. Antiques and country accessories, family-style public dining room, country breakfast. Over 100 shoppes in quaint village. Open April through Christmas.

MAPLE OATMEAL SOUFFLÉ

3/4 cup lowfat milk
1 tablespoon butter
1 cup (1 minute) instant
  oatmeal
1/3 of 8 oz. pkg. of
  reduced calorie cream
  cheese

3/4 teaspoon cinnamon
1/2 teaspoon nutmeg
1/4 teaspoon salt
1/2 cup maple syrup
3 eggs, separated
1/2 - 3/4 cup raisins or
  currants

Preheat oven to 350°. Coat 1 1/2 quart soufflé dish well with nonstick cooking spray, and lightly sugar. Heat milk and butter until little bubbles form around edges. Add oatmeal and cook, while stirring, about 1 minute. Remove from heat and add cream cheese, stirring until melted. Add spices, maple syrup, egg yolks and raisins. Stir to blend. Beat egg whites until peaks form and gently fold into oatmeal mixture until no large white lumps appear. Pour into dish and bake in center of oven for 40 - 45 minutes until set. Serve drizzled with cream. Makes 4 - 5 servings.

Submitted by:

Newtons' 1824 House Inn
Route 100, Box 159
Waitsfield, Vermont 05673
(802) 496-7555
Nicholas & Joyce Newton
$75.00 to $115.00 (dbl. occ.)

Full breakfast
6 rooms, 6 private baths
No pets
No smoking
Mastercard, Visa, Am Ex
AAA 3-Diamond award

Relaxed elegance at beautifully restored, 10 gabled inn, on the Mad River. Oriental rugs, antiques, original art, king featherbeds. Enjoy afternoon refreshment on the porch while listening to classical music. 52 acres to stroll, even a swimming hole. Friendly innkeepers.

MAPLE SYRUP DOUGHNUTS

1 cup maple syrup	1 teaspoon baking
2 eggs	powder
3 tablespoons	1/2 teaspoon nutmeg
shortening	1 teaspoon vanilla
1/2 teaspoon salt	2/3 cup sour milk
1 teaspoon baking soda	Enough flour for dough

Mix all ingredients in order stated. Add only enough flour to make dough workable. Pat out on floured board to 1/2" thickness and cut with floured doughnut cutter. Fry until dough is done on both sides in hot fat heated to 370°.

Submitted by:

The Peeping Cow B&B
Route 106, P.O. Box 178
Reading, Vermont 05062
(802) 484-5036
Nancy & Frank Lynch & Family
$60.00 to $80.00

Continental plus breakfast
3 rooms, 3 private baths
Children, over 10
No pets
No smoking

Homestead, circa 1828, on 30 acre pastoral setting of brook, forest, and stone-walled meadows. Antiques, goosedown comforters, yummy, healthy breakfasts. Well-situated for daytripping to all parts of Vermont. Featured in Christie's 1990 art auction fundraising gala.

MEANDER INN'S FROSTY SUMMER FRUIT SMOOTHIE

2 cups orange juice	1/2 cup half & half
2 cups cranberry juice	2 teaspoons lemon juice
2 bananas	10 ice cubes

Chill 6 glasses in freezer the night before. Blend all ingredients in blender until smooth, and serve at once. Serves 6. Perfect for a warm summer morning!

Submitted by:

The Meander Inn
Route 612 - P.O. Box 443
Nellysford, Virginia 22958
(804) 361-1121
Kathy & Rick Cornelius
$60.00 to $80.00

Full breakfast
5 rooms, 5 private baths
Well-behaved children allowed
No pets
Restricted smoking
Mastercard & Visa

50 acre working farm, near Charlottesville & Wintergreen Resort, on the Rockfish River with panoramic view of Blue Ridge Mountains. Hiking, golf, skiing & fine dining nearby. Hot tub, open woodstove, country breakfast with farm fresh eggs. Owner-run and operated.

MINTED WATERMELON REFRESHER

1/2 watermelon, cut into
chunks, and seeded
1/2 cup fresh mint
leaves

1/4 cup frozen orange
concentrate
Juice of 1 lime
Honey to taste

Remove watermelon from rind, cut into chunks, seed, and place in blender with the mint leaves. This is best done in several batches. Add orange concentrate, lime juice and honey. Let set several hours, or overnight. Stir well before serving. Garnish glasses with sprig of mint. Makes 12 + servings.

Submitted by:

The Inn on South Street
South Street, Box 478A
Kennebunkport, Maine 04046
(207) 967-5151
Jacques & Eva Downs
$75.00 to $105.00

Full breakfast
3 rooms, 3 private baths
Children, over 10
No pets
Restricted smoking
Am Ex

Comfortable elegance in early 19th century home. Spacious guest rooms, one with fireplace, tastefully decorated with period antiques. Sumptuous breakfast, good conversation & views of the river & ocean. On a quiet side street, close to restaurants, shops & beach.

PEACHY STRAWBERRY YOGURT SHORTCAKE

1 1/2 cups baking mix
1/4 cup sugar
3 tablespoons butter
1 cup lowfat vanilla
   yogurt
2 eggs, beaten

Filling:
2 cups sliced peaches
1 cup sliced
   strawberries
2 1/2 cups vanilla
   yogurt

Cut butter into baking mix and sugar. Stir in yogurt and eggs until just moistened. Spread in 9" round pan. Bake at 375° for 30 - 35 minutes. Cool in pan for 15 minutes. Mix filling ingredients together. Split cake in half horizontally. Spread half of the filling on the cut side. Top with second layer of shortcake and remaining half of filling on top. Cut into 8 pieces.

Submitted by:

Anton Boxrud B&B
57 South   600 East
Salt Lake City, Utah 84102
(801) 363-8035
Ray & Margaret Fuller
$39.00 to $59.00

Full breakfast
5 rooms, 2 private baths
Children allowed
No pets
Restricted smoking
Mastercard & Visa

This B&B is restored to the original 1901 plans. Interior is replete with beveled and stained glass windows, burled woodwork, hardwood floors and pocket doors. Homemade specialties and family recipes for breakfast. Downtown is within walking distance.

PEAR JAM

4 cups prepared fruit	1/4 teaspoon nutmeg
(2 quarts fully ripe)	1/4 teaspoon cinnamon
1/4 cup lemon juice	1 bottle liquid pectin
7 1/2 cups sugar	(Certo)

Peel and core pears, grate very fine. Mix fruit, sugar, spices, and lemon juice well, in heavy saucepan. Place over high heat and bring to full rolling boil. Boil hard for 1 minute stirring constantly. Remove from heat and at once stir in pectin (Certo). Skim off foam. Seal jars as for any jam.

Submitted by:

Misty Mountain Lodge	Full breakfast
Stowe Hill Rd., Box 114	9 rooms
Wilmington, Vermont 05363	Children allowed
(802) 464-3961	No pets
Lensey (Buzz)/Elizabeth Cole	Restricted smoking
$30.00 to $42.00	

Small inn, converted farmhouse, with twin, double, and family rooms. Home-cooked meals, served family-style in rustic dining room. Homemade jams and jellies. Cozy living room with large fireplace. Host sings and plays guitar. TV, games and books for the children.

PINEAPPLE-CREAM ENGLISH MUFFINS

8 oz. lowfat cream cheese　　　**1 small can crushed pineapple in own juice**

Drain pineapple. Mix with cream cheese and refrigerate overnight. Serve with warmed whole wheat English muffins. Makes 6 servings.

Submitted by:

Kaia Ranch & Co.
Ulaino Road, P.O. Box 404
Hana, Hawaii 96713
(808) 248-7725
JoLoyce Kaia
$75.00

Continental plus breakfast
2 rooms, 2 private baths
No children
No pets
No smoking
No alcohol

A tropical flower and fruit farm. Guests are welcome to walk, take pictures, and picnic. 2 studios with kitchens. Lanai's and hammocks. Quiet seclusion. Village and swimming 4 miles away.

QUICK PINEAPPLE COMBO

20 oz. can pineapple
  chunks, chilled
2 kiwi fruit, peeled &
  sliced

1 cup seedless red or
  green grapes
8 oz. carton pina colada
  yogurt

Mix fruit together. Carefully fold in yogurt. Chill and serve. Makes 4 servings.

Submitted by:

Oak Spring Farm & Vineyard
Route 1, Box 356
Raphine, Virginia 24472
  (Lexington area)
(703) 377-2398
Pat & Jim Tichenor
$45.00 to $65.00

Continental plus breakfast
3 rooms, 3 private baths
Children, over 16
No pets
No smoking
Mastercard & Visa

Recently restored circa 1826 plantation house featuring modern conveniences, period antiques, family and other accessories collected during world-wide military travels. 40 acre farm & vineyard affords warm hospitality in a picturesque setting in a quiet rural area.

RANCHER'S PORRIDGE

4 cups milk
1/2 cup quick-cooking
  brown rice
1 cup raisins

1/4 cup margarine
4 eggs
1/2 cup brown sugar
2 tablespoons vanilla

Topping:
Spiced cereal mix
Granola

Nuts
Spices

Bring 2 cups of milk, the rice and raisins to boiling. Reduce heat, cover, and simmer approximately 15 minutes. Milk should be reduced to "slurry" stage. Remove from heat, stir in margarine. In separate bowl, blend eggs, remaining milk, sugar and vanilla. Pour combined mixtures into small camp kettle (approximately 8" diameter) or 9" x 9" pan. Bake for 20 minutes at 325°. Then top with spiced cereal topping or granola. Bake an additional 30 minutes or as needed to set custard. Makes 8 servings.

Submitted by:

Trout City Inn
P.O. Box 431
Buena Vista, Colorado 81211
(719) 395-8433
(719) 495-0348 (Winter)
Juel & Irene Kjeldsen
$35.00 to $50.00

Full breakfast
4 rooms, 4 private baths
Children allowed
No pets
No smoking
Mastercard & Visa

Historic railway station on Trout Creek Pass in National Forest. Victorian decor and antiques in depot rooms plus private Pullman car and Drover's caboose. Railroad, trout stream, beaver ponds & gold mine with grand view of canyon and collegiate peaks along Continental Divide.

TROUT CITY INN

ON THE SOUTH PARK LINE

ROMEO INN PEACH DELIGHT

1 large fresh peach, peeled, and cut into chunks

4 cups freshly squeezed orange juice
1/3 cup milk
Dash of vanilla

Mix all ingredients together in a blender until smooth. Serve in fruit juice glasses. Makes 6 - 8 servings.

Submitted by:

Romeo Inn
295 Idaho St.
Ashland, Oregon 97520
(503) 488-0884
Bruce & Margaret Halverson
$105.00 to $175.00

Full breakfast (gourmet)
6 rooms, 6 private baths
Children, over 12
No pets
No smoking
Mastercard & Visa

Elegant Cape Cod in walking distance of town & OR Shakespeare Festival. On 1/2 acre, amid towering ponderosa pines, overlooking Rogue Valley & Cascade Mtns.   Fireplaces, hot tubs, beautiful gardens, pool & spa. King-sized beds, hand-stitched Amish quilts, room phones, c/a. Rated 3-star "Excellent" by Mobil Travel Guide.

ROYAL GRANOLA

10 cups old-fashioned
  oats
1/2 lb. shredded un-
  sweetened coconut
1/2 cup sesame seeds
2 cups sunflower seeds
  (roasted & salted)
3 cups chopped almonds
  & walnuts
1 cup wheat germ (opt.)

Syrup:
1 1/2 cups brown
  sugar
1 1/2 cups water
1 1/2 cups oil
1/2 cup honey
1/2 cup molasses
1 1/2 teaspoons salt
2 teaspoons cinnamon
3 teaspoons vanilla

In very large bowl combine oats, coconut, seeds, nuts, and wheat germ. Blend well. In large saucepan combine syrup ingredients. Heat until sugar is dissolved, but do not boil. Pour syrup over dry ingredients and stir until well-coated. Spread onto 4 large cookie sheets. Bake at 300° for 30 - 40 minutes. Stir 2 - 3 times during baking. Store in airtight containers. Makes 20 cups.

Submitted by:

Royal Hotel
18239 Main Street
Jamestown, California 95327
(209) 984-5271
Bob & Nancy Bosich
$35.00 to $85.00

Continental plus breakfast
19 rooms, 12 private baths
Children allowed
No pets
No smoking
Mastercard, Visa, Am Ex

Historic inn 125 miles NE of San Francisco, 70 miles from Yosemite National Park. Specialized Gold Rush, western, WWI and WWII bookstore. Local gold panning, steam-powered train rides, wineries, & "oodles" of antique shops in foothills of the Sierras, known as California Gold Country!

SPICED PEAR COMPOTE

3 - 1 lb. cans pear slices in syrup	1/4 teaspoon nutmeg
1 cup firmly packed brown sugar	1/4 teaspoon allspice
1/2 teaspoon cinnamon	1/4 cup lemon or orange juice

Drain syrup from pears and reserve 1 cup syrup. Mix syrup with sugar, spices and fruit juice. Add pears and mix gently, covering pears with syrup. Let stand overnight in refrigerator for full flavor to develop. Serve in small compote dishes. This compote may also be served warm. Makes 6 servings.

Submitted by:

Maplewood Inn & Antiques
Route 22A South
Fair Haven, Vermont 05743
(802) 265-8039 or
1-800-253-7729
Cindy & Doug Baird
$70.00 (dbl.) to $105.00 (sui.)

Continental plus breakfast
5 rooms, 5 private baths
Children, over 5
No pets, can arrange boarding
Restricted smoking
Mastercard, Visa, Discover

Romantic, antique-filled haven, 1843 Greek Revival is on VT Historic Register. Rooms have TV & telephone, 3 have fireplaces. Gathering Room for reading or games, & parlor. Richly appointed, a/c. Bike, canoe rentals & antique shop on-site. Near lakes, skiing, museums, shops and restaurants.

SPICY HASH BROWNS

2 small potatoes,
   washed
Pinch of red pepper
   flakes
Pinch of thyme

Pinch of caraway seeds
1 teaspoon paprika
Salt & pepper to taste
Oil for frying

Grate potatoes, with skin on. Mix in remaining ingredients except oil.
Taste to make sure properly seasoned. Heat large skillet to smoking
point. Coat pan generously with oil, and immediately squeeze water
out of grated potatoes with fist. Place in pan. Cook on both sides,
forming a square with a spatula, until golden brown, and place on rack
in 350° oven for 15 minutes. Cut in half to make triangle. Makes 2
servings.

Submitted by:

Roundtop Bed & Breakfast
Box 258, R.D. #2
Wrightsville, Penn. 17368
(717) 252-3169
Tyler & Jodi Sloan
$50.00 to $75.00

Full breakfast
6 rooms, 1 private bath
Children allowed
No pets
Smoking allowed
Mastercard & Visa

Romantic 1880 stone home, 800 feet above the Susquehanna
River. Spectacular views, a true "getaway", but only 5 minutes from a
renowned French restaurant. Unique setting on over 100 acres of
woodland.

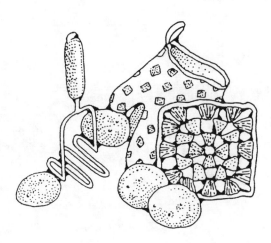

SPORTSMAN'S HIGH CELEBRATION SURPRIZE

2 cups milk	1 tablespoon vanilla
1/4 cup sugar	10 - 12 ice cubes
6 oz. frozen orange juice concentrate	1/8 teaspoon nutmeg (opt.)

Mix all ingredients together in a blender and blend on high speed until the ice is gone. Serve immediately in wine glasses. This is served for birthdays, anniversaries, honeymoons, any special occasion. Makes 6 servings.

Submitted by:

Sportsman's High Bed
  & Breakfast
750. Deer Street
West Yellowstone, Montana
  59758
(800) 272-4227
$65.00 to $85.00

Full breakfast
5 rooms, 5 private baths
Children, over 9
No pets
No smoking
Mastercard & Visa

Spacious country-style home with wraparound porch, nestled on 3 acres of aspen and pines. Spectacular views await, only 8 miles from the west entrance of Yellowstone Park. Antique-filled guest rooms are lovingly decorated with country colors and fabrics. Feather pillows, terry robes, outdoor hot tub. Come, & be treated as a friend!

STRAWBERRY BUTTER

1 cup unsalted butter, (2 sticks, softened) 1/2 cup sifted confectioner's sugar	1 - 10 oz. carton frozen sliced strawberries, thawed and drained (reserve juice)

Whip the butter until fluffy. Beat in the sugar and add the strawberries. Gradually beat in the reserved strawberry juice. Store in refrigerator. This butter freezes well. Serve on hot biscuits or rolls. Makes 1 3/4 cups.

Origin: Handed down by my great-grandmother, Minnie Webb.

Submitted by:

Hamilton Place	Full breakfast
105 E. Mason Avenue	3 rooms, 3 private baths
Holly Springs, Miss. 38635	Children allowed
(601) 252-4368	No pets
Linda & Jack Stubbs	Smoking allowed
$55.00 to $65.00	Mastercard & Visa

Built in 1838, on National Register, and 3 blocks from historic town square, in Holly Springs, which is steeped in history & tradition. All rooms furnished in antiques. Swimming pool and hot tub for guests.

THAT GOOD GRANOLA

8 cups old-fashioned oatmeal	8 oz. cashews
1 1/2 cups wheat germ	1/2 cup honey
1 cup sunflower seeds	1/2 cup apple juice
1 cup sesame seeds	1/2 cup oil
1 cup brown sugar	1/2 cup crunchy peanut butter
8 oz. wide coconut	2 teaspoons vanilla
8 oz. slivered almonds	

Optional:

All Bran cereal	Peanuts
Grape Nuts cereal	Walnuts
Raisins	Dates

Mix oatmeal, wheat germ, sunflower seeds, sesame seeds, brown sugar, coconut, almonds and cashews in large container. Mix moist ingredients and bring to a boil. Add second mixture to first mixture. Blend. Spread mixture on 2 or 3 cookie sheets. Bake at 200° for approximately 2 hours. Optional: After baking you may add one cup of each of the following: All Bran, Grape Nuts, raisins, peanuts, walnuts, dates. Makes approximately 6 lbs. of granola.

Submitted by:

Hostess House	Full breakfast
5758 NE Emerson	2 rooms
Portland, Ore. 97218	No children
(503) 282-7892	Pets allowed
Milli Laughlin	No smoking
$35.00 to $45.00	

Warmth and hospitality in a contemporary setting. Breakfast served in dining room overlooking a deep, terraced yard. Large deck for relaxing, reading or writing. A quiet residence adjacent to public transportation. Near main highway arterials and airport.

WILLIAM CATLIN HOUSE
FRIED APPLE RINGS

3 apples
Lemon juice if needed
1 tablespoon butter
  for frying

1/4 cup sugar
1/2 teaspoon ground
  cinnamon
1 - 2 tablespoons water

Core and slice apples 1/4" thick. Toss apple slices in lemon juice if not cooking immediately. Melt butter in 10" nonstick frying pan. Cook until tender, about 5 minutes on each side. Mix sugar and cinnamon, more or less, to taste, and sprinkle over apples. Add water. Steam apples in mixture about 1 minute on each side. Serve with pancakes or French Toast or as a side dish. Makes 6 servings.

Submitted by:

The William Catlin House
2304 E. Broad Street
Richmond, VA 23223
(804) 780-3746
Robert & Josie Martin
$70.00 to $140.00

Full breakfast
5 rooms, 3 private baths
Children, over 10
No pets
Restricted smoking
Mastercard, Visa & Discover

Richmond's first and oldest B&B. 1845 restored home decorated entirely with antiques, reproductions, canopy & poster beds, oriental rugs, and crystal chandeliers. Central air-conditioning, fireplaces, and lots of Southern hospitality. Room rates include all taxes.

WILLIAM KLINGER'S STRAWBERRY SOUP

1 - 15 oz. pkg. frozen strawberries	1 tablespoon vanilla
1 - 15 oz. carton sour cream	1 tablespoon sugar
1 tablespoon grenadine syrup	3 oz. sifted powdered sugar
1 tablespoon lemon juice	3 pints whipping cream
	Garnish: Strawberry halves & mint leaves

In blender mix strawberries and sour cream, beat slowly till well mixed. While mixing, add grenadine syrup, lemon juice, vanilla, and sugars. When very smooth, add whipping cream, mix on high for 5 seconds. Chill and shake well before serving. Use a strawberry half with a mint leaf as garnish. Makes 8 - 1/2 cup servings.

Origin: I serve soups with my breakfasts, and love to create good recipes.

Submitted by:

William Klinger Inn
108 East Second Street
Hermann, Missouri 65041
(314) 486-5930
Laverne Rickher
$86.83 to $121.37

Full breakfast
7 rooms, 7 private baths
No children
No pets
No smoking
Mastercard & Visa

Over 100 years old, the original owner was William Klinger. 2 large suites, 1 with queen canopy bed. Victorian era antiques throughout. An elegant inn to pamper you for relaxation. Private patio, walking district area, 4 wineries.

INDEX OF INNS

More B&B Cookbooks from Winters Publishing

The Indiana Bed & Breakfast Association Cookbook and Directory
Features recipes from 75 inns throughout the state of Indiana, with complete information about each inn. 96 pgs. $9.95

Overnight Sensations
Recipes From Virginia's Finest Bed & Breakfasts
Features recipes from 90 inns throughout the state of Virginia, with complete information about each inn. 112 pgs. $9.95

Pure Gold - Colorado Treasures
Recipes From Bed & Breakfast Innkeepers of Colorado
Features more than 100 recipes from 54 inns throughout the state of Colorado, with complete information about each inn. 96 pgs. $9.95

Inn-describably Delicious
Recipes From The Illinois Bed & Breakfast Association Innkeepers
Features recipes from 82 inns throughout the state of Illinois, with complete information about each inn. 112 pgs. $9.95

Just Inn Time for Breakfast
A Cookbook from the Michigan Lake To Lake B & B Association
Features recipes from 93 inns throughout the state of Michigan, with complete information about each inn. 128 pgs. $10.95

American Mornings
Favorite Breakfast Recipes From Bed & Breakfast Inns
Features breakfast recipes from 302 inns throughout the country, with complete information about each inn. 320 pgs. $12.95

Check for availability at your local bookstore, or indicate the quantity of the book(s) that you wish to order below. <u>MAIL THIS ORDER TO</u>:

Winters Publishing, P.O. Box 501, Greensburg, IN 47240.

Qty.

_____	*Indiana B&B Assn. Cookbook*	$ 9.95 each _____
_____	*Overnight Sensations*	$ 9.95 each _____
_____	*Pure Gold - Colorado Treasures*	$ 9.95 each _____
_____	*Inn-describably Delicious*	$ 9.95 each _____
_____	*Just Inn Time for Breakfast*	$10.95 each _____
_____	*American Mornings*	$12.95 each _____

Shipping Charge $ 2.00 each _____

5% Sales Tax (Indiana residents <u>ONLY</u>)   _____

TOTAL _____

Please send to:

Name: _____

Address: _____

City: _____ State: _____ Zip: _____